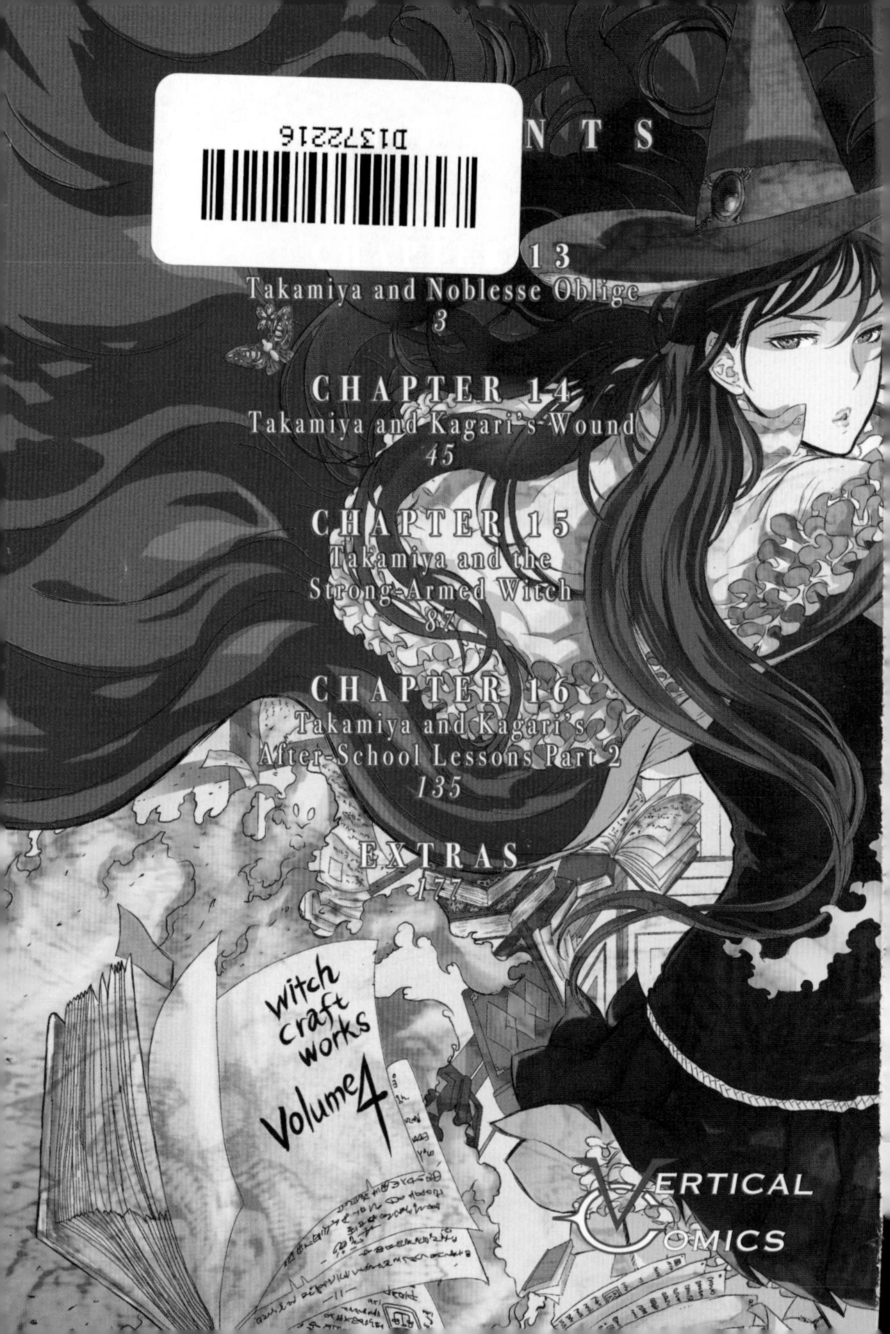
witch craft works
Volume 4
VERTICAL COMICS

NTS

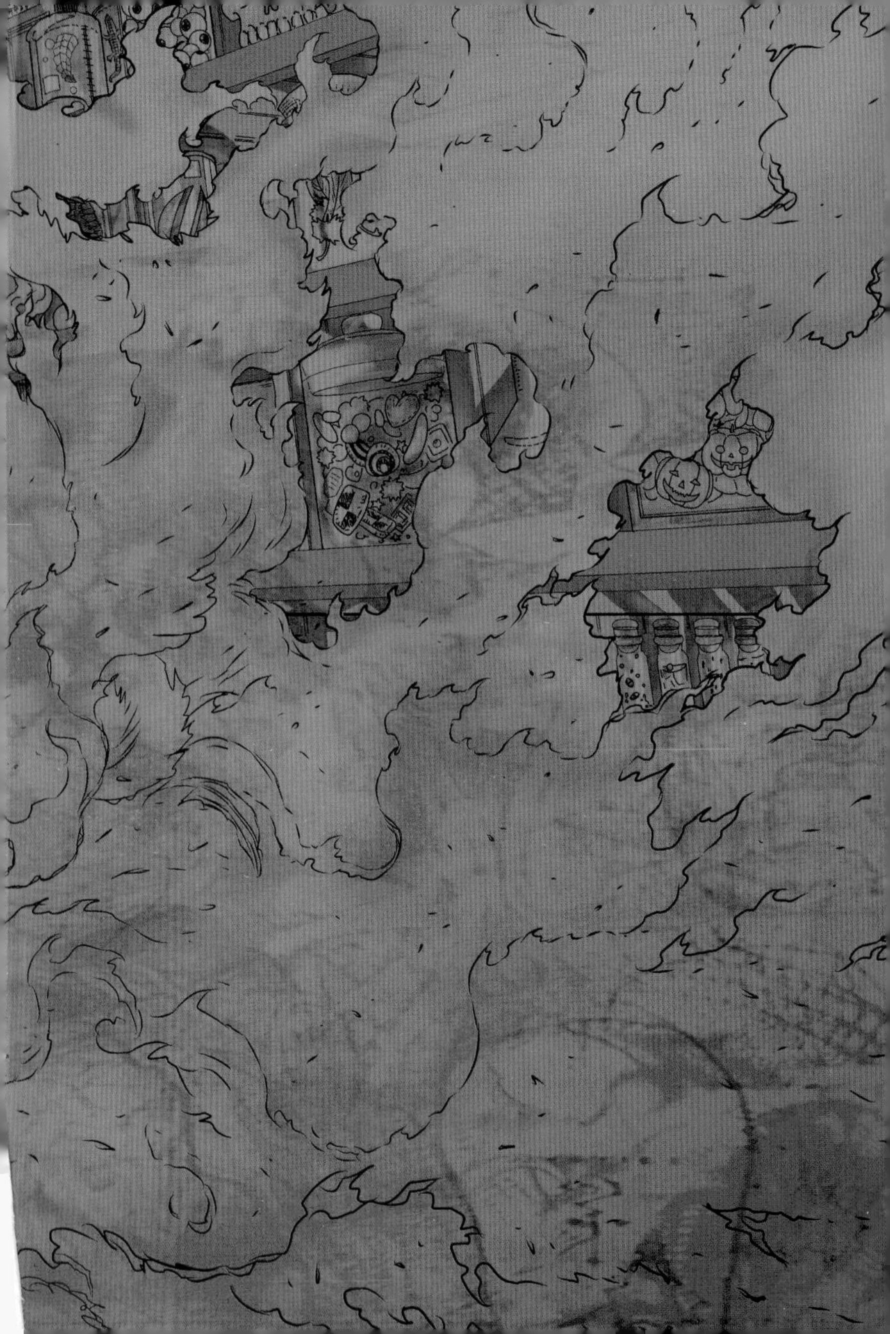

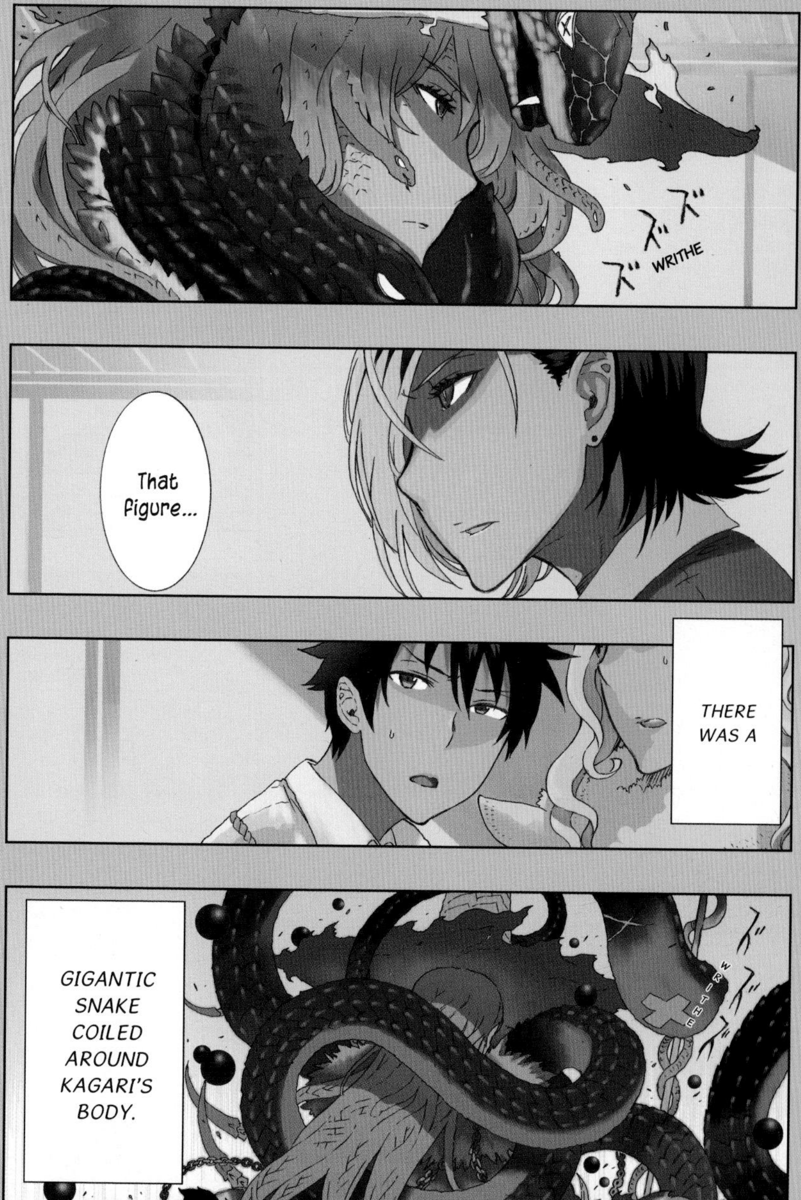
ズズズ
WRITHE
That figure...
THERE WAS A
GIGANTIC SNAKE COILED AROUND KAGARI'S BODY.
WRITHE

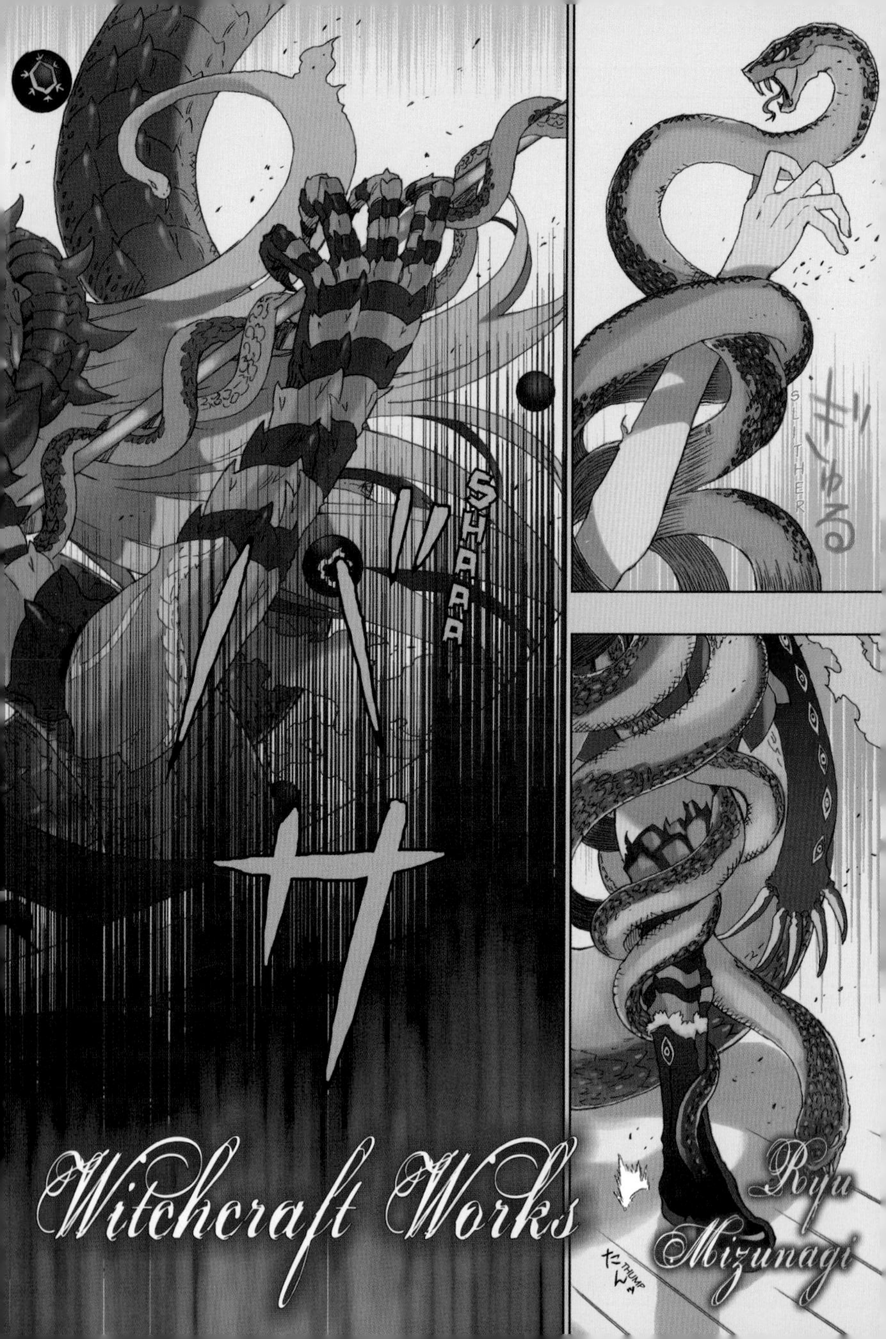
SLITHER
THUMP
SHAAA
Witchcraft Works
Ryu Mizunagi

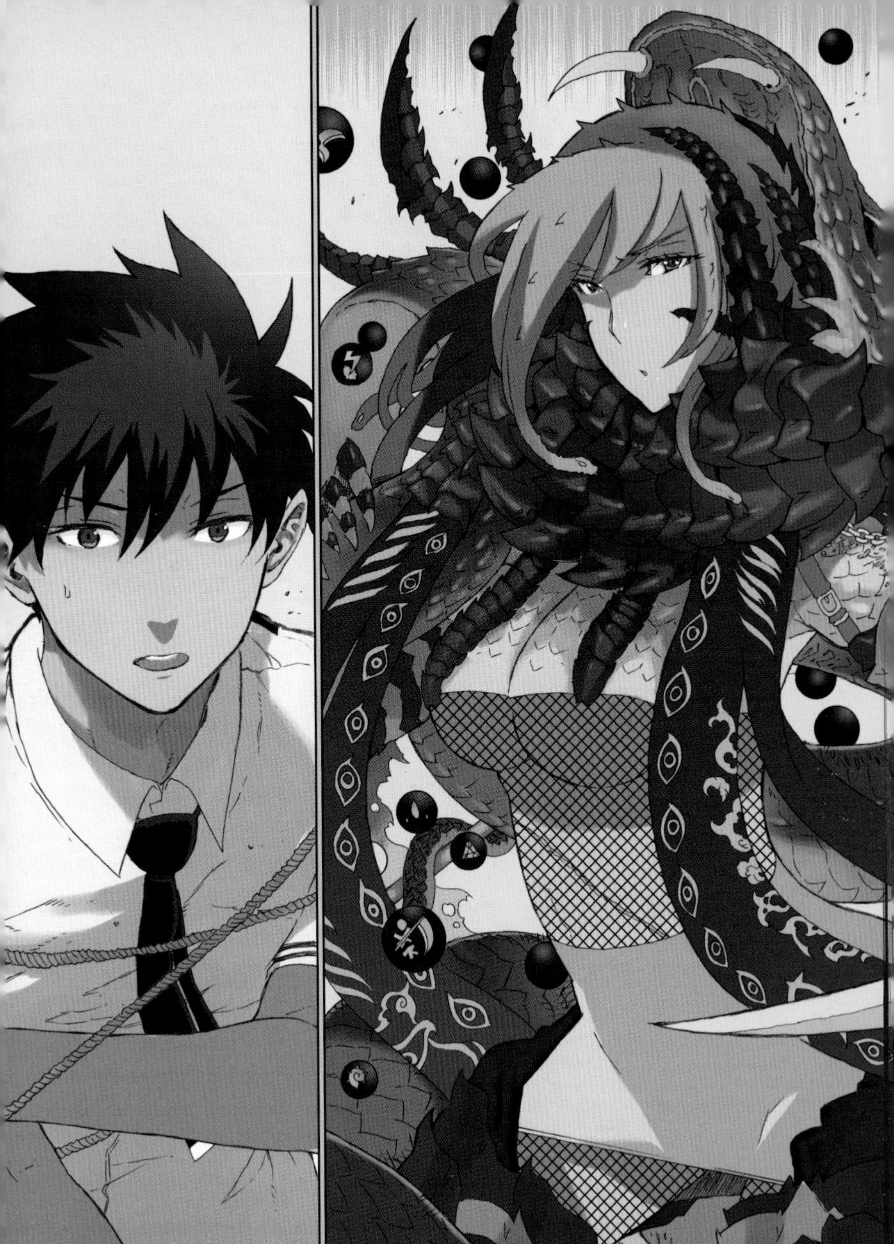

CHAPTER 13 Takamiya and Noblesse Oblige

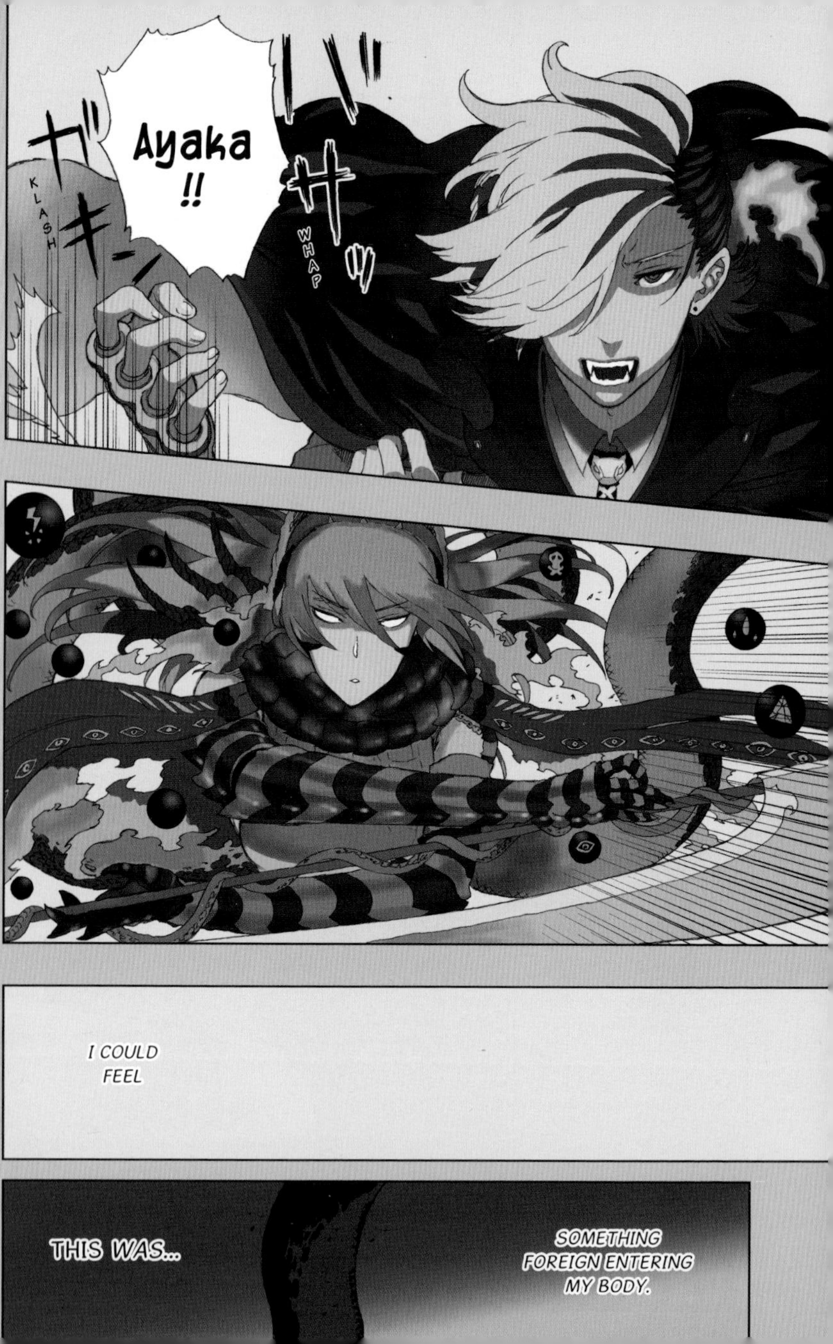
WHAP
Ayaka !!
KLASH
I COULD FEEL
SOMETHING FOREIGN ENTERING MY BODY.
THIS WAS...

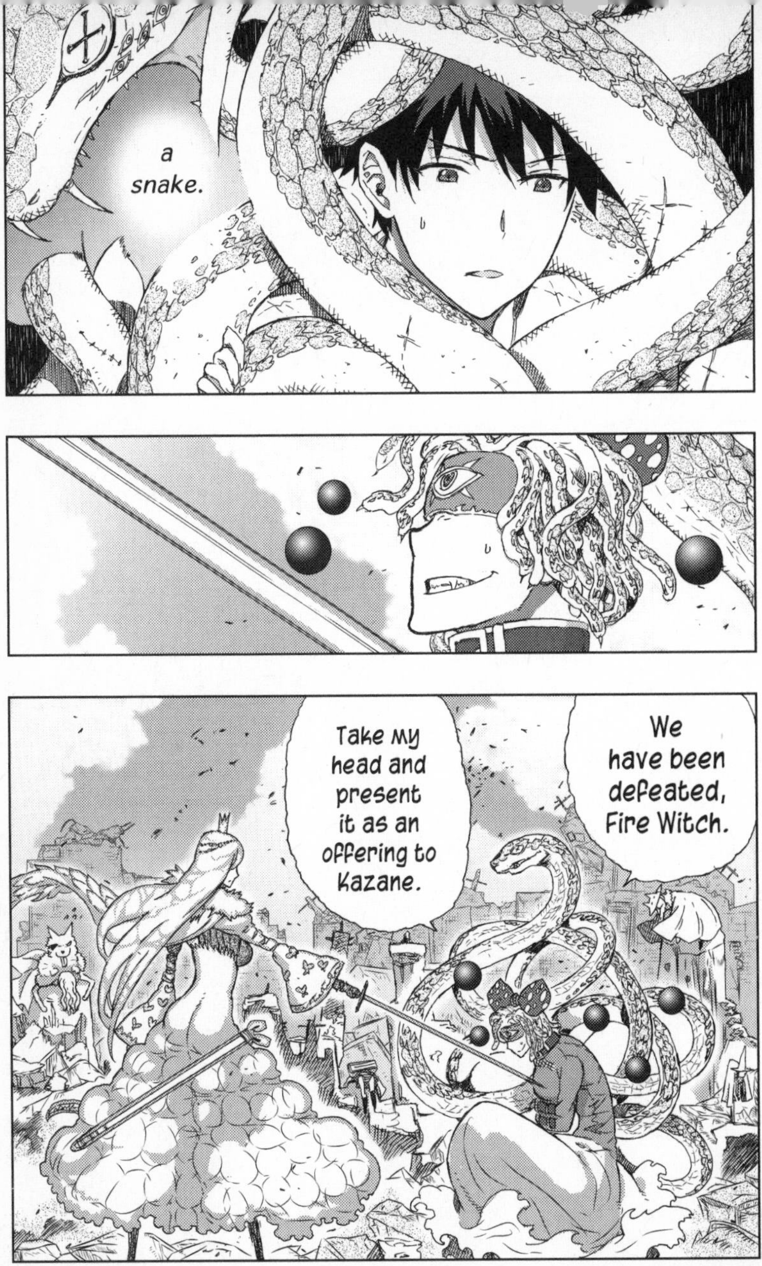
a snake.
We have been defeated, Fire Witch.
Take my head and present it as an offering to Kazane.

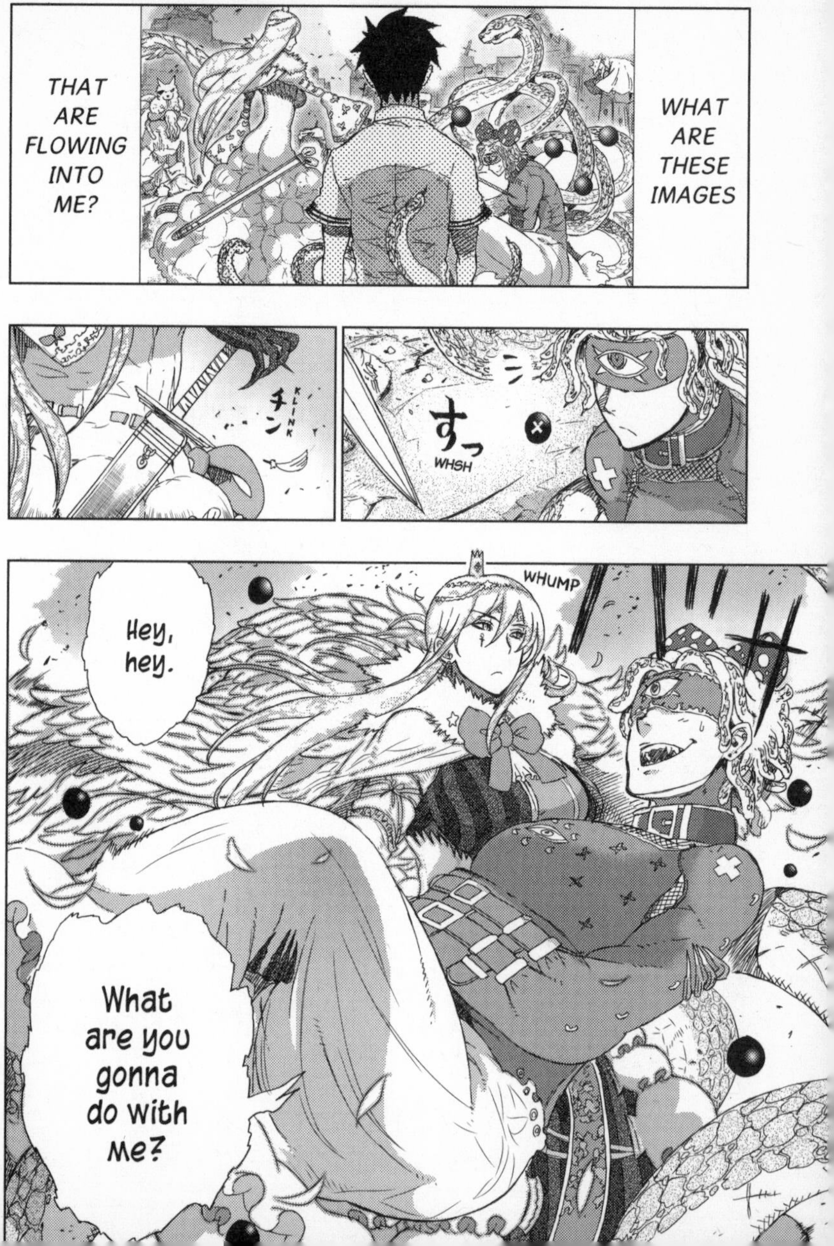
WHAT ARE THESE IMAGES
THAT ARE FLOWING INTO ME?
すっ
WHSH
チン
KLINK
WHUMP
Hey, hey.
What are you gonna do with me?

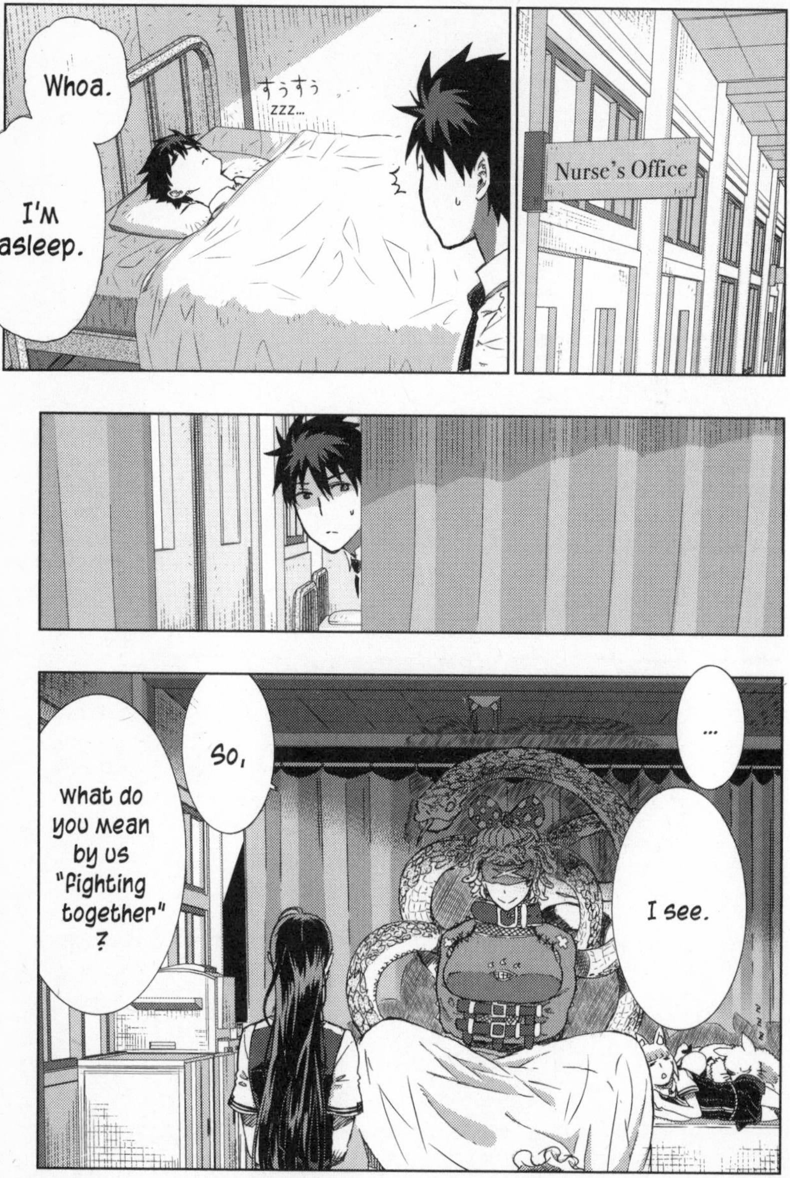
Nurse's Office
すうすう
zzz...
Whoa.
I'M asleep.
...
I see.
So,
what do you mean by us "fighting together"?

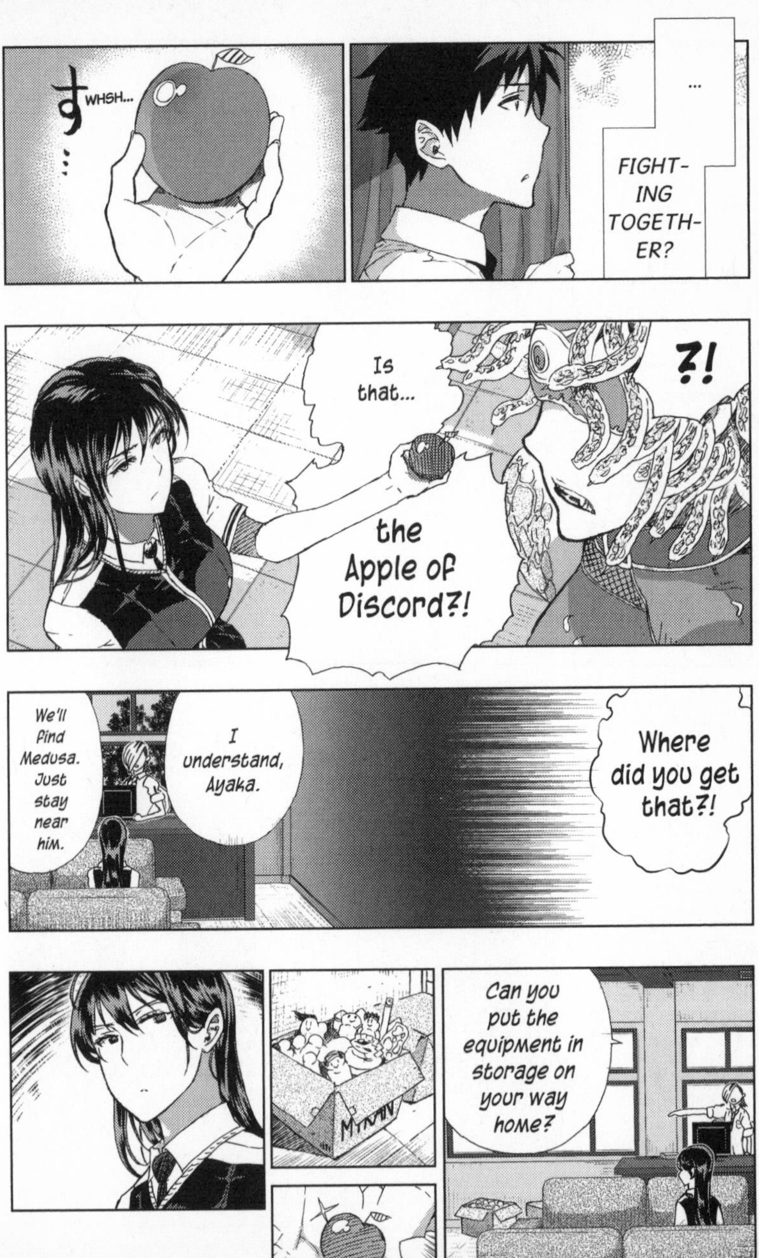
...
FIGHT-ING TOGETH-ER?
す WHSH...
?!
Is that...
the Apple of Discord?!
Where did you get that?!
I understand, Ayaka.
We'll find Medusa. Just stay near him.
Can you put the equipment in storage on your way home?

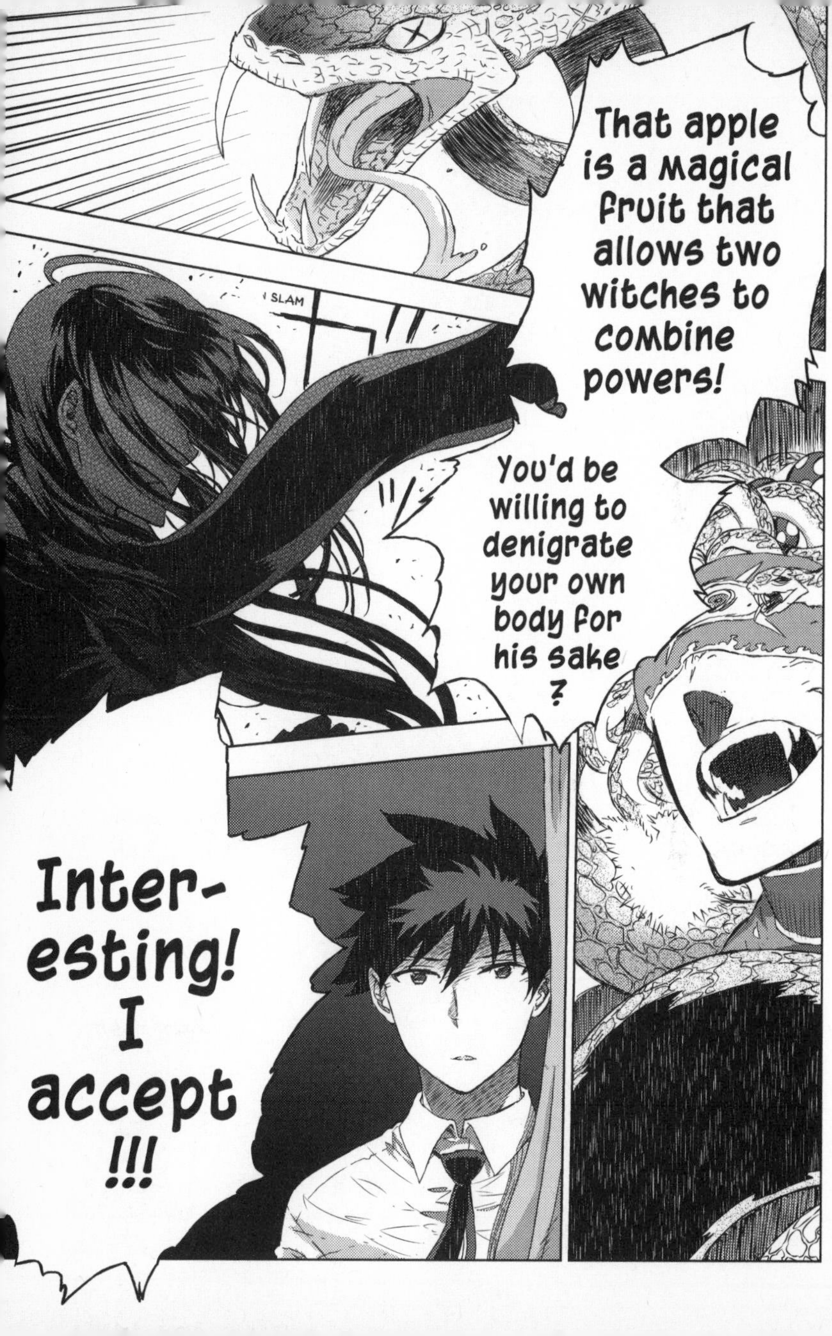
That apple is a magical fruit that allows two witches to combine powers!
SLAM
You'd be willing to denigrate your own body for his sake?
Inter-esting! I accept!!!

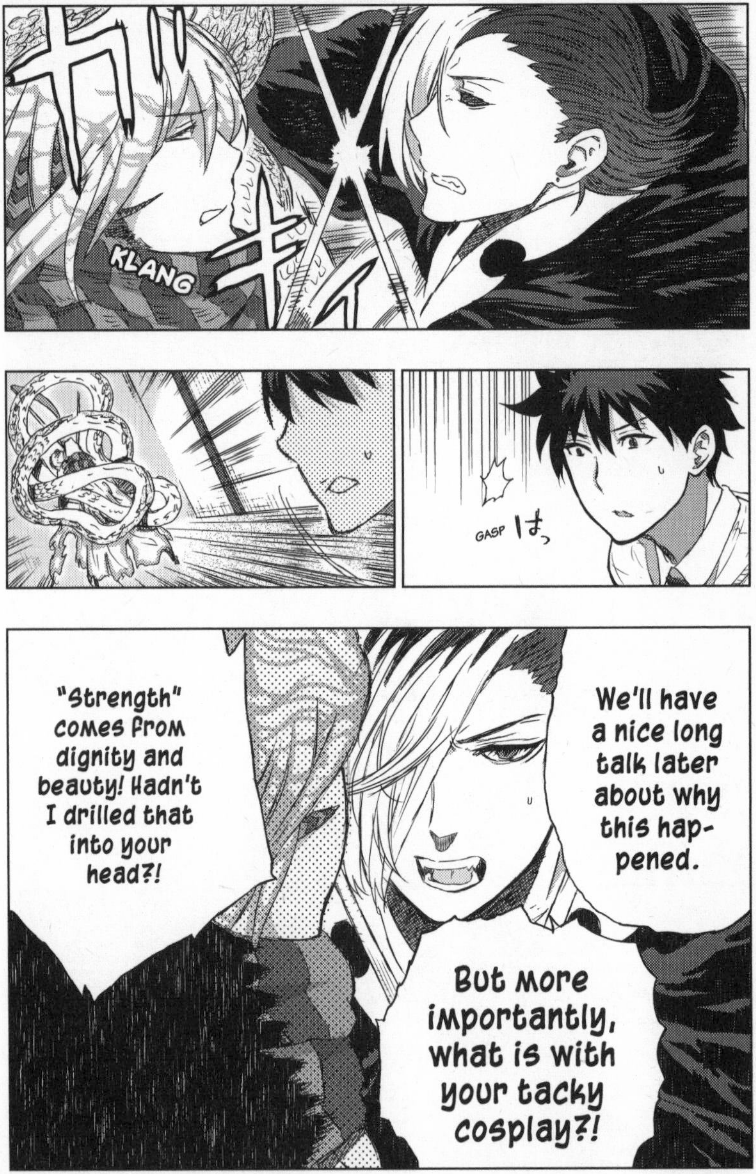
KLANG
GASP はっ
We'll have a nice long talk later about why this hap-pened.
"Strength" comes from dignity and beauty! Hadn't I drilled that into your head?!
But more importantly, what is with your tacky cosplay?!

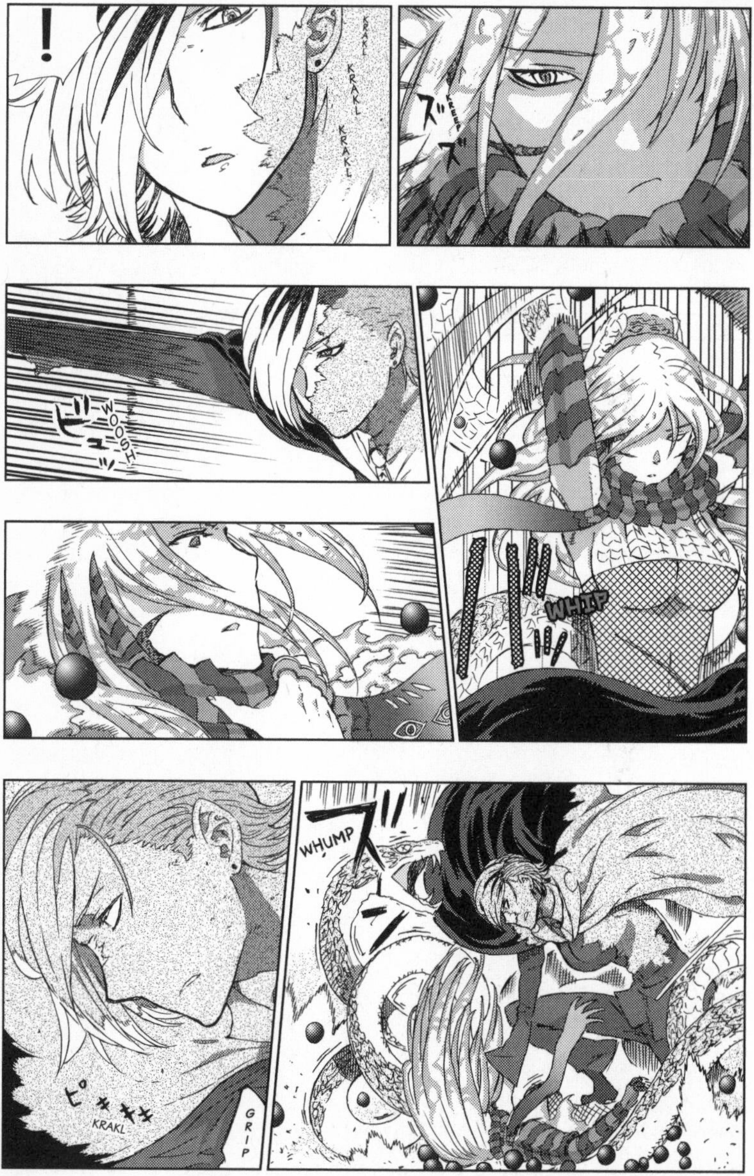
ズズ
KREEP
!
KRAKL
KRAKL
KRAKL
WHIP
ビュッ
WOOSH
ズ
WHUMP
GRIP
ピキキ
KRAKL

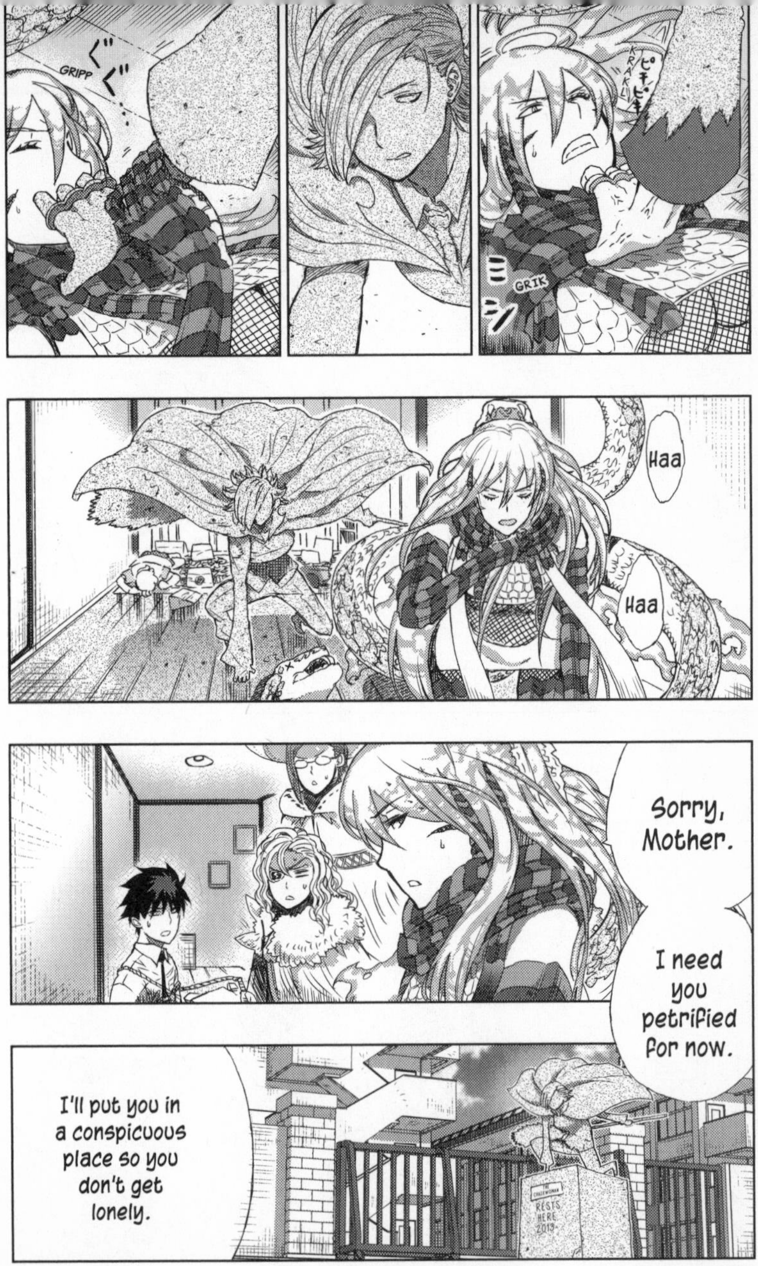
ピキピキ
KRAKLIK
ミシ
GRIK
ぐぐ
GRIPP
Haa
Haa
Sorry, Mother.
I need you petrified for now.
I'll put you in a conspicuous place so you don't get lonely.
THE CHAIRWOMAN
RESTS HERE 2013

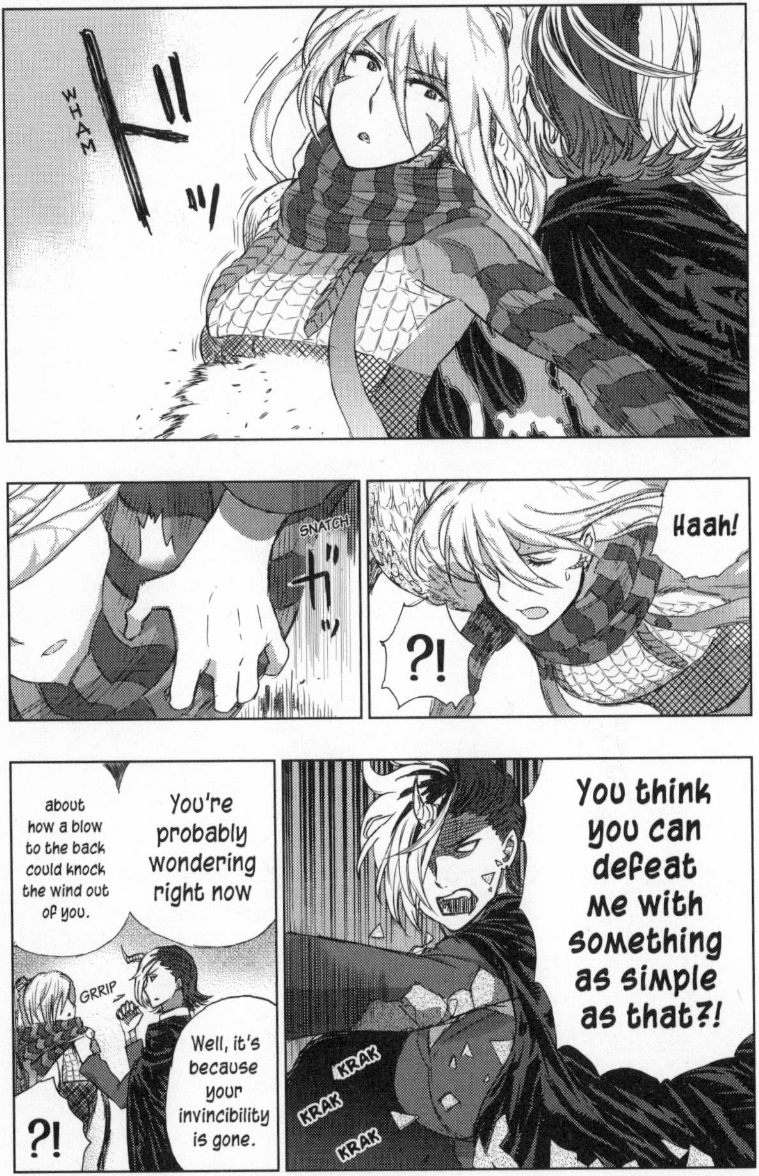

WHAM
Haah!
?!
SNATCH
You think you can defeat me with something as simple as that?!
KRAK
KRAK
KRAK
KRAK
You're probably wondering right now
about how a blow to the back could knock the wind out of you.
GRRIP
Well, it's because your invincibility is gone.
?!

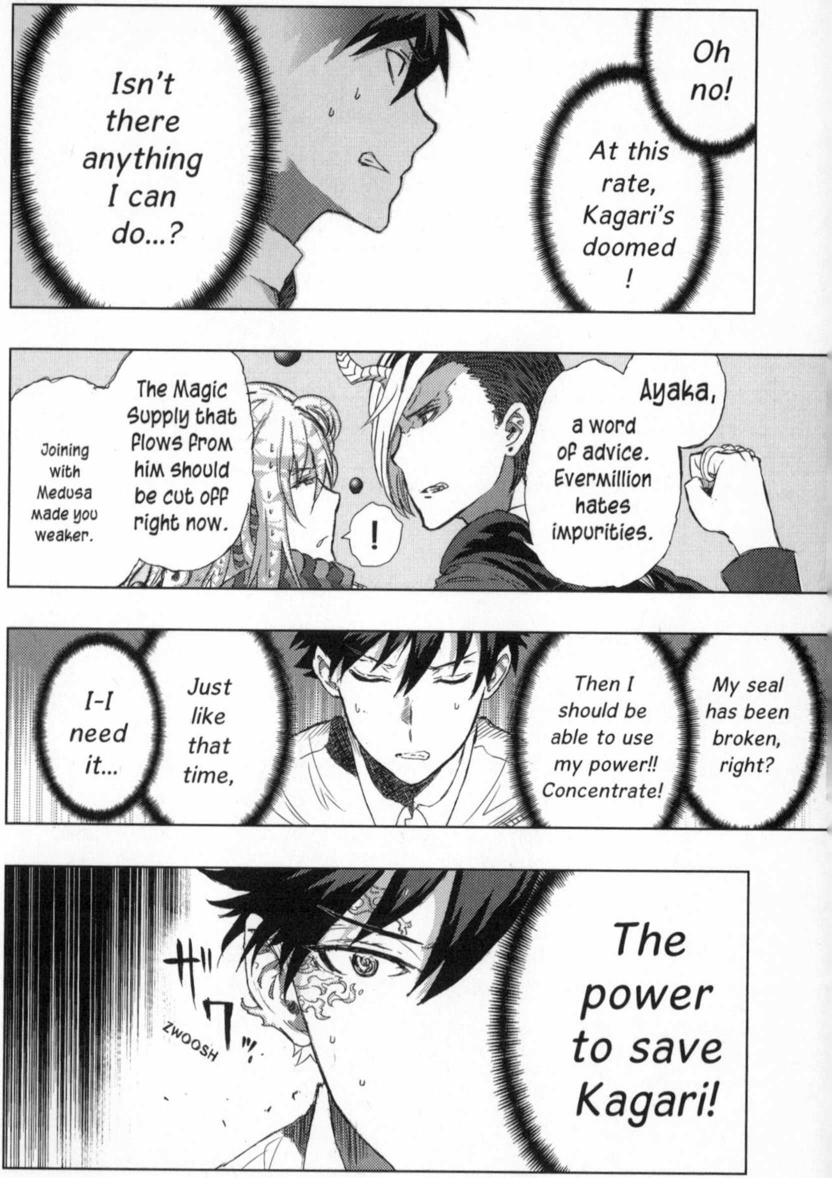
Oh no!
At this rate, Kagari's doomed !
Isn't there anything I can do...?
Ayaka, a word of advice. Evermillion hates impurities.
!
The Magic Supply that flows from him should be cut off right now.
Joining with Medusa made you weaker.
My seal has been broken, right?
Then I should be able to use my power!! Concentrate!
Just like that time,
I-I need it...
The power to save Kagari!
ザワッ
ZWOOSH

No,
Takamiya!
That
power—

GASP

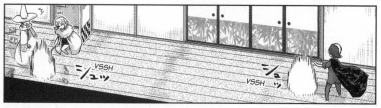

VSSH ニュッ

VSSH ニュッ

POP ぱっ

POP ぱっ

Huh?

SLITHER

PING

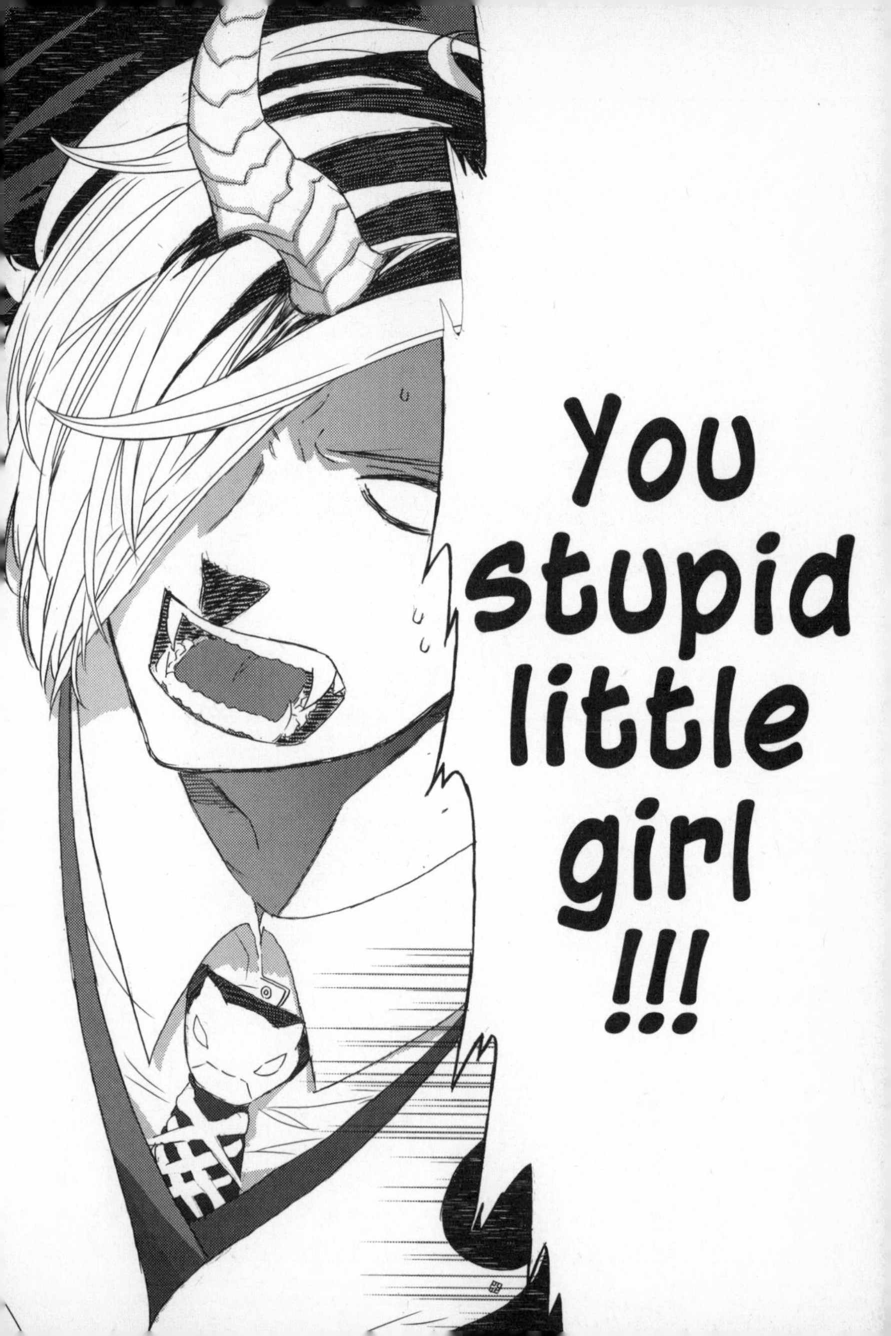
You stupid little girl !!!

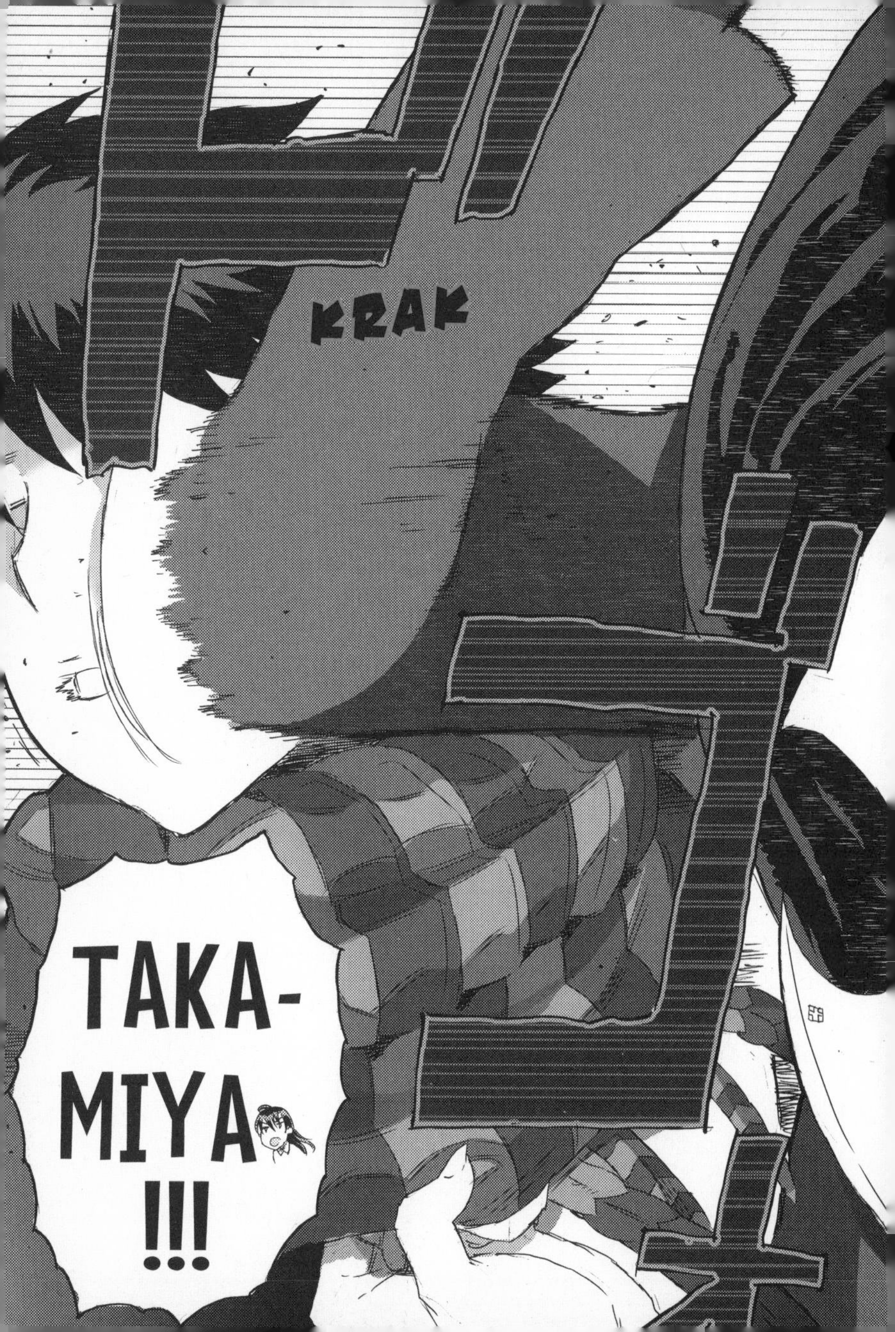
KRAK
TAKA-
MIYA
!!!

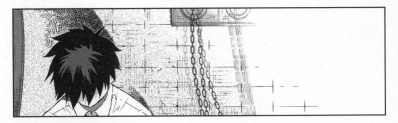

...

STING

HMM
?

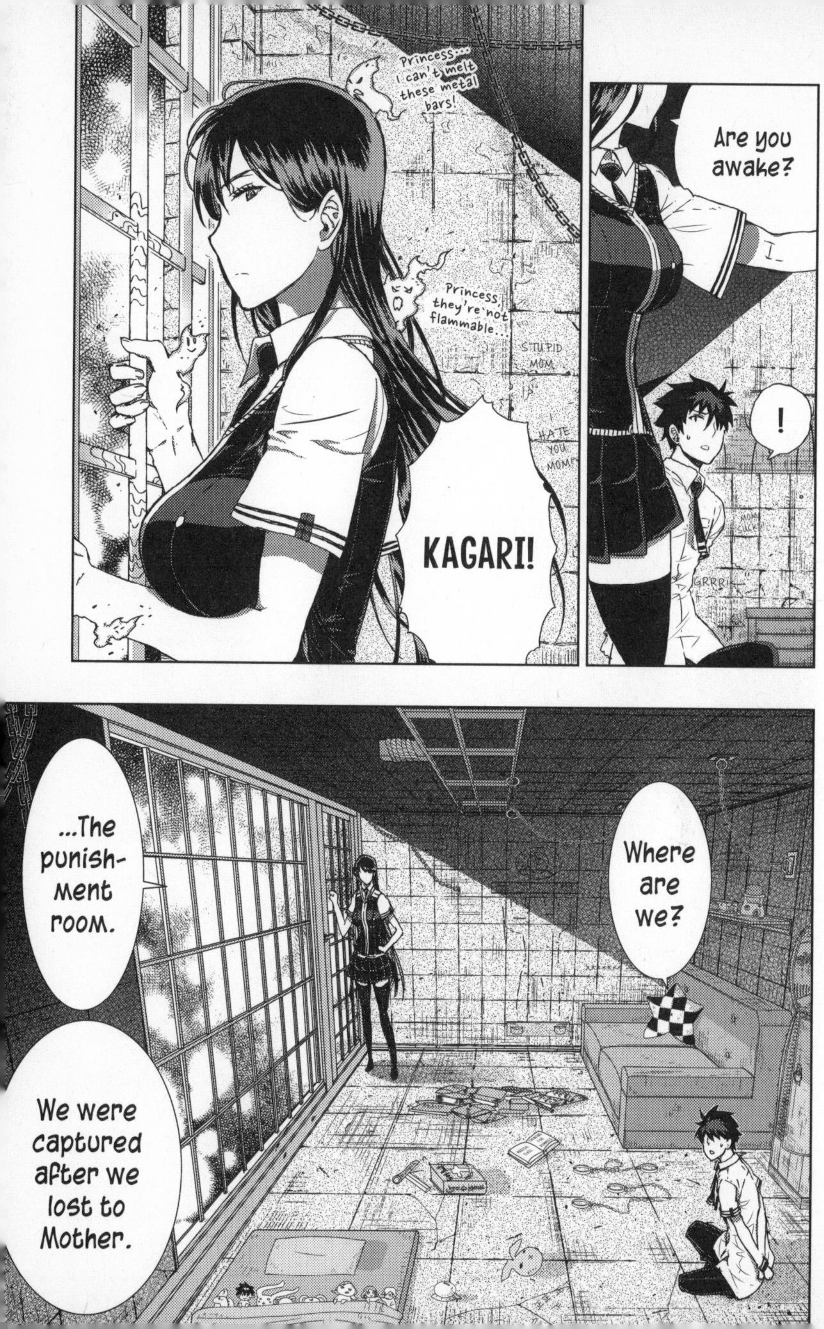

Are you awake?
!
GRRR!
Princess... I can't melt these metal bars!
Princess, they're not flammable...
STUPID MOM
HATE YOU MOM
KAGARI!
Where are we?
...The punish-ment room.
We were captured after we lost to Mother.

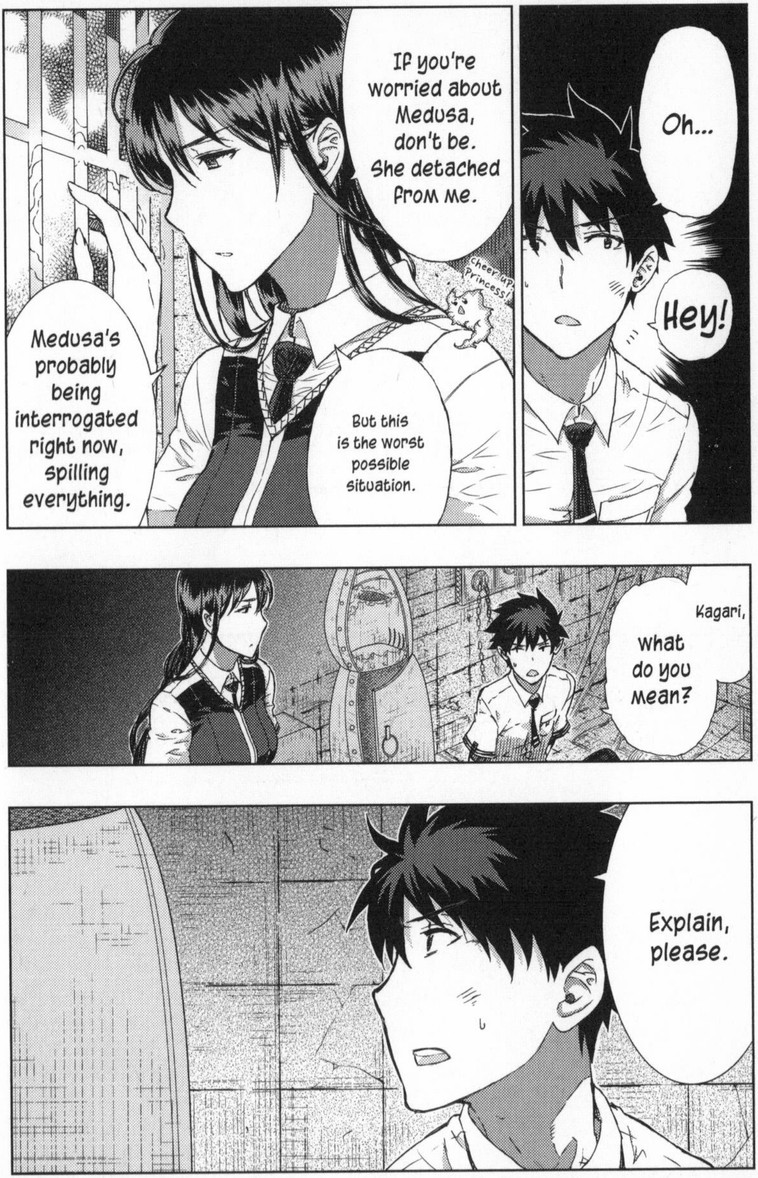
Oh...
Hey!
If you're worried about Medusa, don't be. She detached from me.
Cheer up, Princess!
But this is the worst possible situation.
Medusa's probably being interrogated right now, spilling everything.
Kagari, what do you mean?
Explain, please.

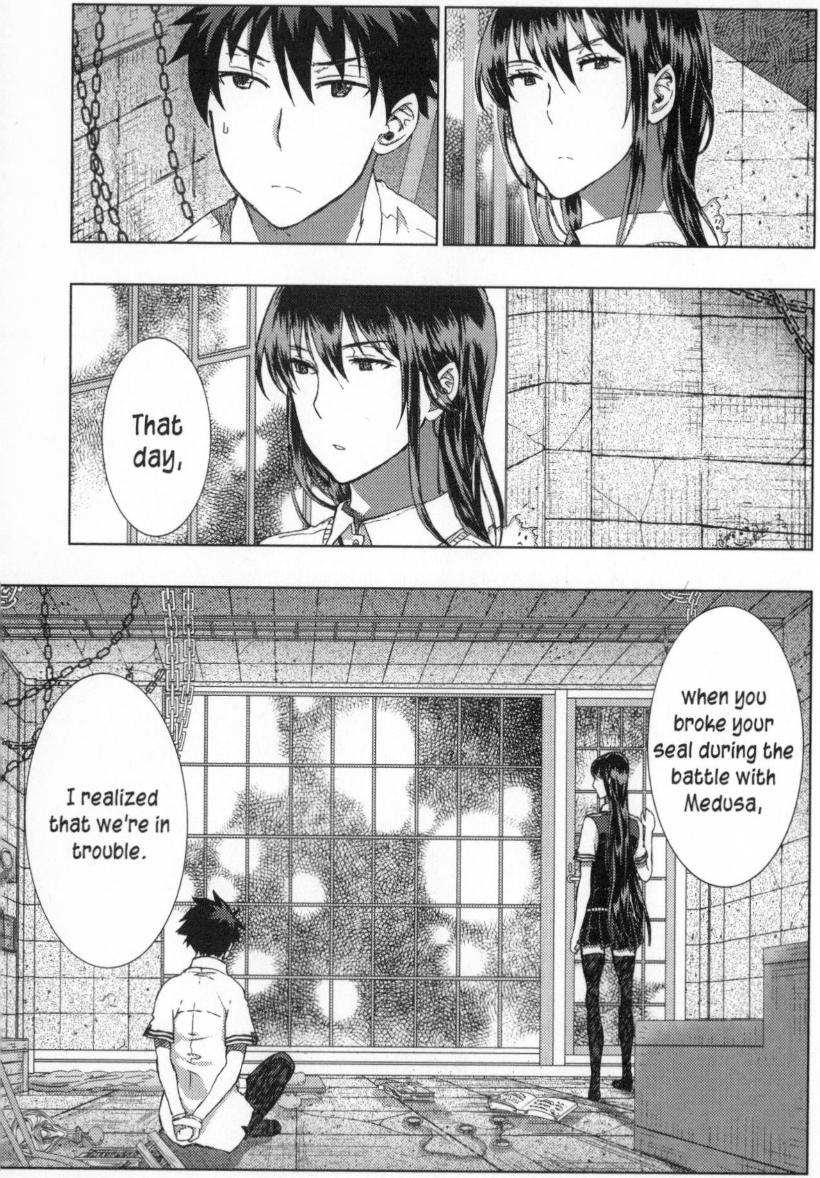
That day,
When you broke your seal during the battle with Medusa,
I realized that we're in trouble.

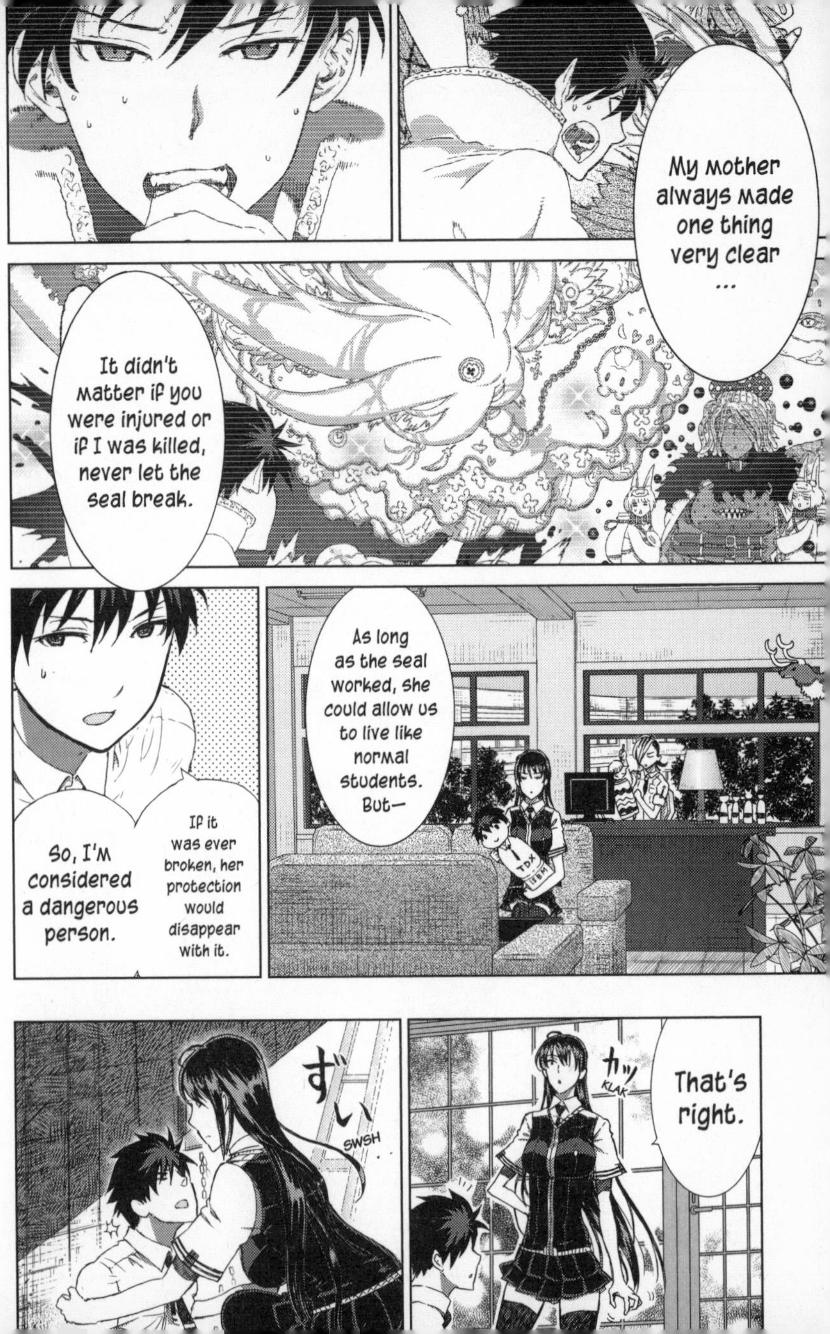
My mother always made one thing very clear ...
It didn't matter if you were injured or if I was killed, never let the seal break.
As long as the seal worked, she could allow us to live like normal students. But—
If it was ever broken, her protection would disappear with it.
So, I'm considered a dangerous person.
That's right.
カッ
KLAK
ずい
SWSH

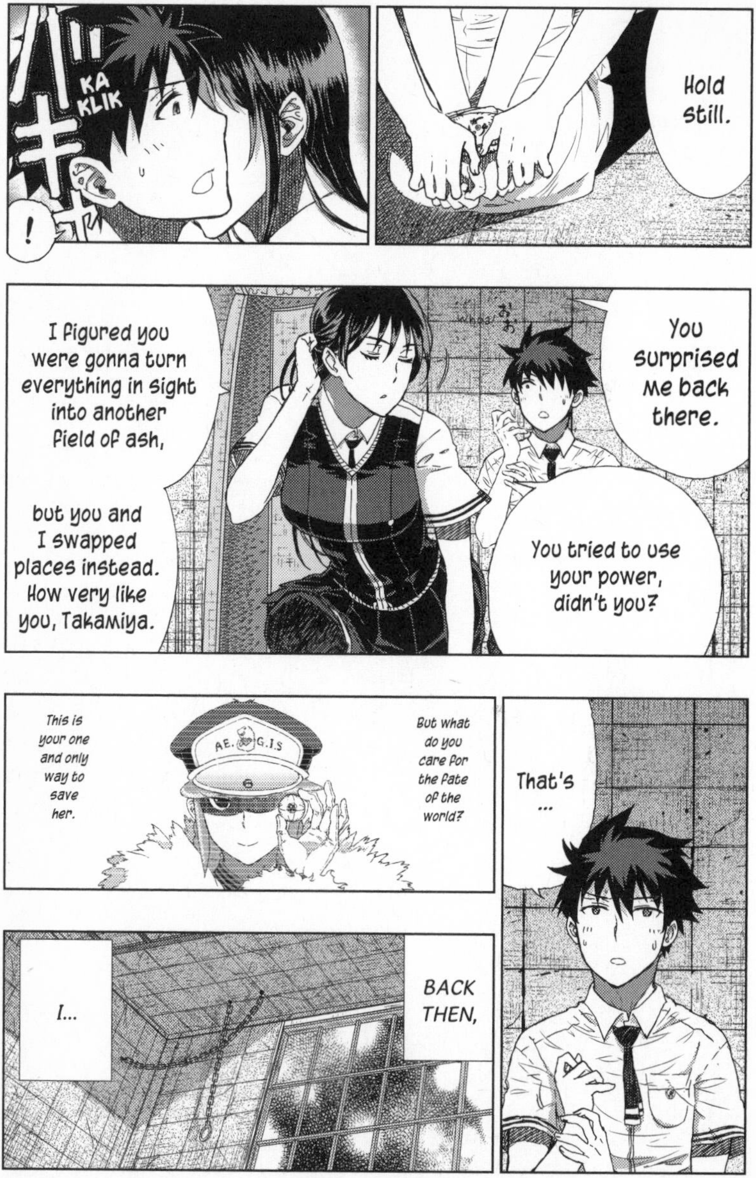
Hold still.
KA KLIK
!
whoa!
You surprised me back there.
You tried to use your power, didn't you?
I figured you were gonna turn everything in sight into another field of ash,
but you and I swapped places instead. How very like you, Takamiya.
That's ...
But what do you care for the fate of the world?
This is your one and only way to save her.
AE.G.I.S
BACK THEN,
I...

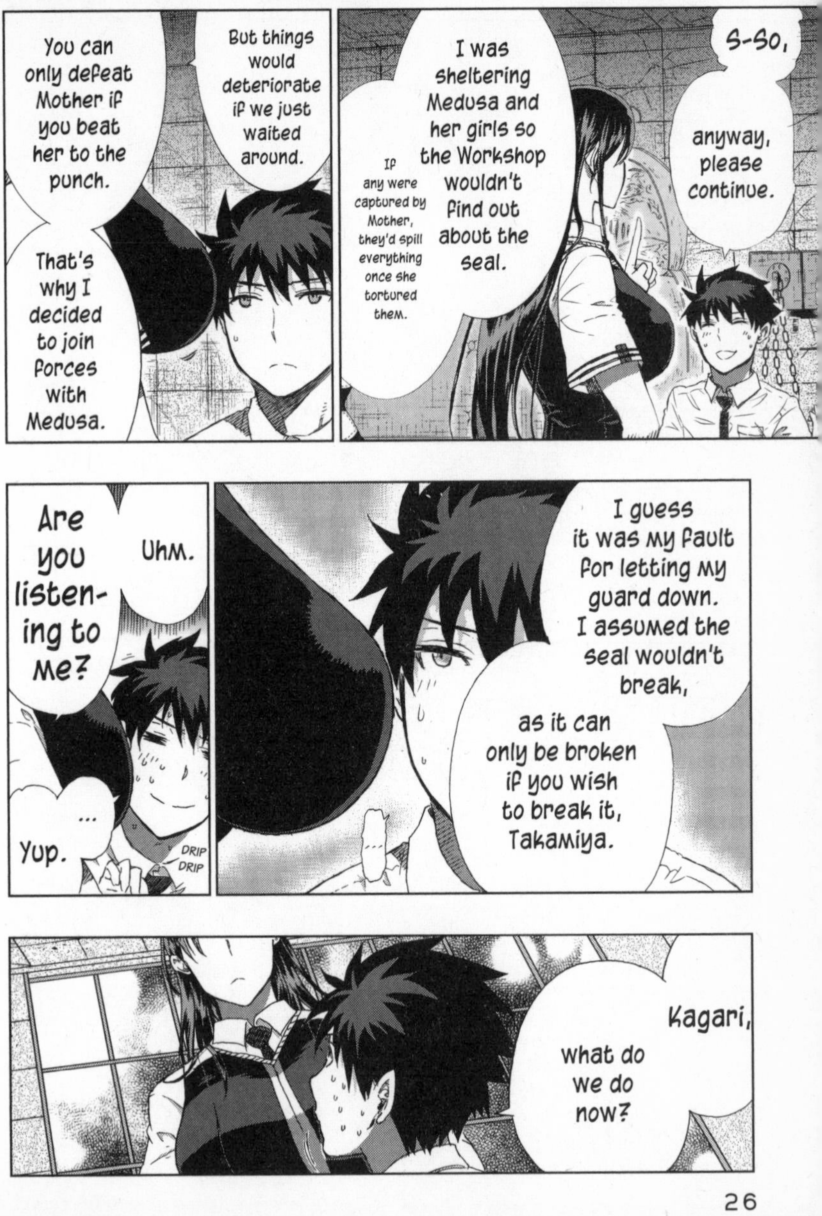
S-So,
anyway, please continue.
I was sheltering Medusa and her girls so the Workshop wouldn't find out about the seal.
If any were captured by Mother, they'd spill everything once she tortured them.
But things would deteriorate if we just waited around.
You can only defeat Mother if you beat her to the punch.
That's why I decided to join forces with Medusa.
I guess it was my fault for letting my guard down. I assumed the seal wouldn't break,
as it can only be broken if you wish to break it, Takamiya.
Uhm.
Are you listen-ing to me?
... Yup.
DRIP DRIP
Kagari,
what do we do now?

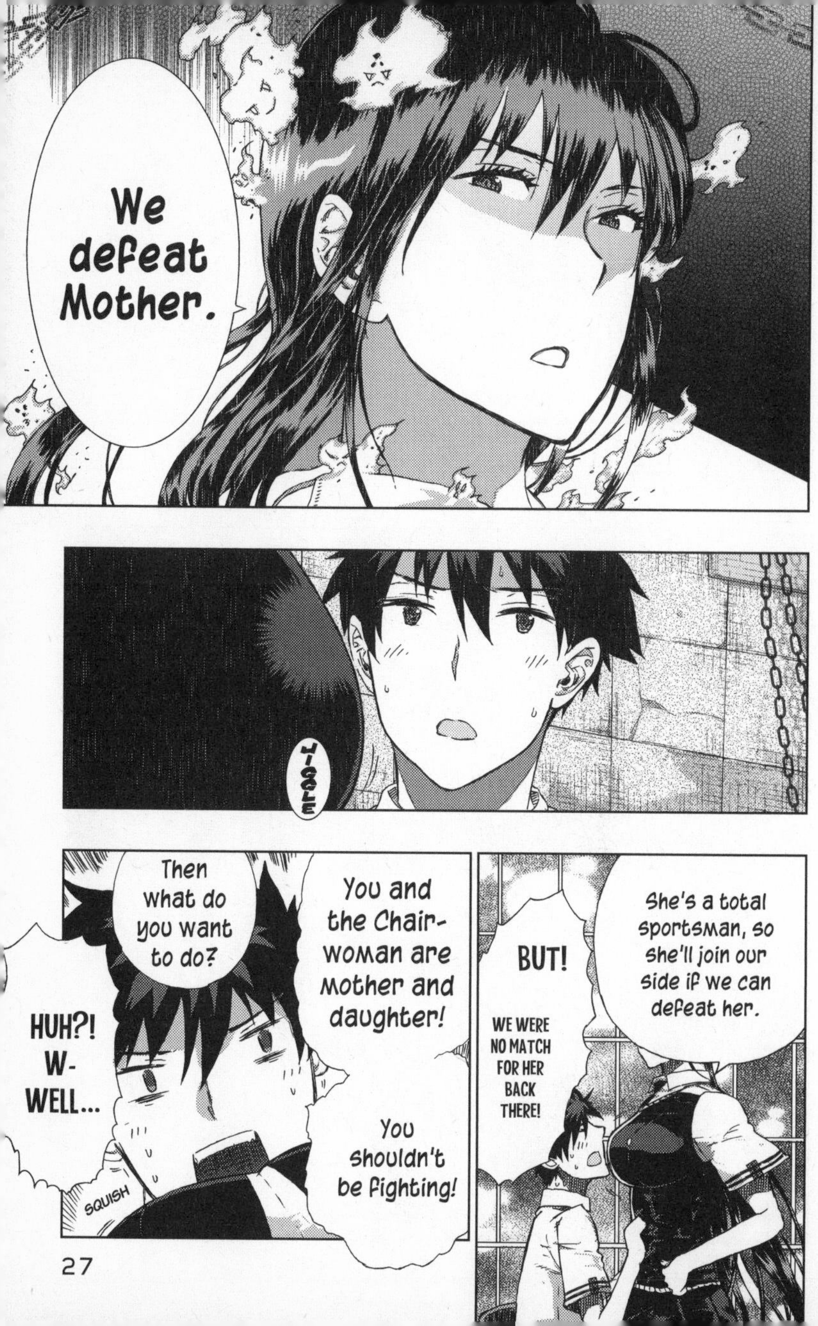
We defeat Mother.
JIGGLE
She's a total sportsman, so she'll join our side if we can defeat her.
BUT!
WE WERE NO MATCH FOR HER BACK THERE!
You and the Chair-woman are mother and daughter!
Then what do you want to do?
You shouldn't be fighting!
HUH?! W-WELL...
SQUISH

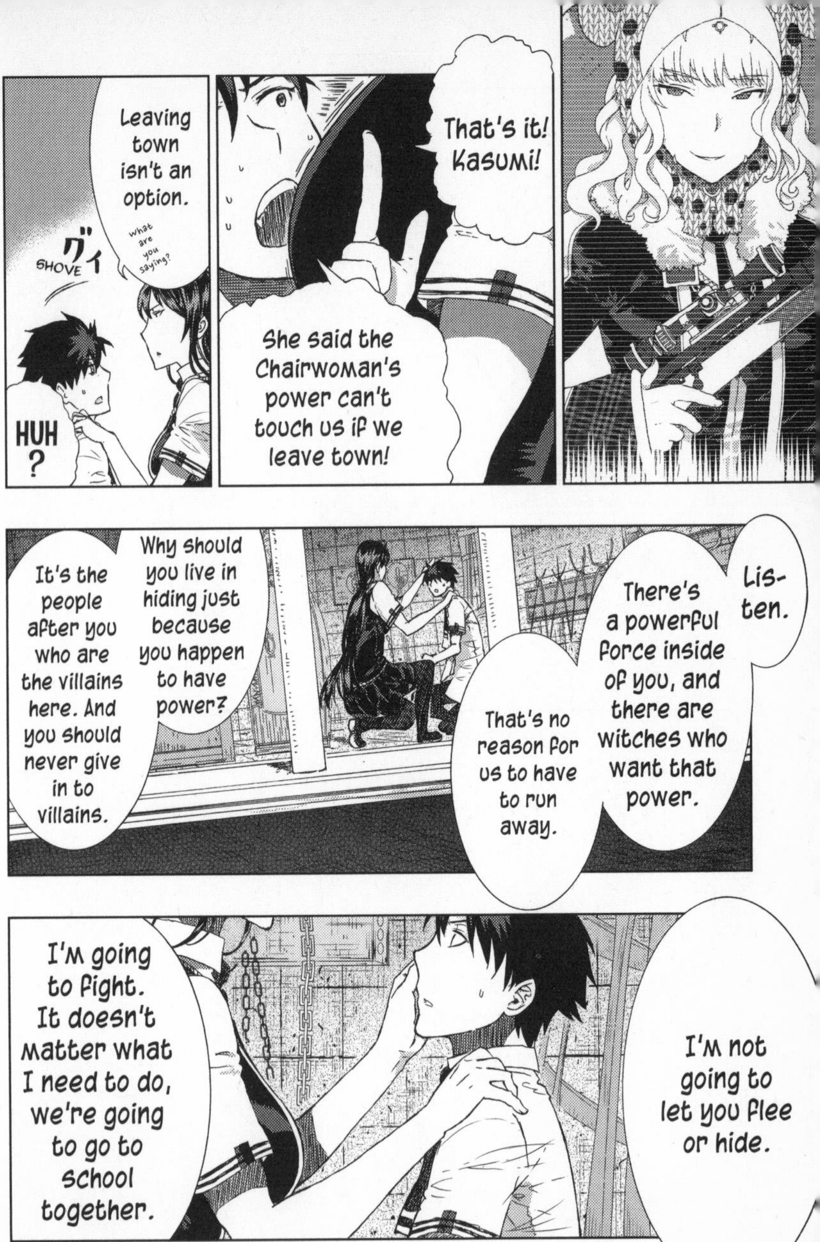
That's it! Kasumi!
She said the Chairwoman's power can't touch us if we leave town!
Leaving town isn't an option.
What are you saying?
グイ SHOVE
HUH?
Lis- ten.
There's a powerful force inside of you, and there are witches who want that power.
That's no reason for us to have to run away.
Why should you live in hiding just because you happen to have power?
It's the people after you who are the villains here. And you should never give in to villains.
I'm not going to let you flee or hide.
I'm going to fight. It doesn't matter what I need to do, we're going to go to school together.

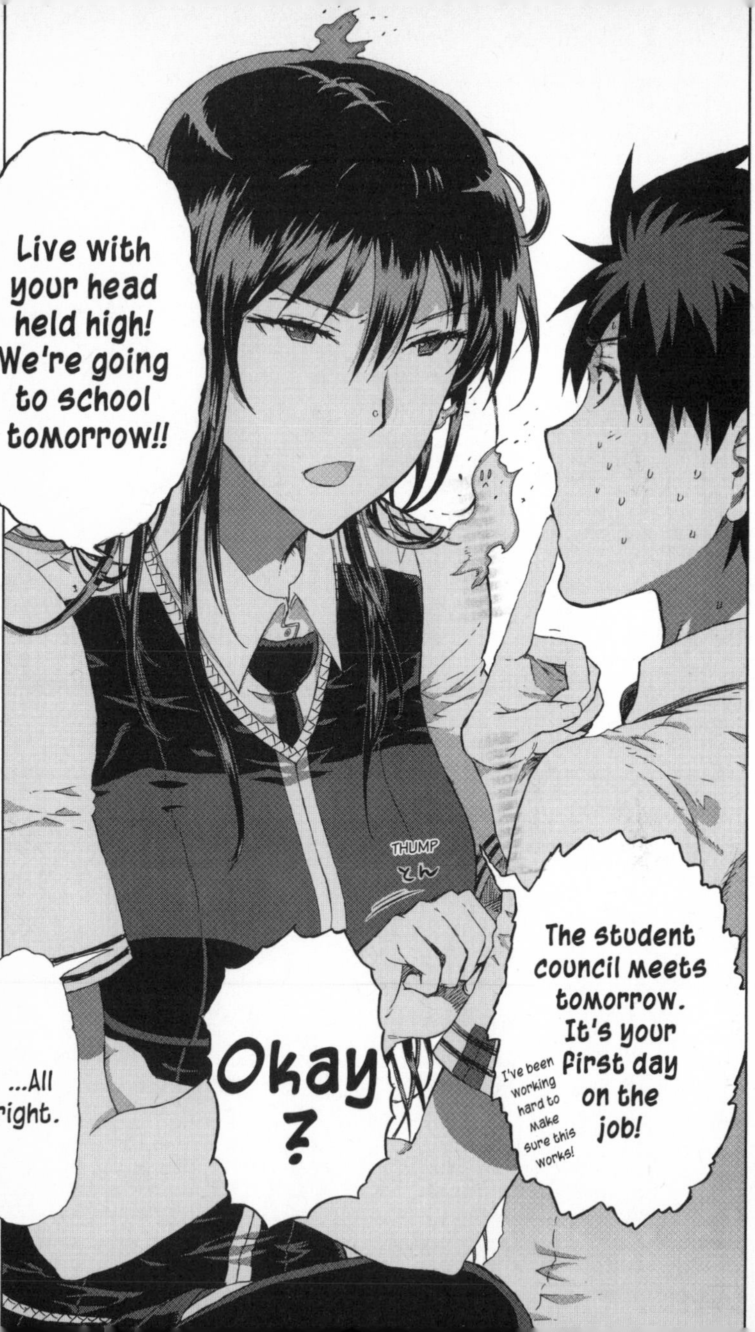
Live with your head held high! We're going to school tomorrow!!
THUMP
とん
The student council meets tomorrow. It's your first day on the job!
I've been working hard to make sure this works!
Okay?
...All right.

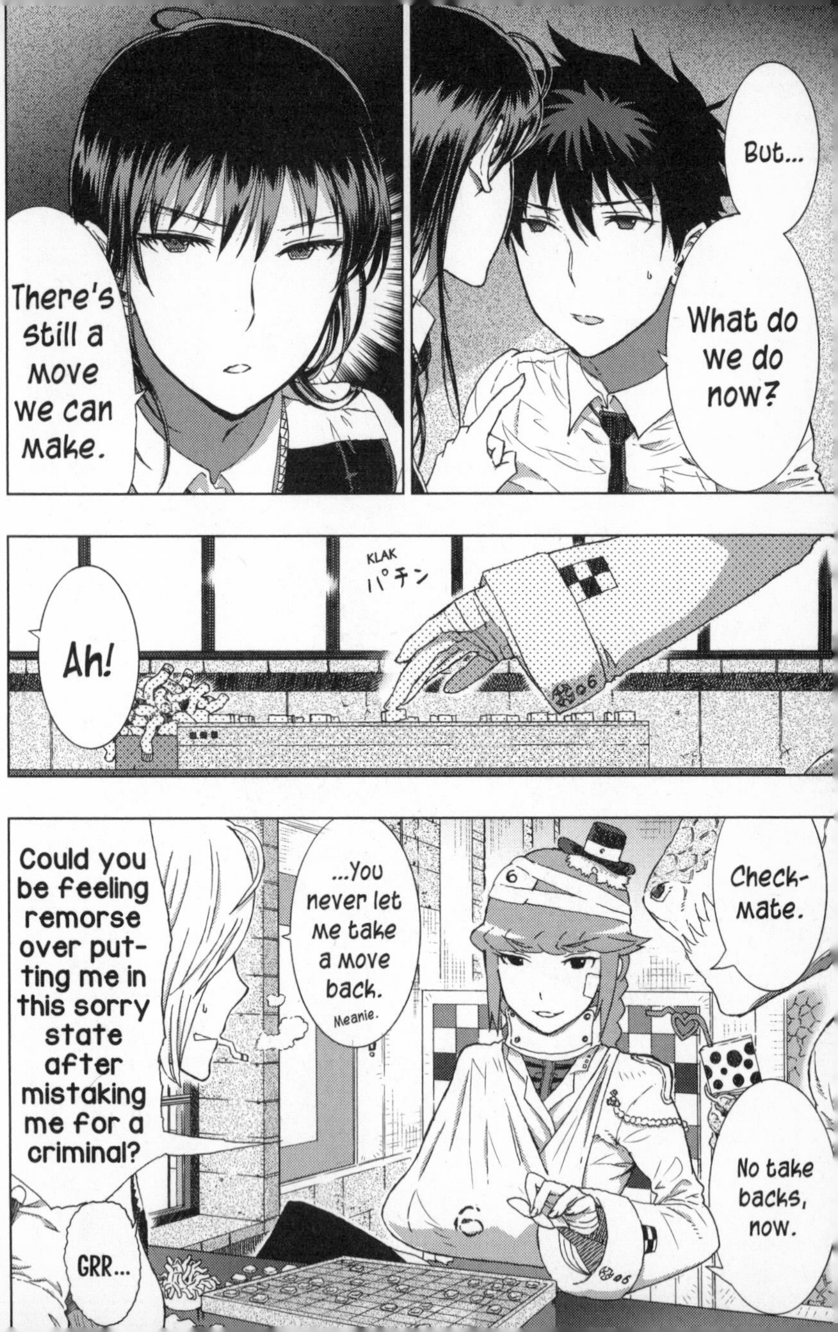
But...
What do we do now?
There's still a move we can make.
KLAK
パチン
Ah!
Check-mate.
...You never let me take a move back.
Meanie.
Could you be feeling remorse over putting me in this sorry state after mistaking me for a criminal?
No take backs, now.
GRR...

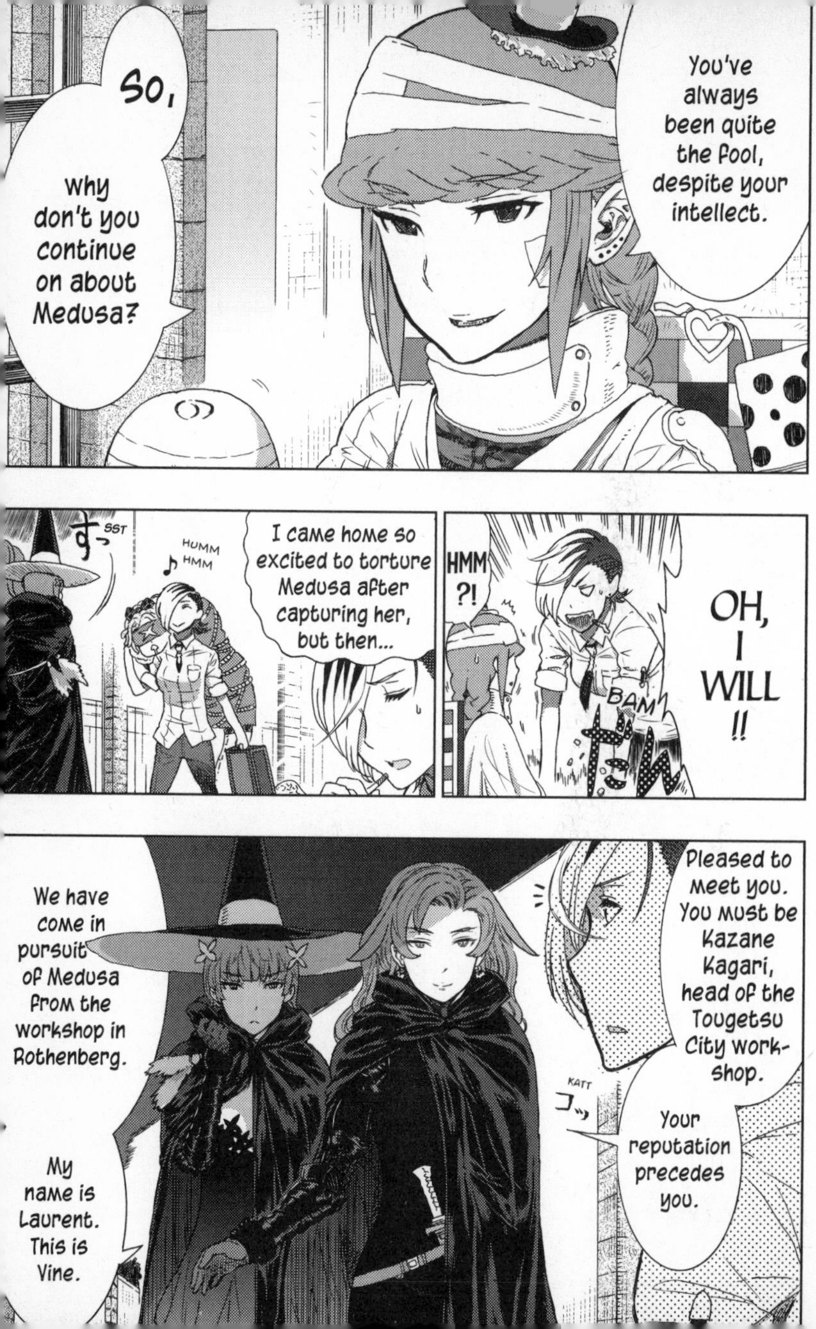
You've always been quite the fool, despite your intellect.
So, why don't you continue on about Medusa?
HMM ?!
OH, I WILL !!
BAM
I came home so excited to torture Medusa after capturing her, but then...
HUMM HMM
SST
Pleased to meet you. You must be Kazane Kagari, head of the Tougetsu City workshop.
KATT
Your reputation precedes you.
We have come in pursuit of Medusa from the workshop in Rothenberg.
My name is Laurent. This is Vine.

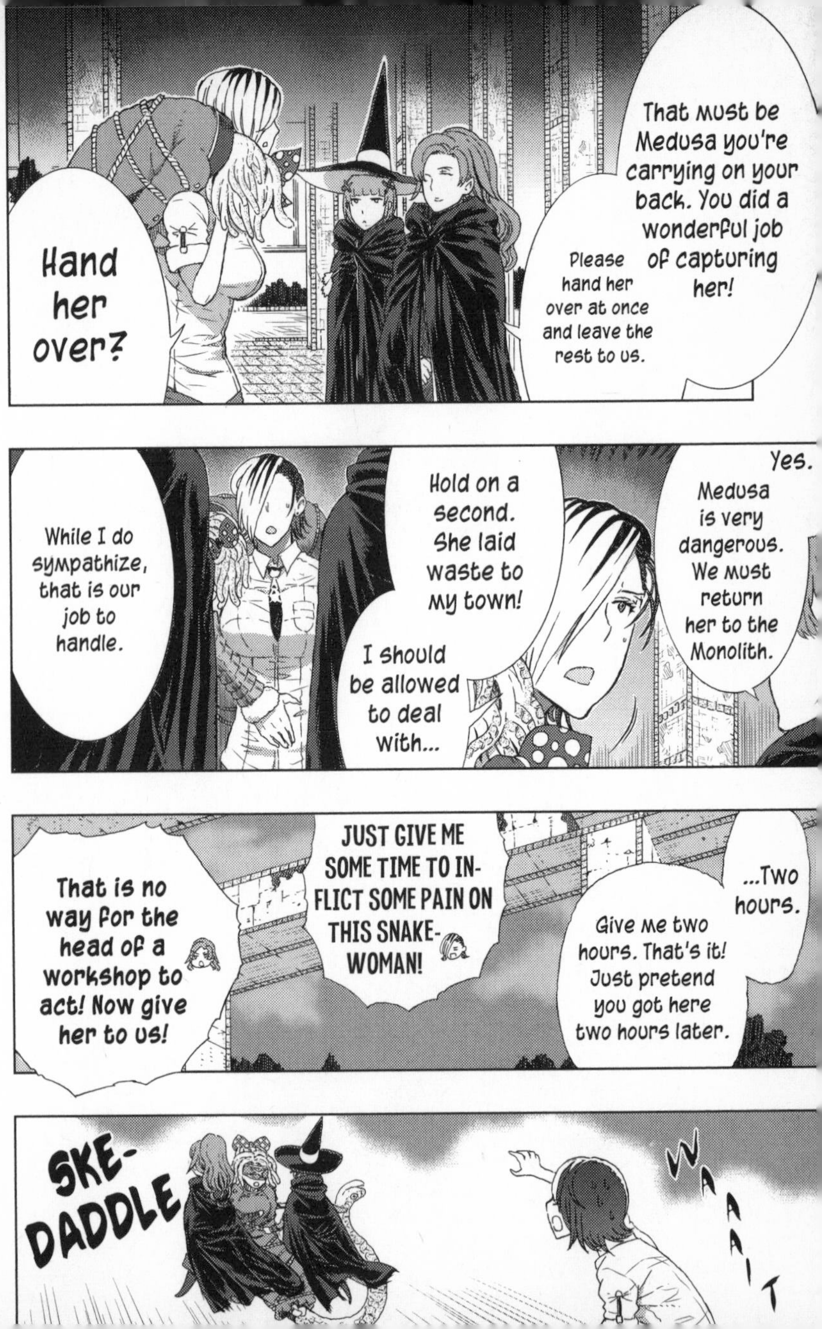
That must be Medusa you're carrying on your back. You did a wonderful job of capturing her!
Please hand her over at once and leave the rest to us.
Hand her over?
Yes. Medusa is very dangerous. We must return her to the Monolith.
Hold on a second. She laid waste to my town!
I should be allowed to deal with...
While I do sympathize, that is our job to handle.
...Two hours.
Give me two hours. That's it! Just pretend you got here two hours later.
JUST GIVE ME SOME TIME TO IN-FLICT SOME PAIN ON THIS SNAKE-WOMAN!
That is no way for the head of a workshop to act! Now give her to us!
WAAAIT
SKE-DADDLE

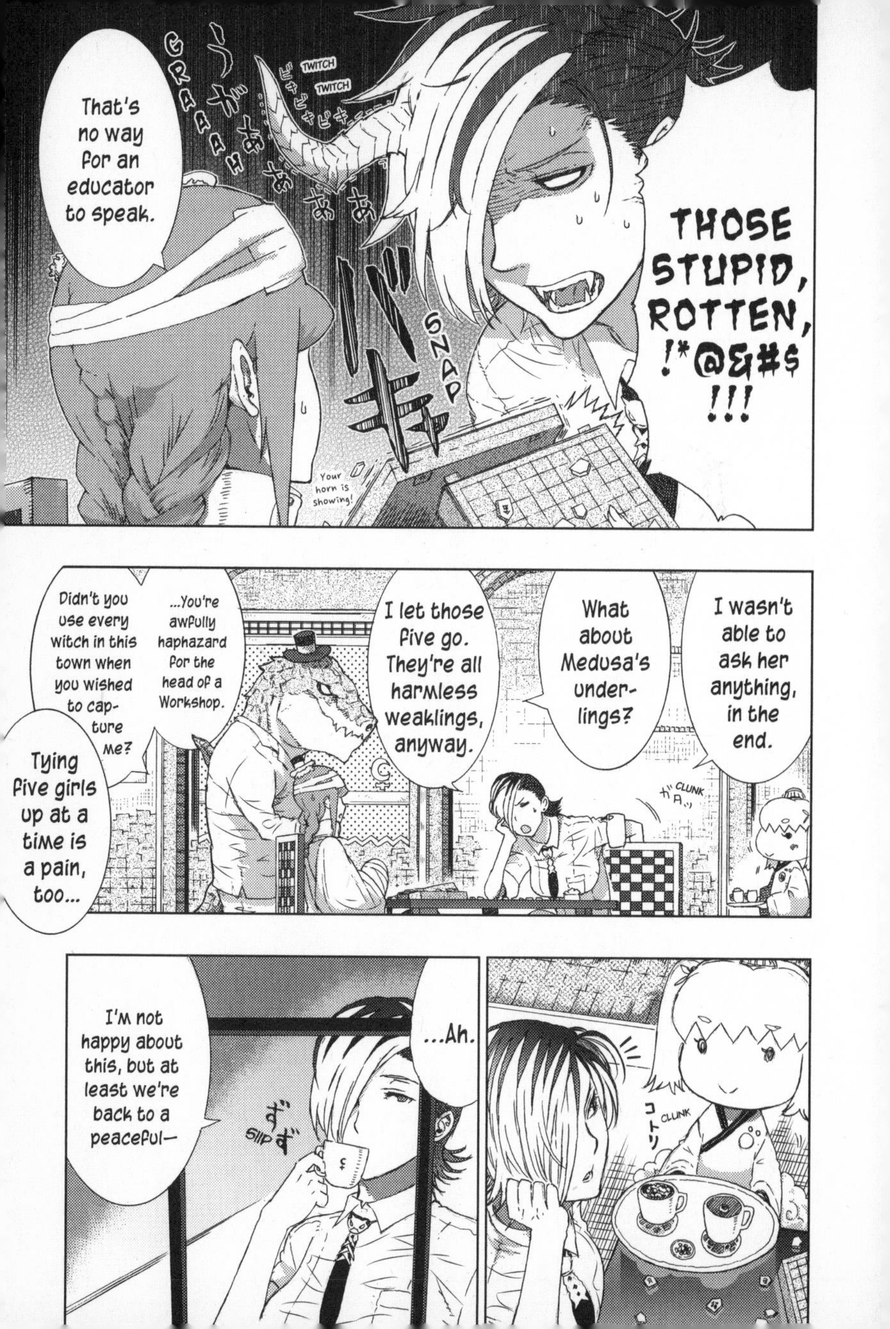
THOSE STUPID, ROTTEN, !*@&#$!!!
TWITCH TWITCH
GRAAAH
SNAP
That's no way for an educator to speak.
Your horn is showing!
I wasn't able to ask her anything, in the end.
CLUNK
What about Medusa's underlings?
I let those five go. They're all harmless weaklings, anyway.
...You're awfully haphazard for the head of a Workshop.
Didn't you use every witch in this town when you wished to capture me?
Tying five girls up at a time is a pain, too...
CLUNK
...Ah.
SLIP
I'm not happy about this, but at least we're back to a peaceful—

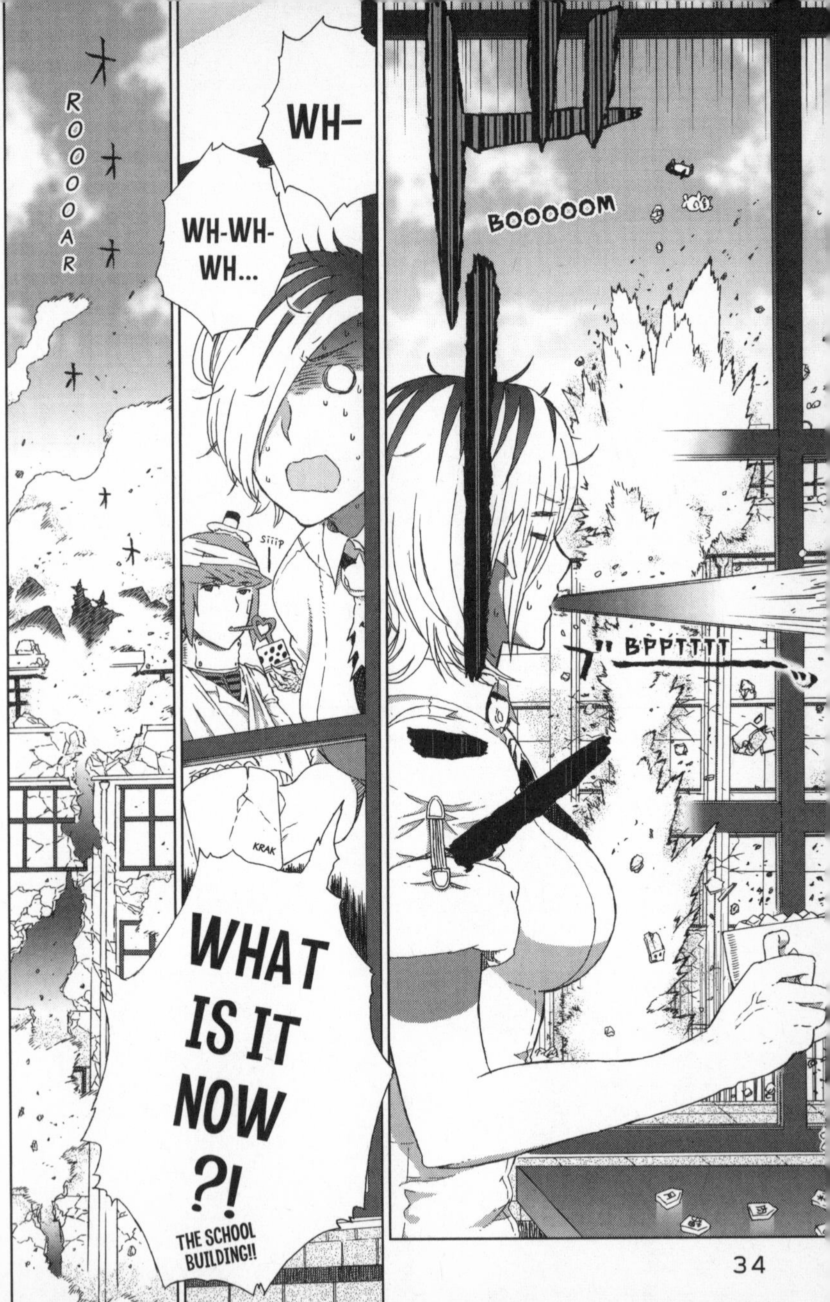
BOOOOOM
BPPTTTT
WH—
WH-WH-WH...
siiip
KRAK
WHAT IS IT NOW?!
THE SCHOOL BUILDING!!
ROOOOOAR

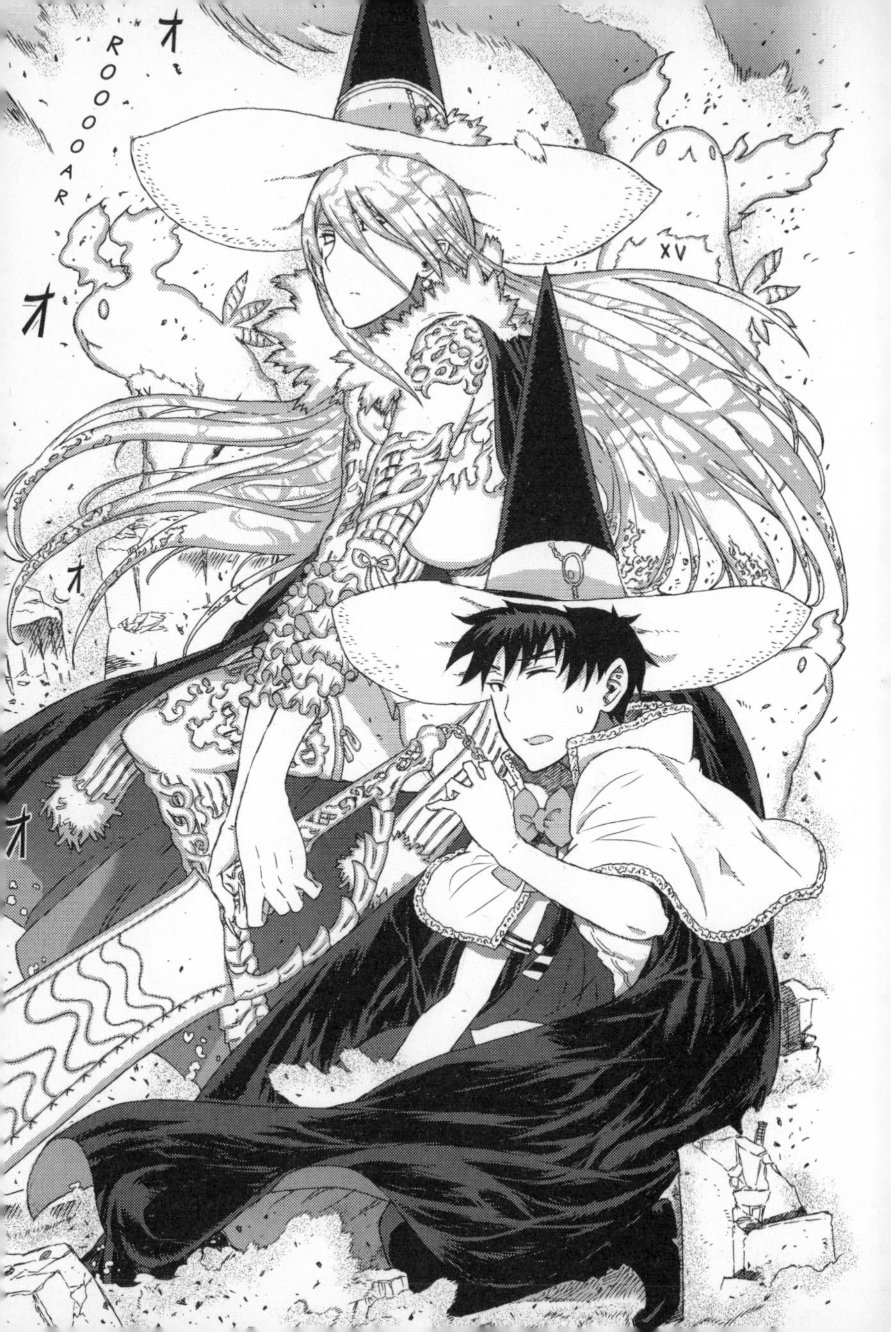
ROOOOAR
オ
オ
オ
オ
XV

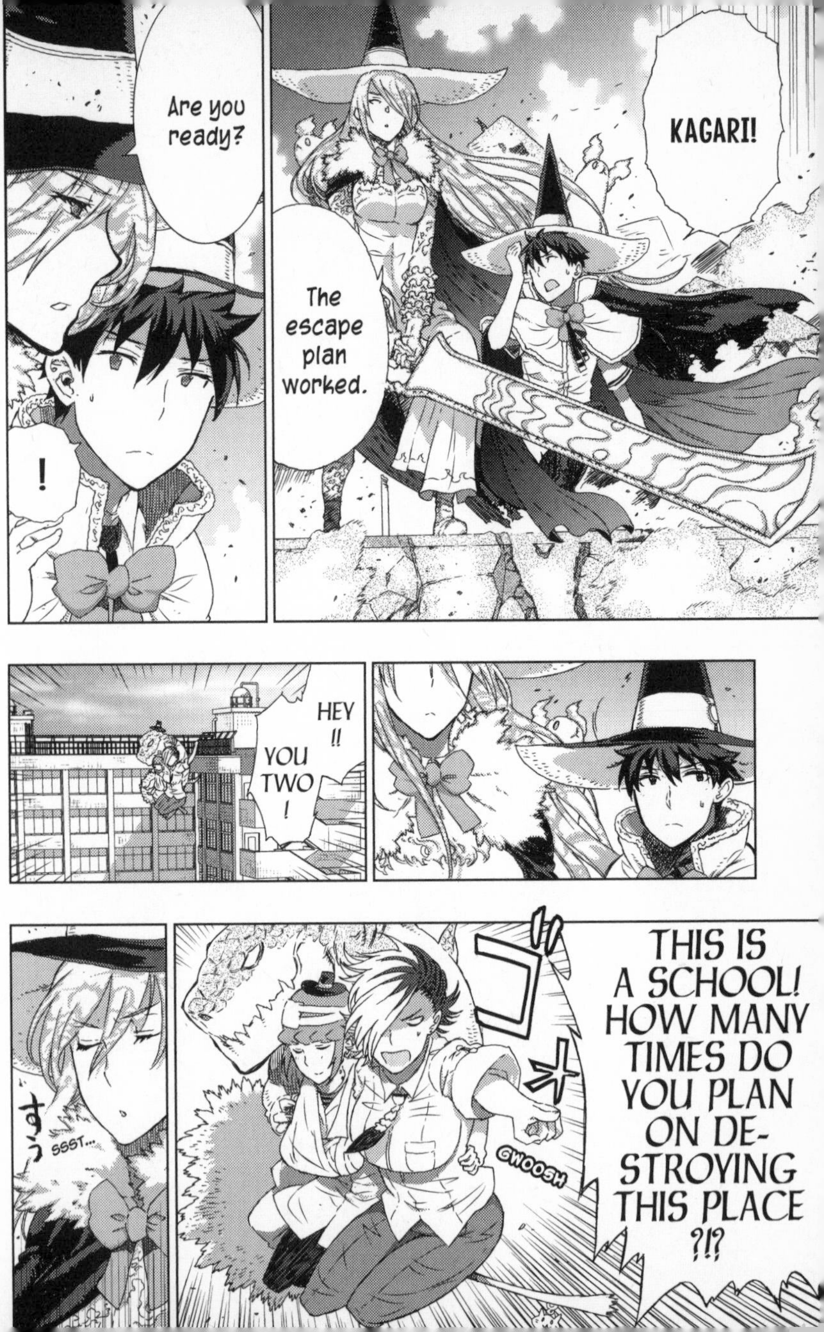
KAGARI!
The escape plan worked.
Are you ready?
!
HEY !!
YOU TWO !
THIS IS A SCHOOL! HOW MANY TIMES DO YOU PLAN ON DE-STROYING THIS PLACE ?!?
ゴオ
GWOOSH
すぅ
SSST...

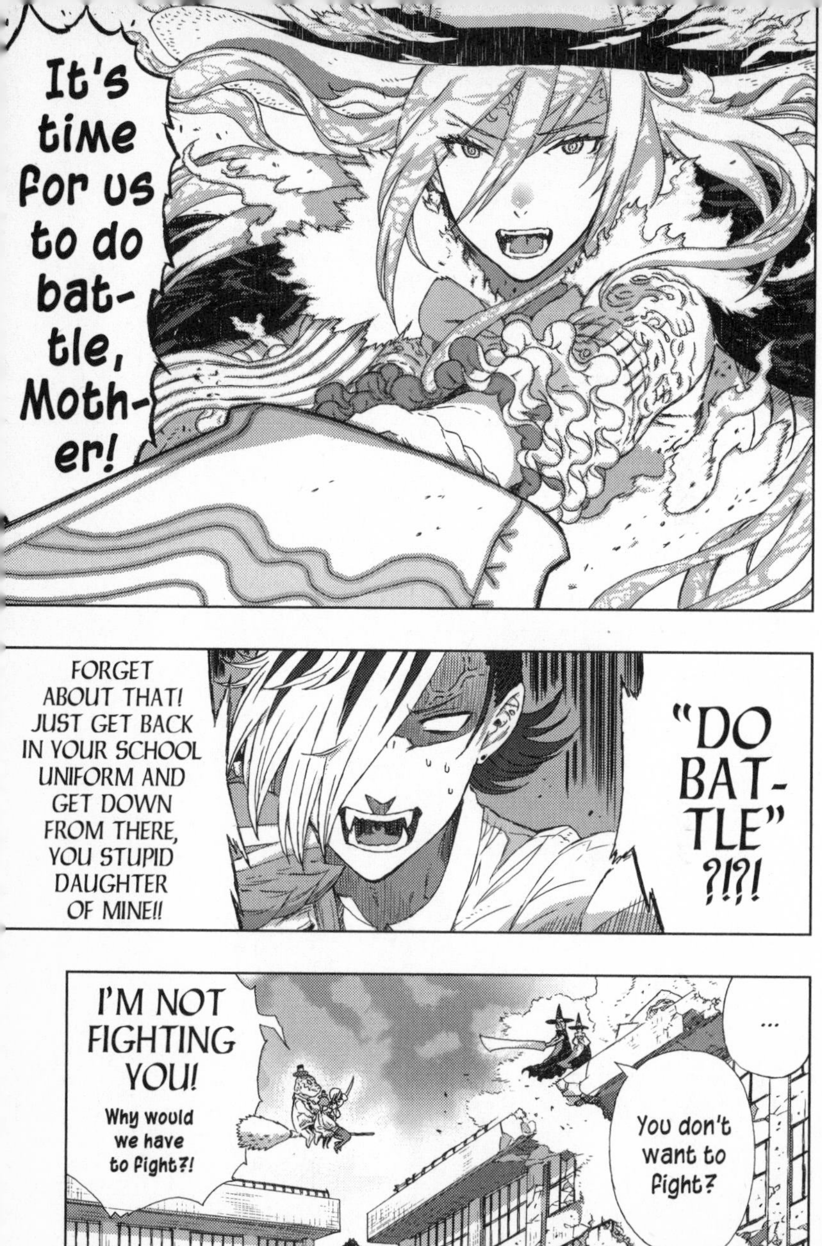
It's time for us to do bat-tle, Moth-er!
"DO BAT-TLE" ?!?!
FORGET ABOUT THAT! JUST GET BACK IN YOUR SCHOOL UNIFORM AND GET DOWN FROM THERE, YOU STUPID DAUGHTER OF MINE!!
...
I'M NOT FIGHTING YOU!
Why would we have to fight?!
You don't want to fight?

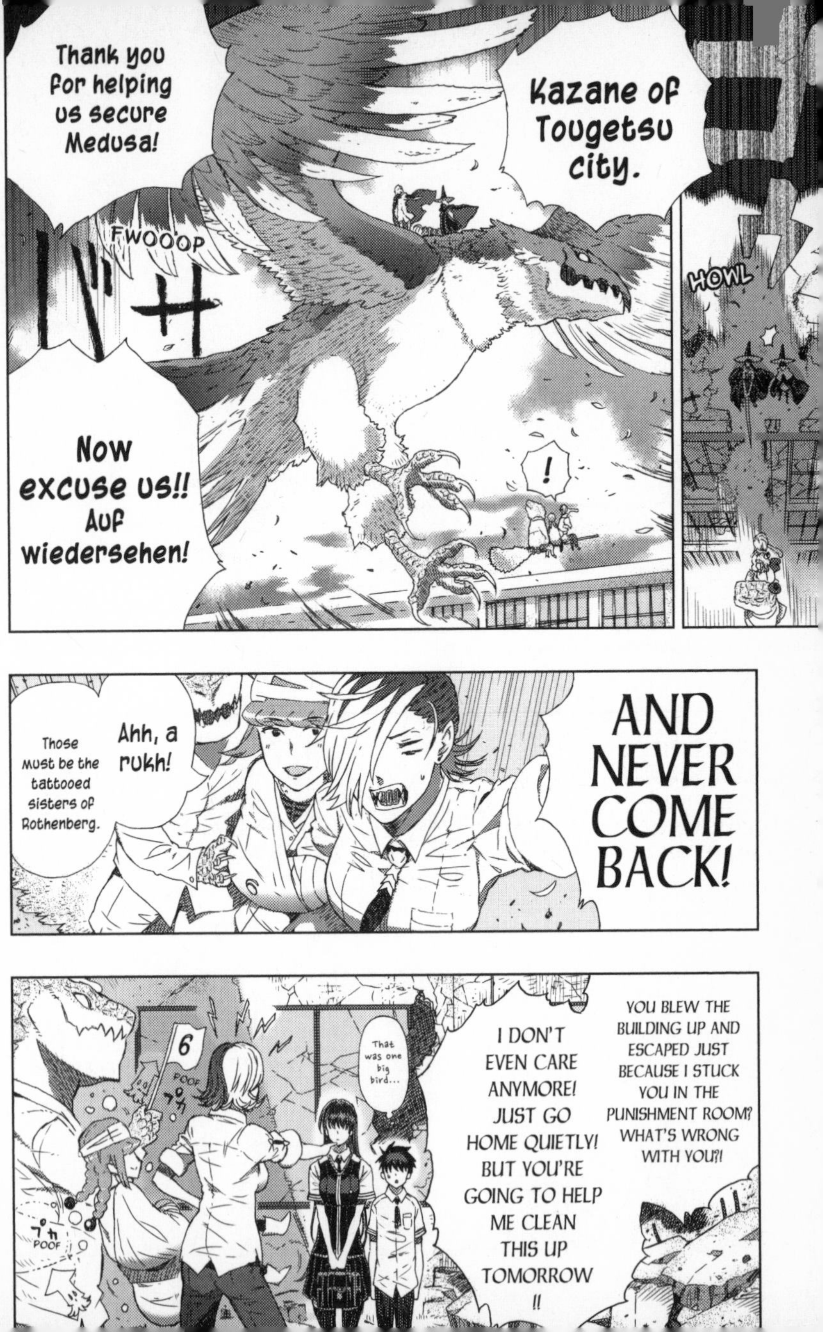
HOWL
Kazane of Tougetsu city.
Thank you for helping us secure Medusa!
FWOOOP
!
Now excuse us!! Auf wiedersehen!
AND NEVER COME BACK!
Ahh, a rukh!
Those must be the tattooed sisters of Rothenberg.
YOU BLEW THE BUILDING UP AND ESCAPED JUST BECAUSE I STUCK YOU IN THE PUNISHMENT ROOM? WHAT'S WRONG WITH YOU?!
I DON'T EVEN CARE ANYMORE! JUST GO HOME QUIETLY! BUT YOU'RE GOING TO HELP ME CLEAN THIS UP TOMORROW!!
That was one big bird...
6
POOF
POOF

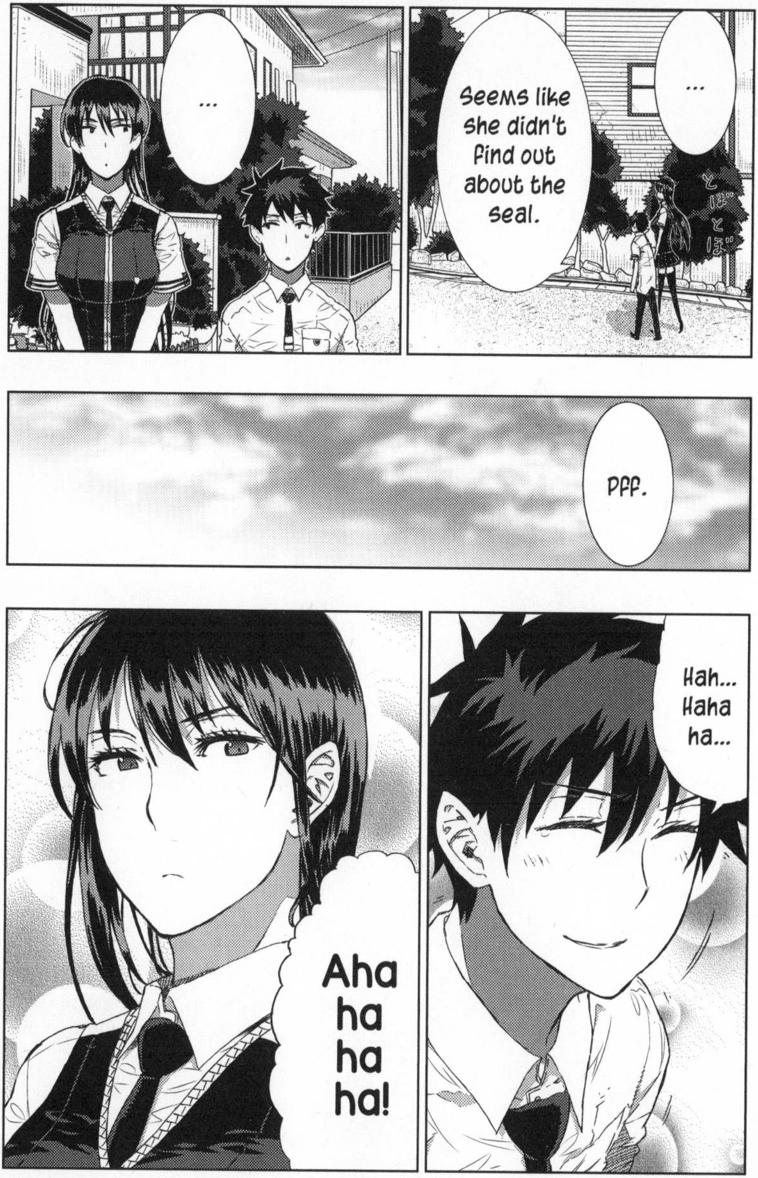
...
Seems like she didn't find out about the seal.
とぼとぼ
...
Pff.
Hah... Haha ha...
Aha ha ha ha!

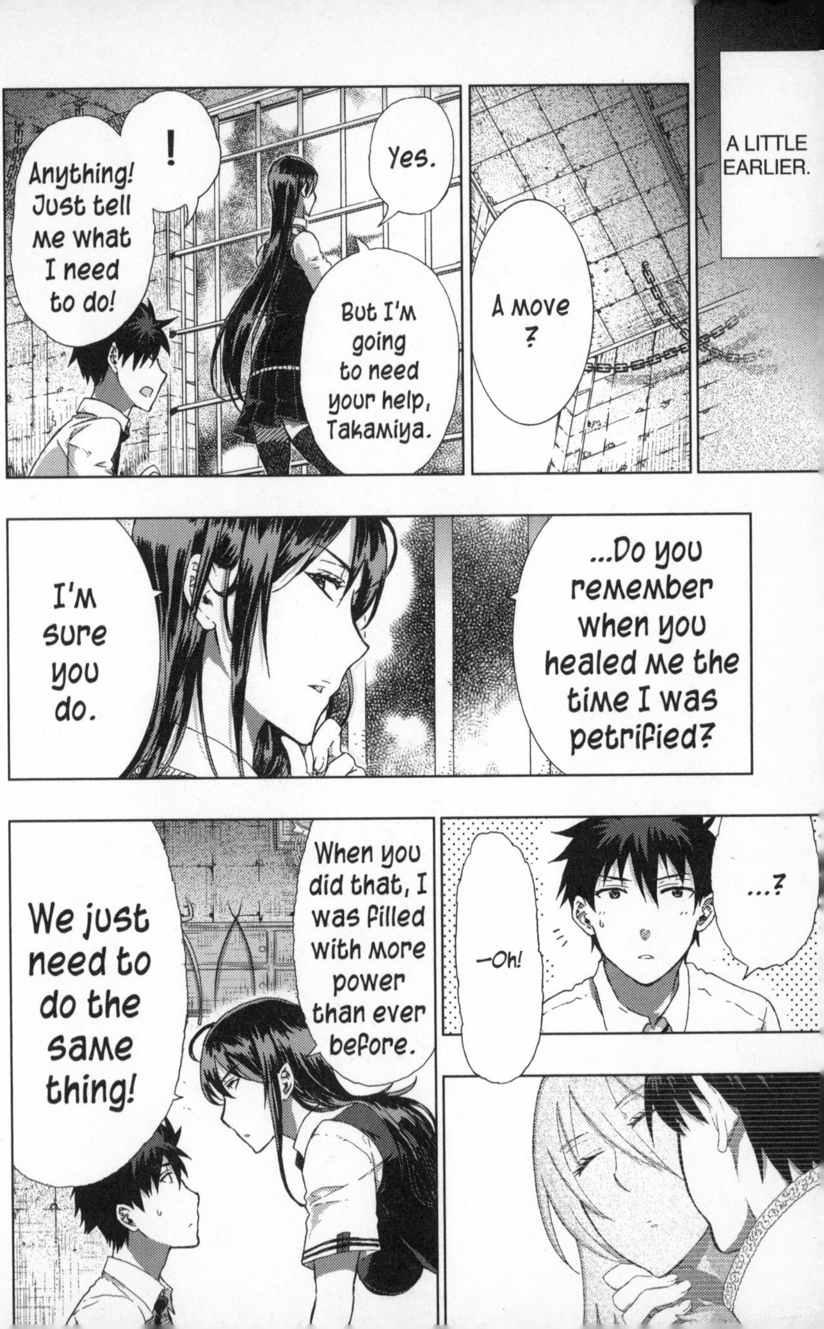

A LITTLE EARLIER.
A move?
Yes.
But I'm going to need your help, Takamiya.
!
Anything! Just tell me what I need to do!
...Do you remember when you healed me the time I was petrified?
I'm sure you do.
...?
—Oh!
When you did that, I was filled with more power than ever before.
We just need to do the same thing!

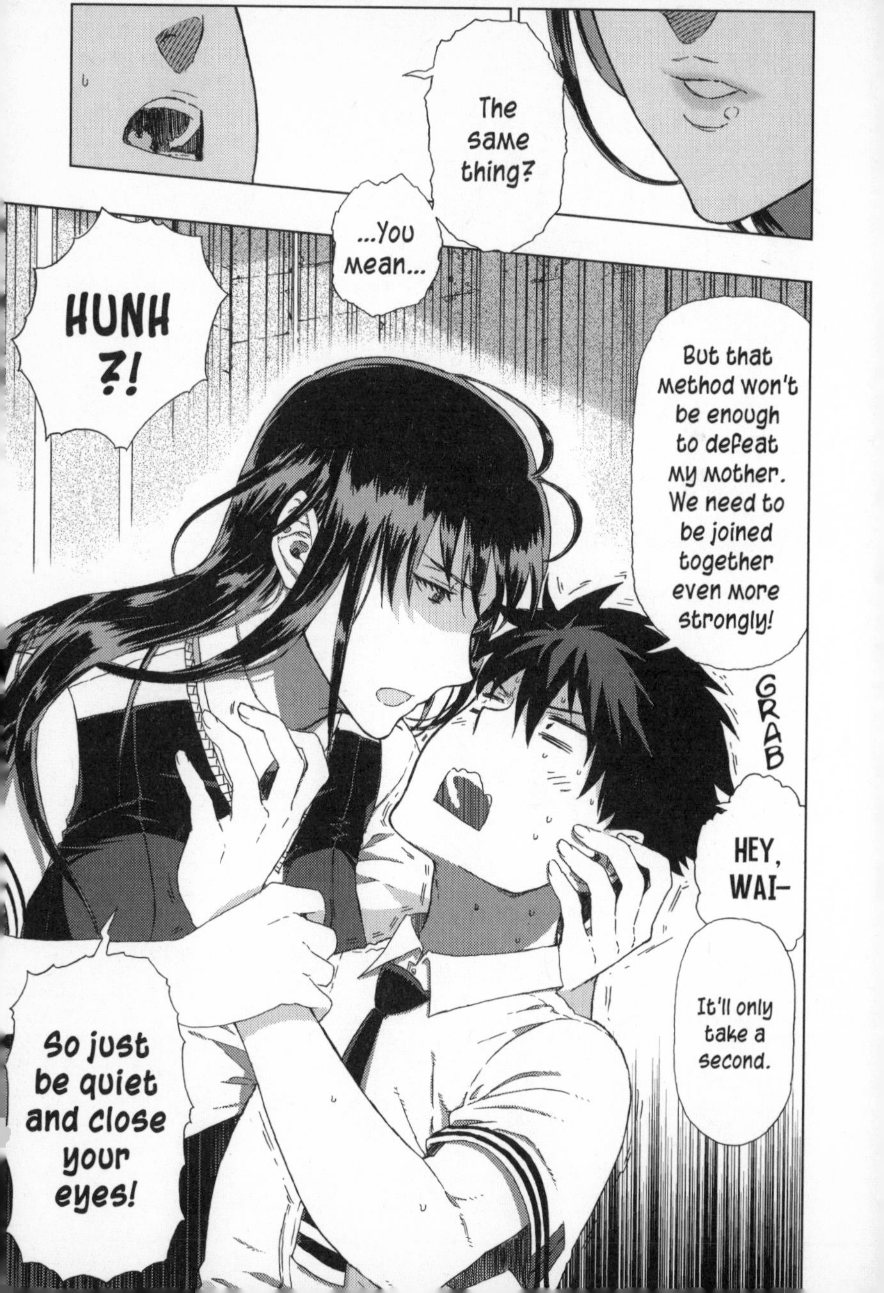
The same thing?
...You mean...
But that method won't be enough to defeat my mother. We need to be joined together even more strongly!
HUNH ?!
GRAB
HEY, WAI-
It'll only take a second.
So just be quiet and close your eyes!

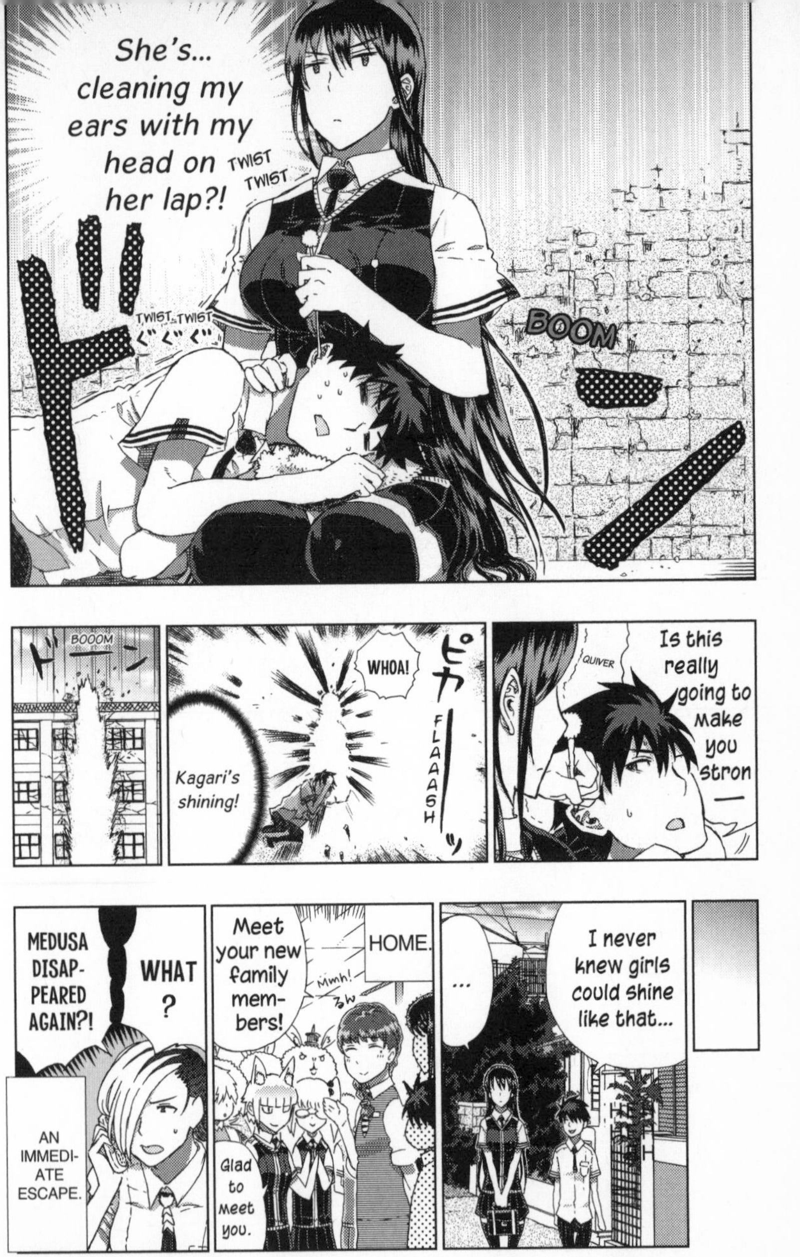
She's... cleaning my ears with my head on her lap?!
TWIST TWIST
TWIST TWIST
ぐ゛ぐ゛ぐ゛
BOOM
QUIVER
Is this really going to make you stron—
ピカ
FLAAAASH
ッ
WHOA!
Kagari's shining!
BOOOM
ドーン
I never knew girls could shine like that...
...
HOME.
Meet your new family members!
Mmh!
るん
Glad to meet you.
WHAT?
MEDUSA DISAPPEARED AGAIN?!
AN IMMEDIATE ESCAPE.

CHAPTER 13: *END*

How Girls Work

Try shining for me, Kasumi.

Huh?

Witchcraft Works

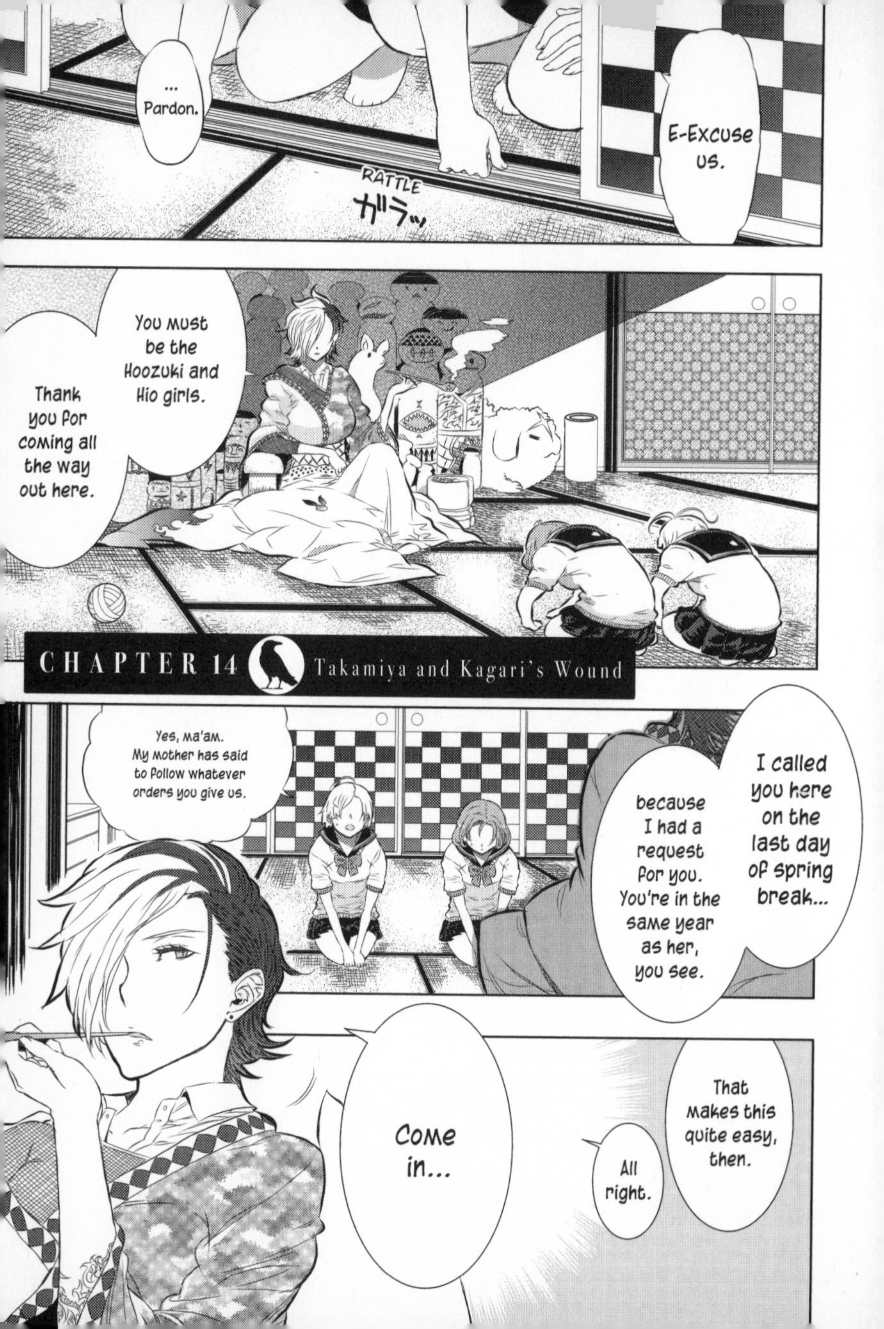
E-Excuse us.
RATTLE
ガラッ
... Pardon.
You must be the Hoozuki and Hio girls.
Thank you for coming all the way out here.
CHAPTER 14 Takamiya and Kagari's Wound
I called you here on the last day of spring break...
because I had a request for you. You're in the same year as her, you see.
Yes, ma'am. My mother has said to follow whatever orders you give us.
That makes this quite easy, then.
All right.
Come in...

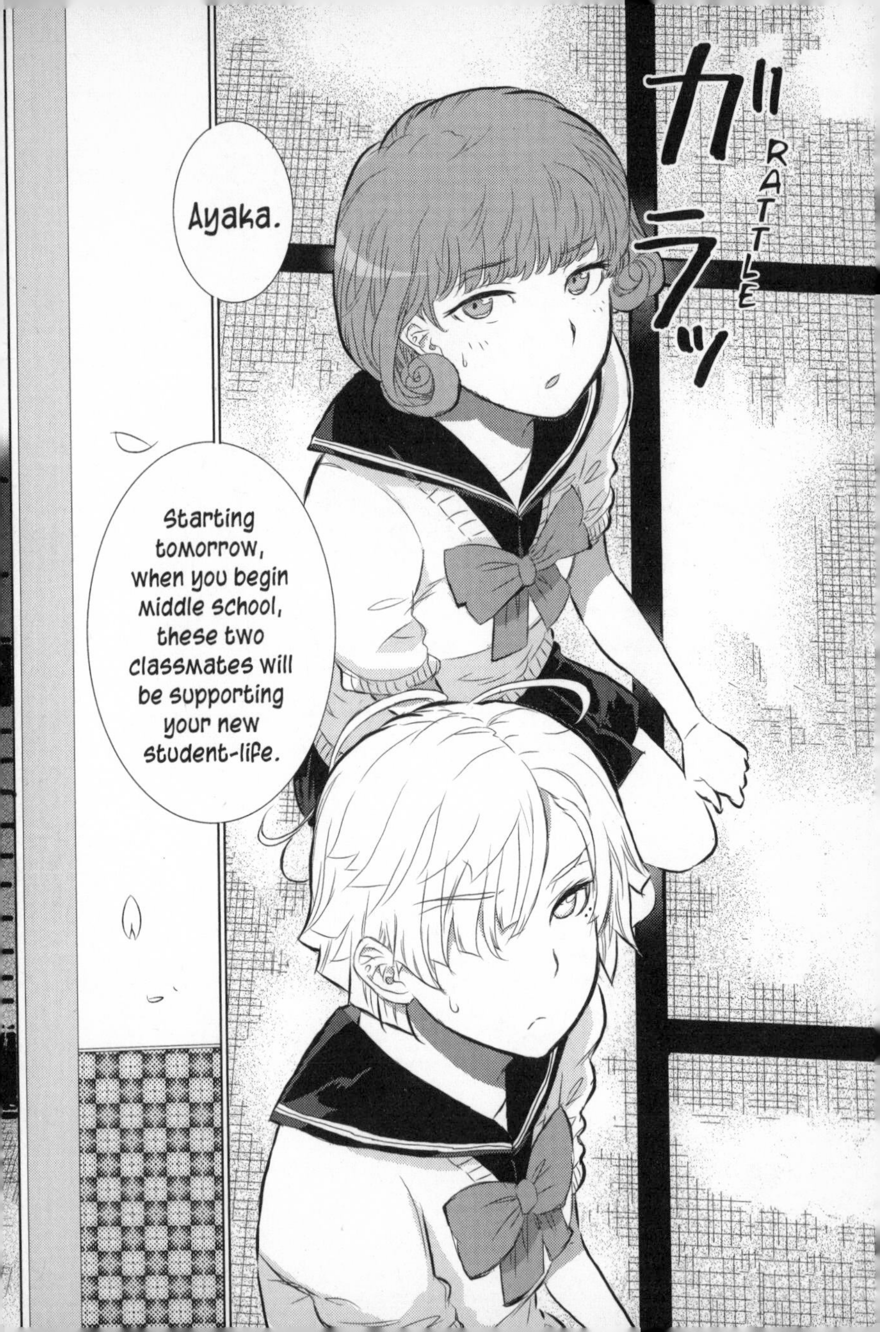
ガラッ
RATTLE
Ayaka.
Starting tomorrow, when you begin middle school, these two classmates will be supporting your new student-life.

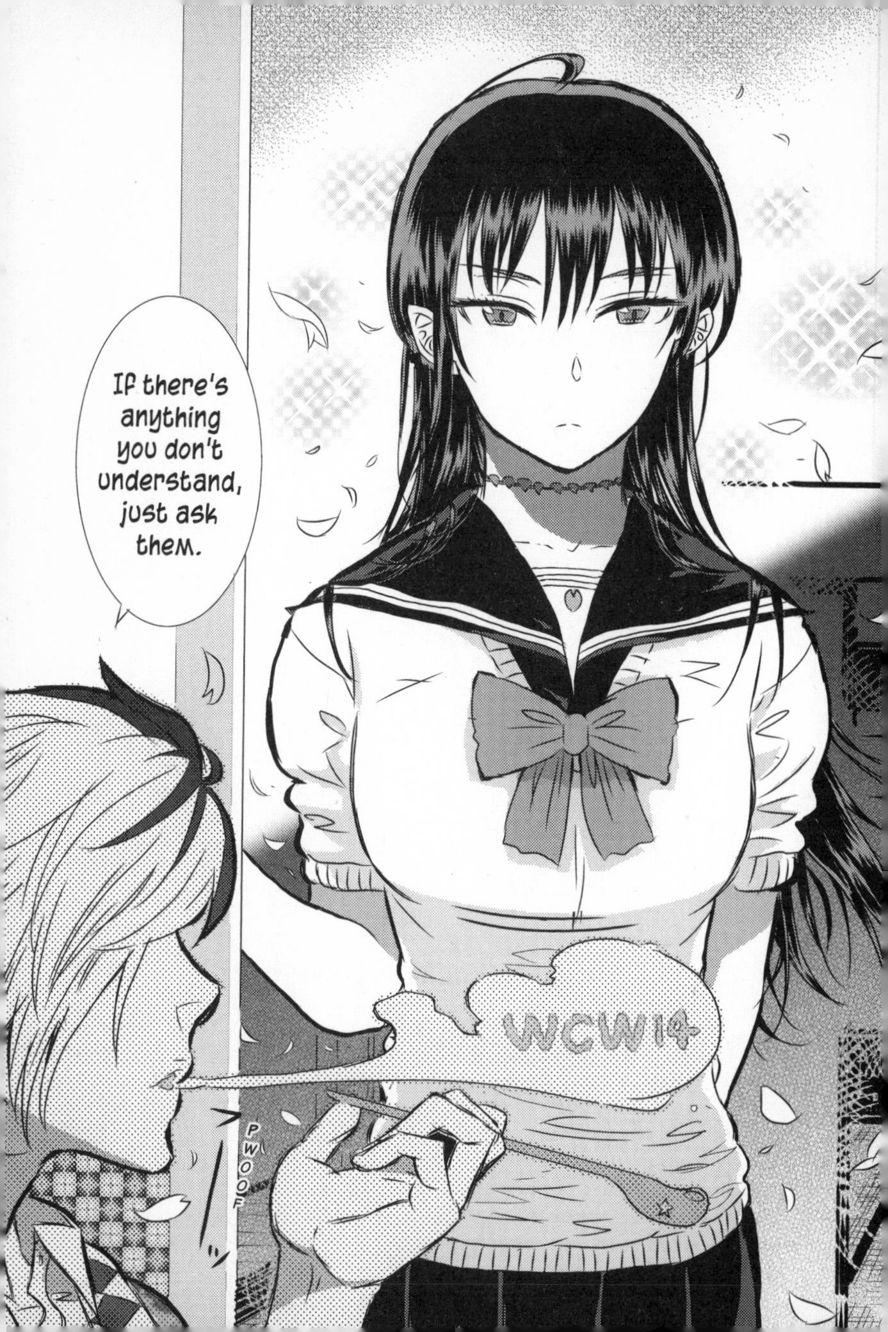
If there's anything you don't understand, just ask them.
WCW14
PWOOF

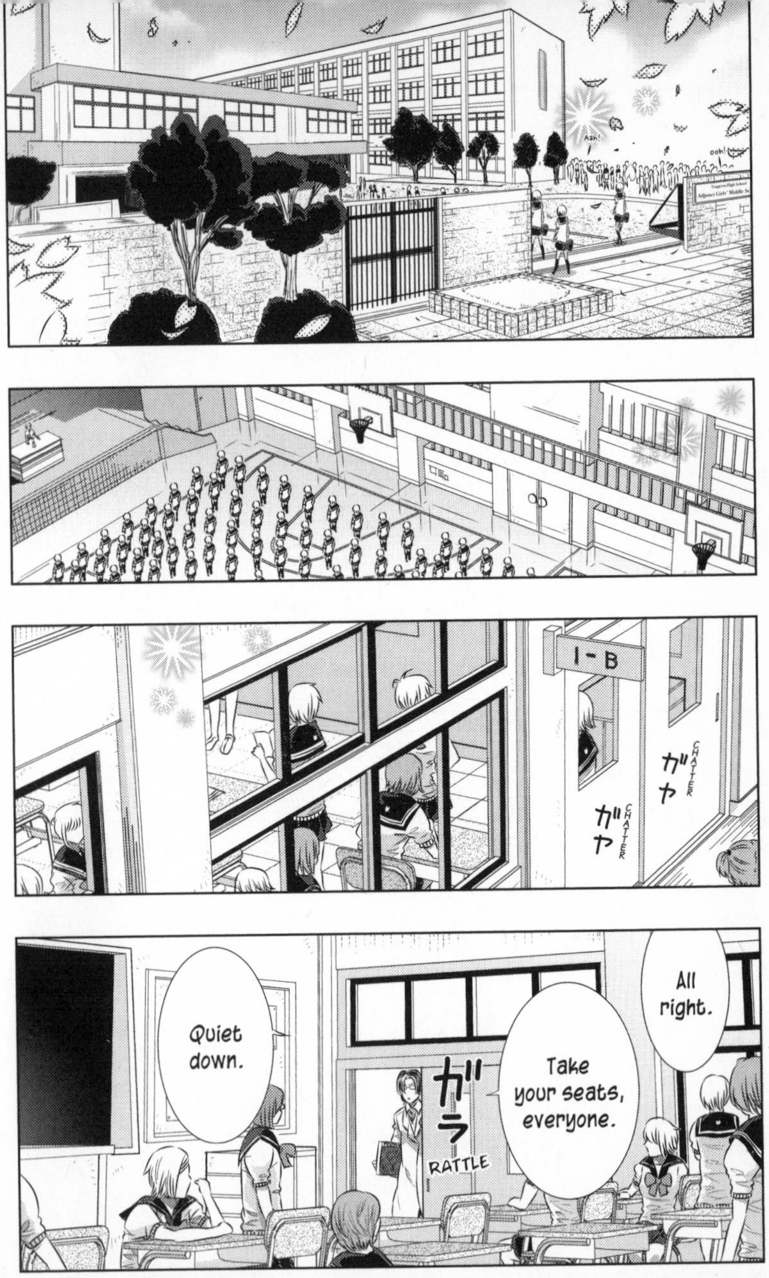
ooh!
Aah!
ガヤ
CHATTER
ガヤ
CHATTER
All right.
Take your seats, everyone.
ガラ
RATTLE
Quiet down.

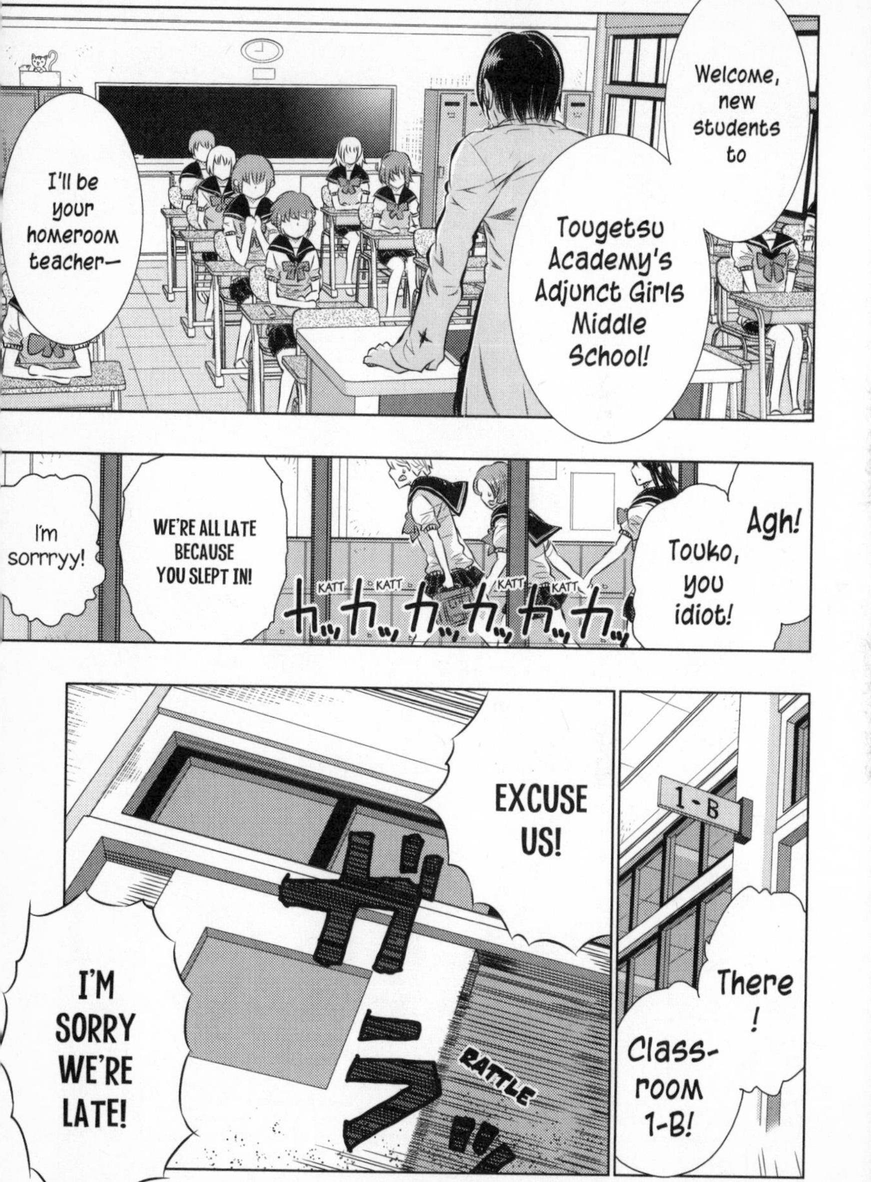
Welcome, new students to
Tougetsu Academy's Adjunct Girls Middle School!
I'll be your homeroom teacher—
Agh! Touko, you idiot!
KATT KATT KATT KATT
WE'RE ALL LATE BECAUSE YOU SLEPT IN!
I'm sorrryy!
1-B
There! Classroom 1-B!
EXCUSE US!
RATTLE
I'M SORRY WE'RE LATE!

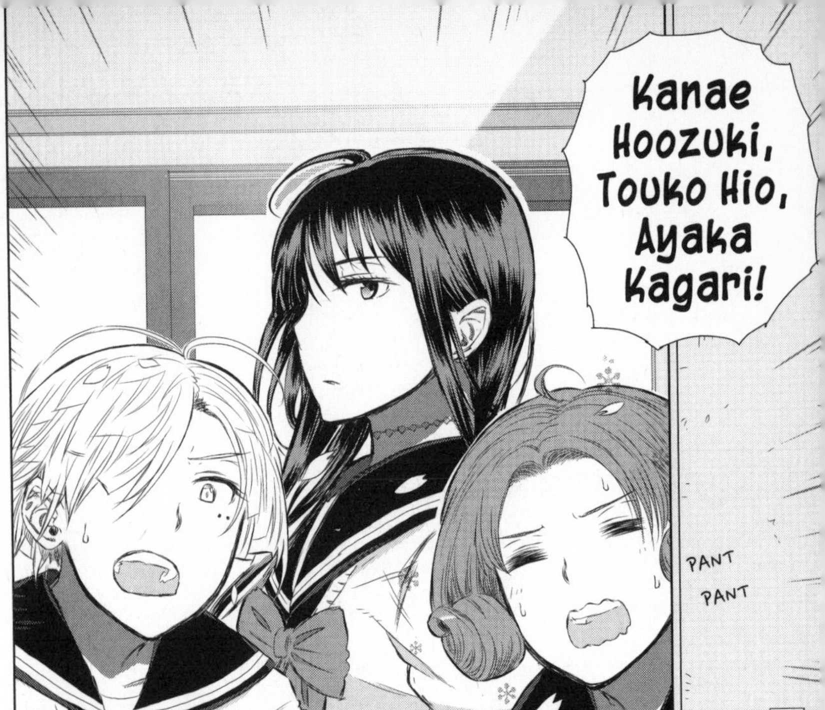
Kanae Hoozuki, Touko Hio, Ayaka Kagari!
PANT PANT
All pres-ent!
ばーん!
BAM!
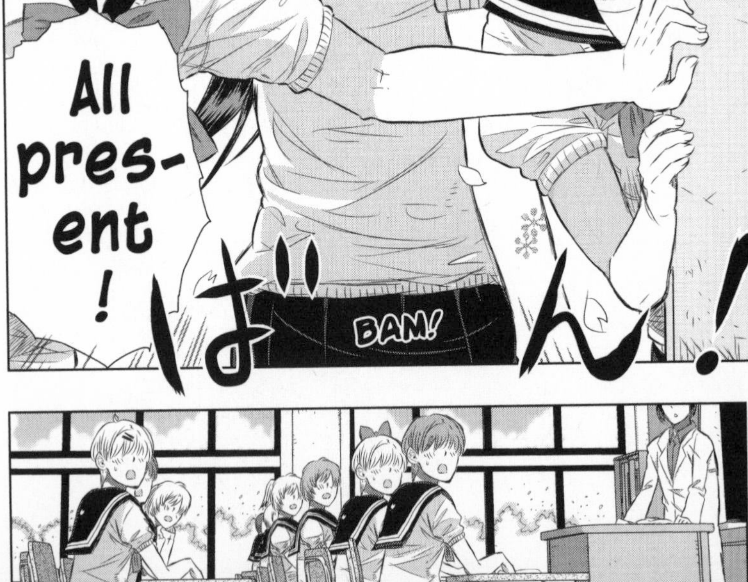

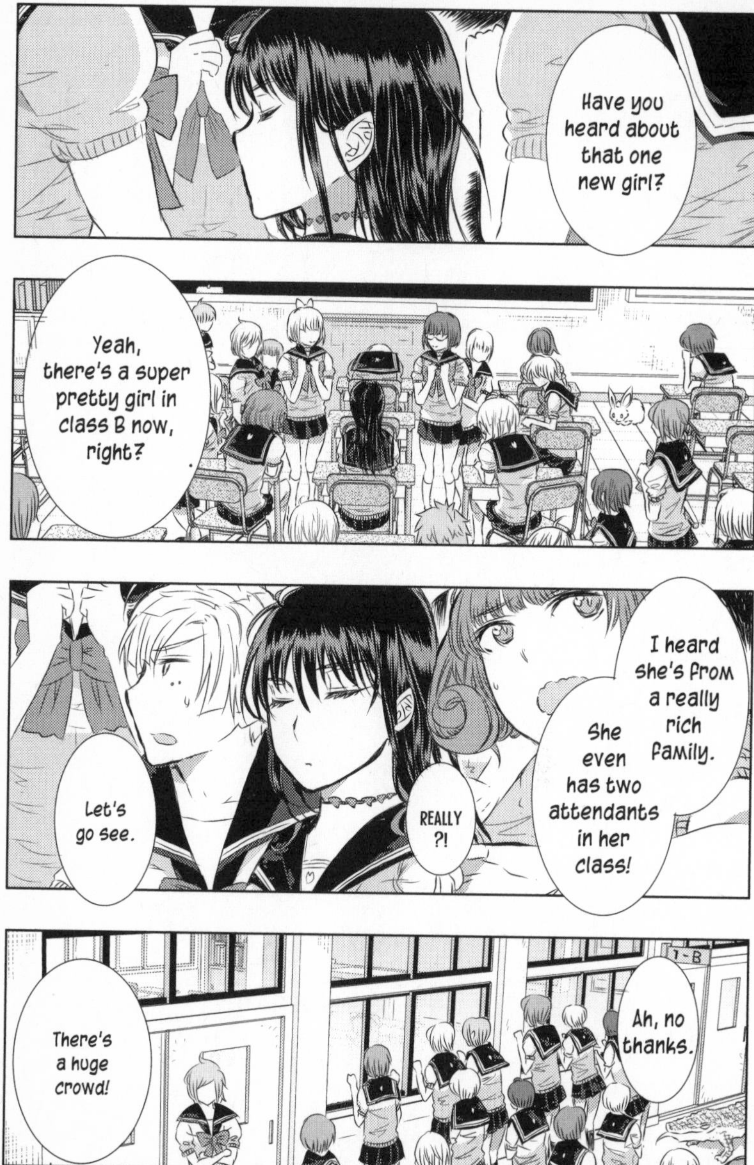
Have you heard about that one new girl?
Yeah, there's a super pretty girl in class B now, right?
I heard she's from a really rich family.
She even has two attendants in her class!
REALLY ?!
Let's go see.
1-B
Ah, no thanks.
There's a huge crowd!

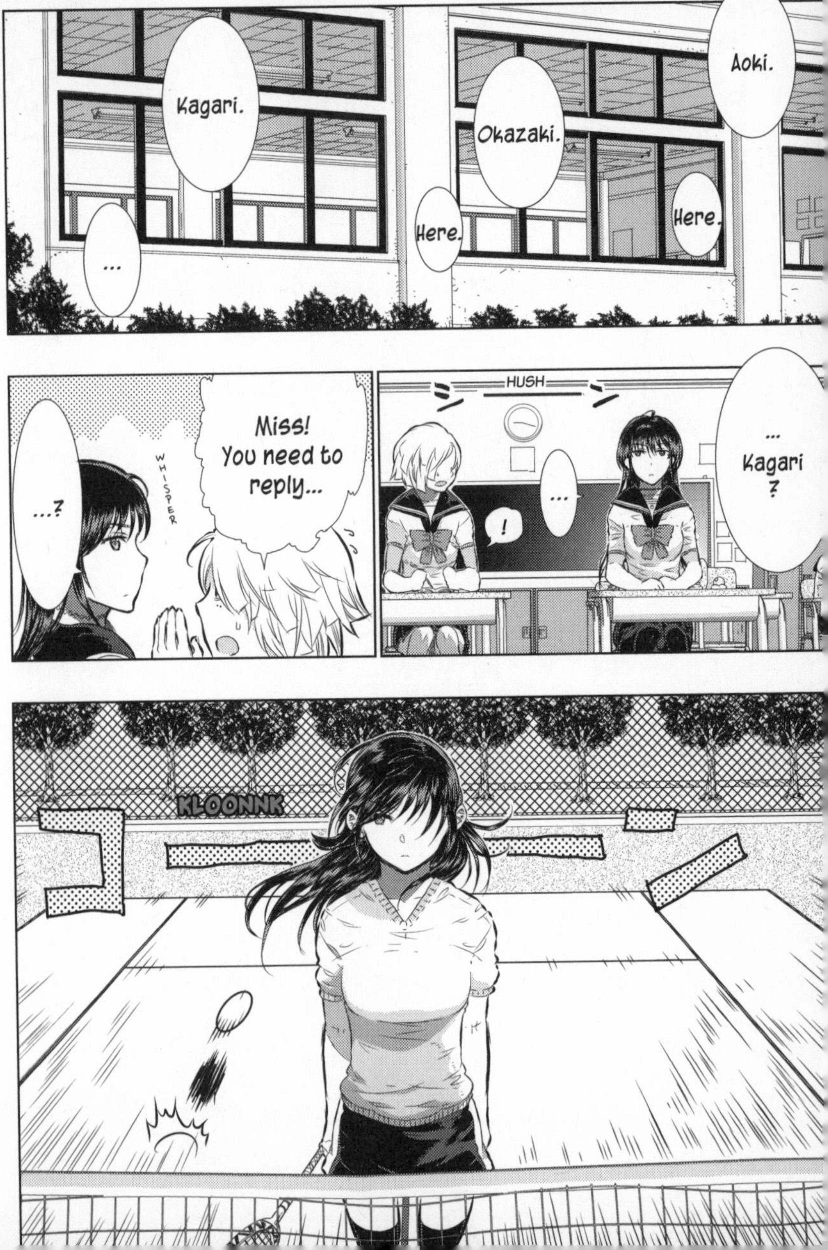
Aoki.
Here.
Okazaki.
Here.
Kagari.
...
... Kagari?
HUSH
...
!
Miss! You need to reply...
WHISPER
...?
KLOONNK

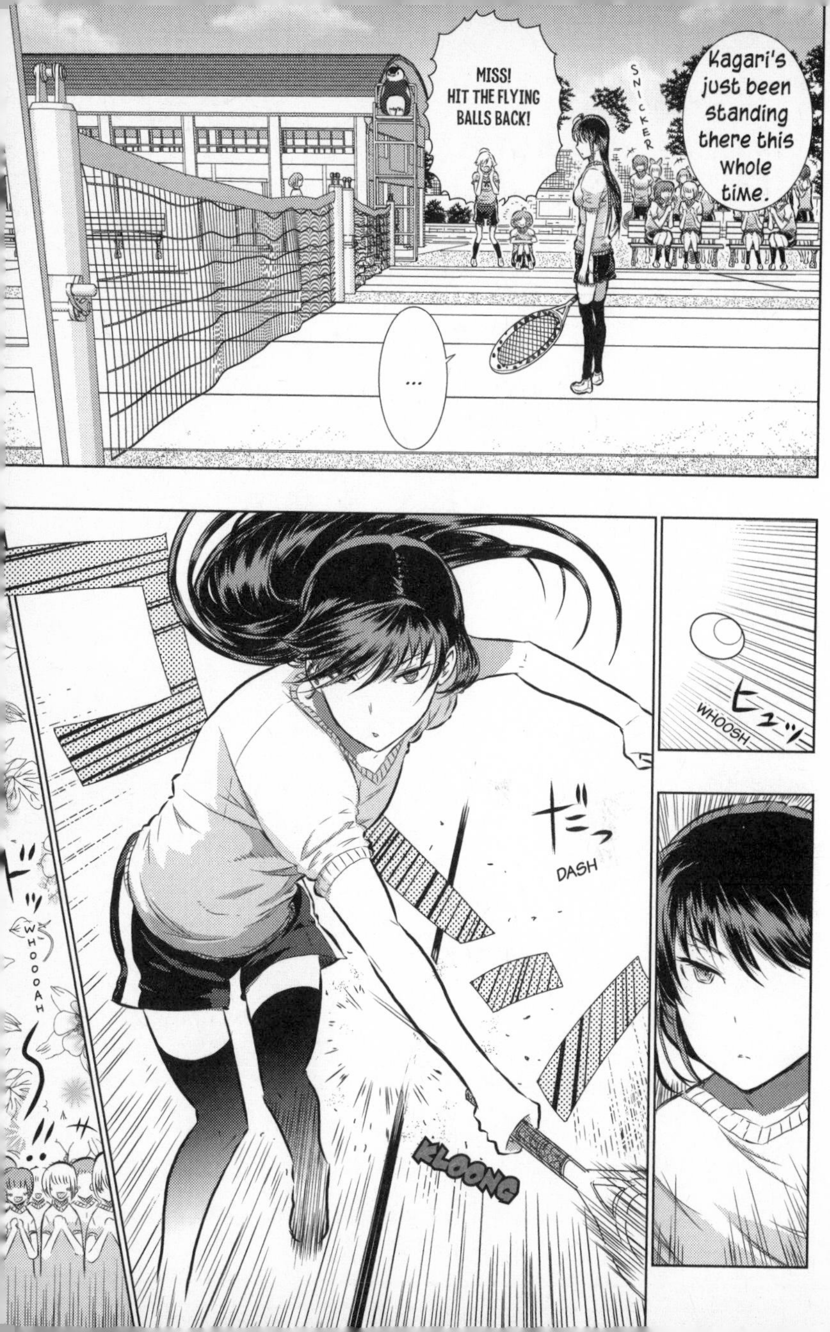
Kagari's just been standing there this whole time.
SNICKER
MISS! HIT THE FLYING BALLS BACK!
...
ヒュッ
WHOOSH
ダッ
DASH
KLOONG
WHOOOOAH

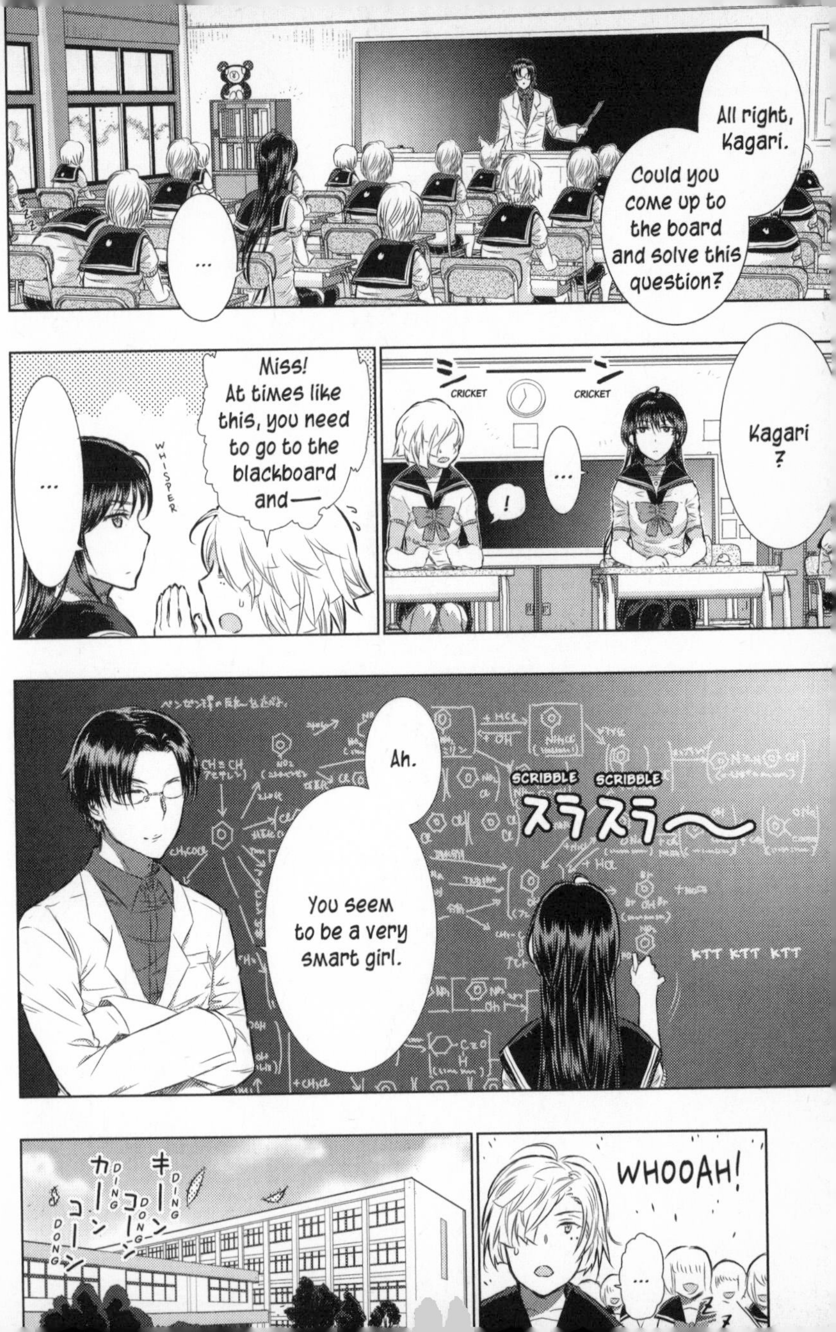
All right, Kagari.
Could you come up to the board and solve this question?
...
Kagari?
CRICKET
CRICKET
...
!
Miss! At times like this, you need to go to the blackboard and—
WHISPER
...
Ah.
SCRIBBLE SCRIBBLE
スラスラ〜
You seem to be a very smart girl.
KTT KTT KTT
WHOOAH!
...
キーンコーン
DING DONG
カーンコーン
DING DONG

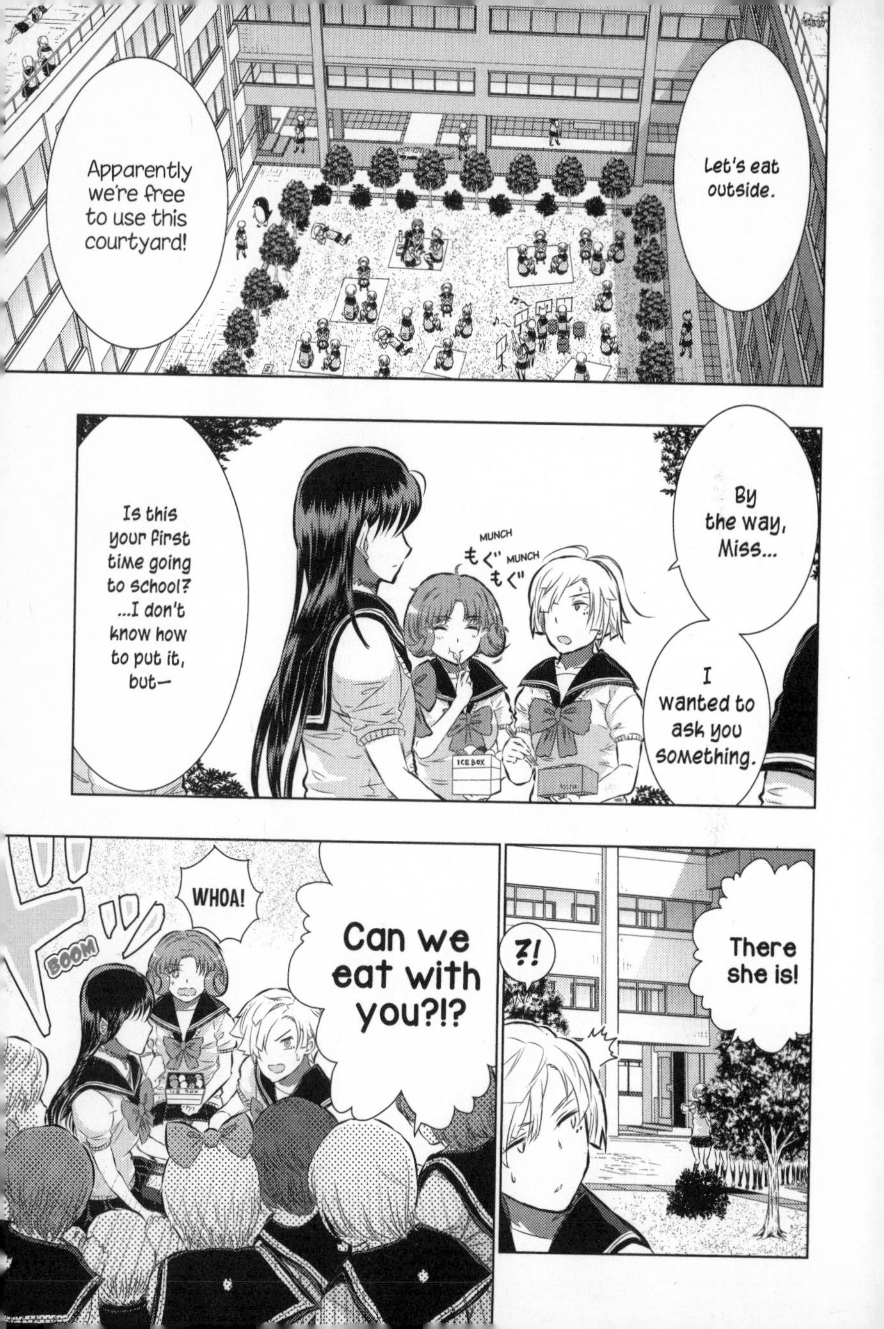
Let's eat outside.
Apparently we're free to use this courtyard!
By the way, Miss...
I wanted to ask you something.
MUNCH もぐ
MUNCH もぐ
Is this your first time going to school? ...I don't know how to put it, but—
ICE BOX
There she is!
?!
Can we eat with you?!?
WHOA!
BOOM

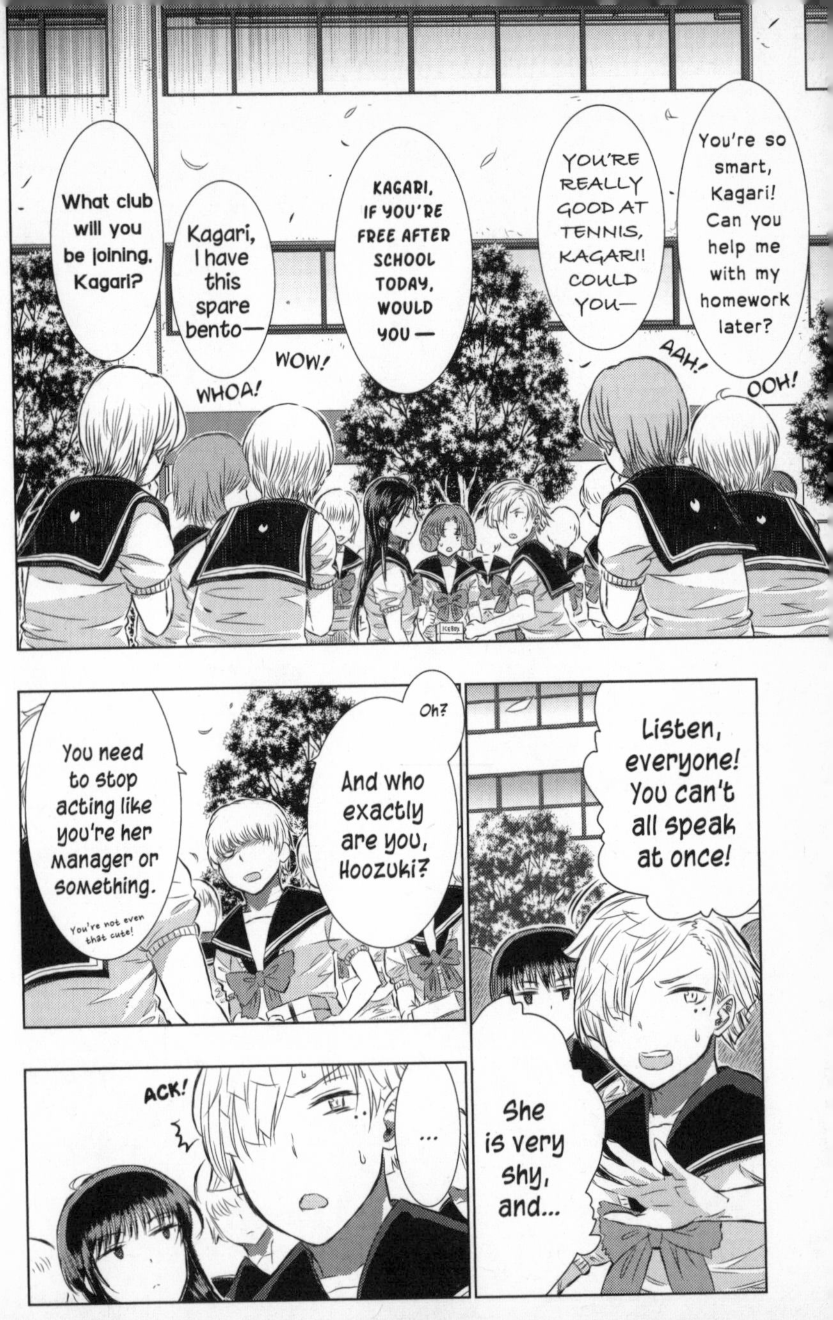
You're so smart, Kagari! Can you help me with my homework later?
OOH!
AAH!
YOU'RE REALLY GOOD AT TENNIS, KAGARI! COULD YOU—
KAGARI, IF YOU'RE FREE AFTER SCHOOL TODAY, WOULD YOU —
WOW!
Kagari, I have this spare bento—
WHOA!
What club will you be joining. Kagari?
Listen, everyone! You can't all speak at once!
She is very shy, and...
Oh?
And who exactly are you, Hoozuki?
You need to stop acting like you're her manager or something.
You're not even that cute!
...
ACK!

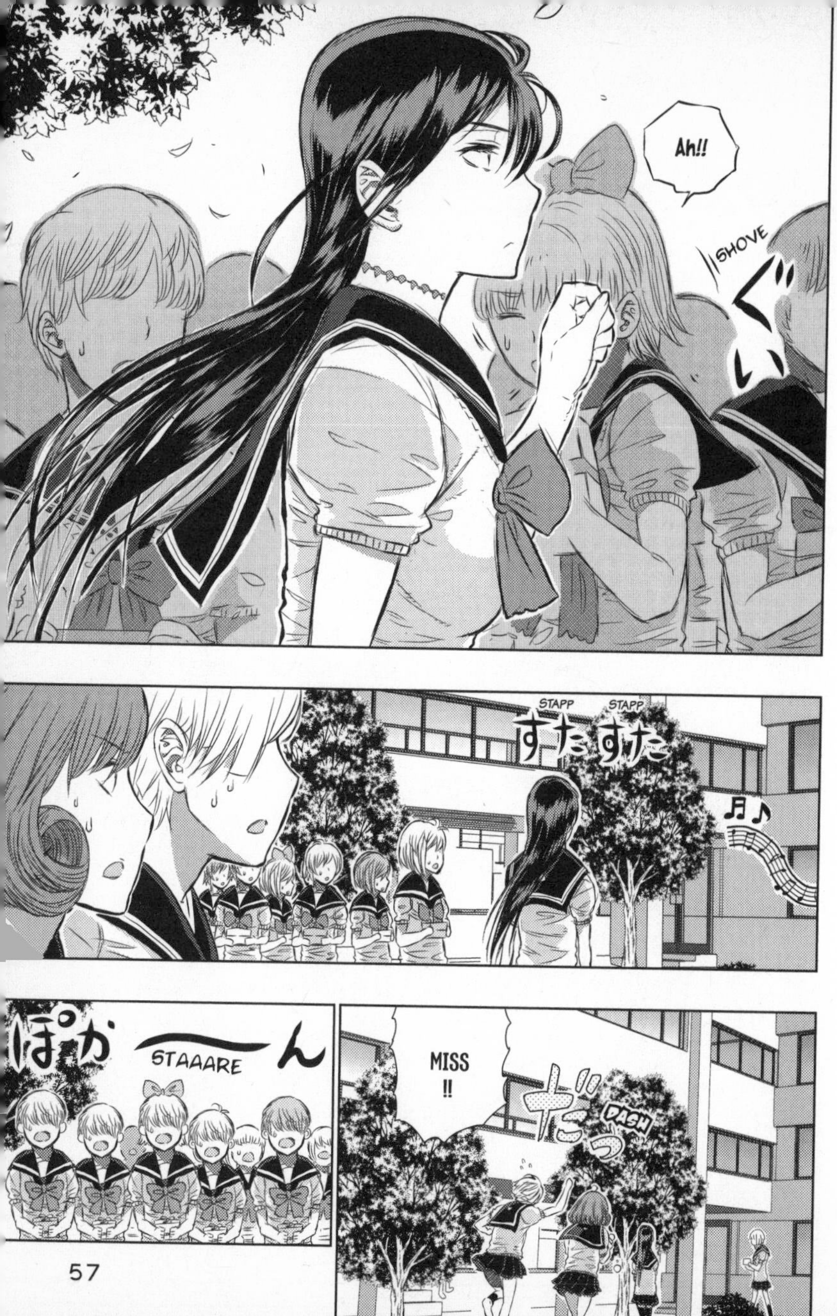
Ah!!
SHOVE
ぐい
STAPP STAPP
すたすた
MISS !!
だっ
DASH
ぽかーん
STAAARE

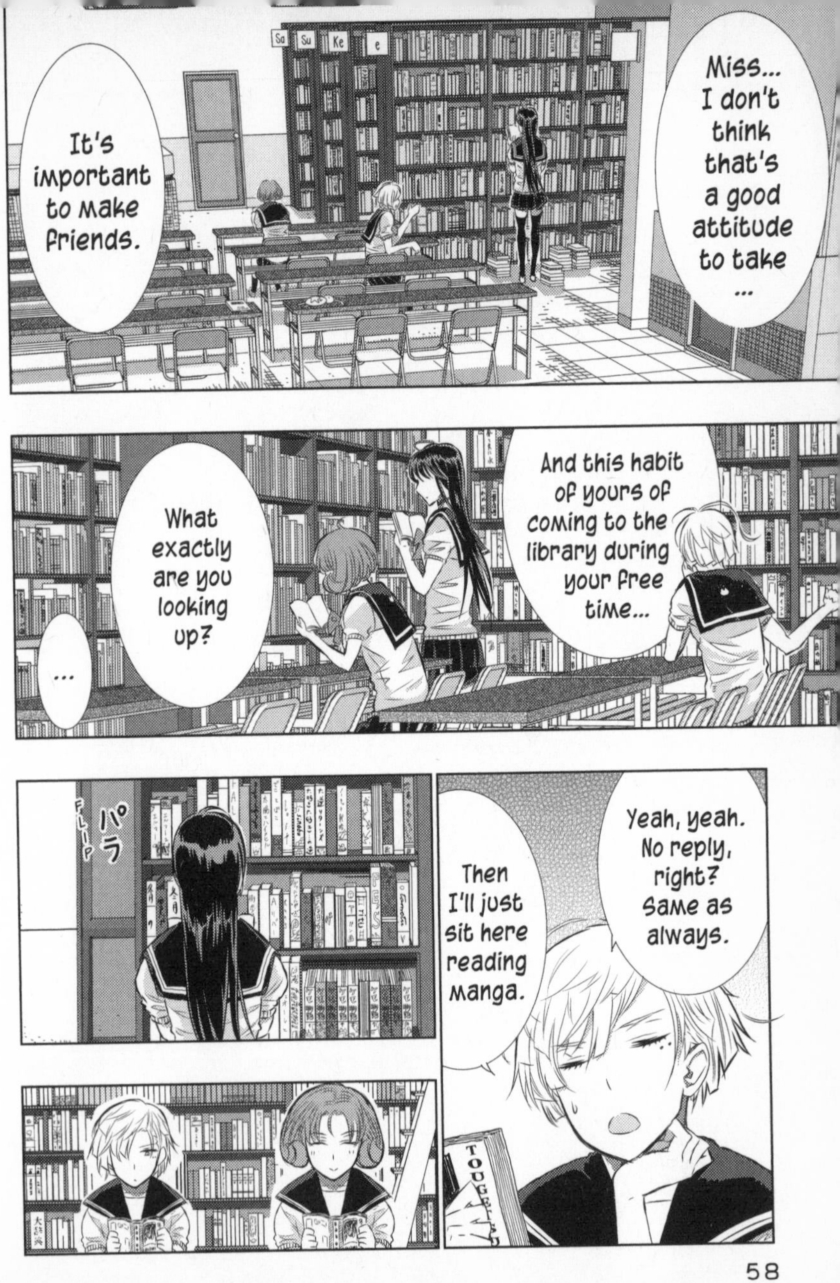
Miss... I don't think that's a good attitude to take ...
It's important to make friends.
And this habit of yours of coming to the library during your free time...
What exactly are you looking up?
...
Yeah, yeah. No reply, right? Same as always.
Then I'll just sit here reading manga.
パラ
FLIP

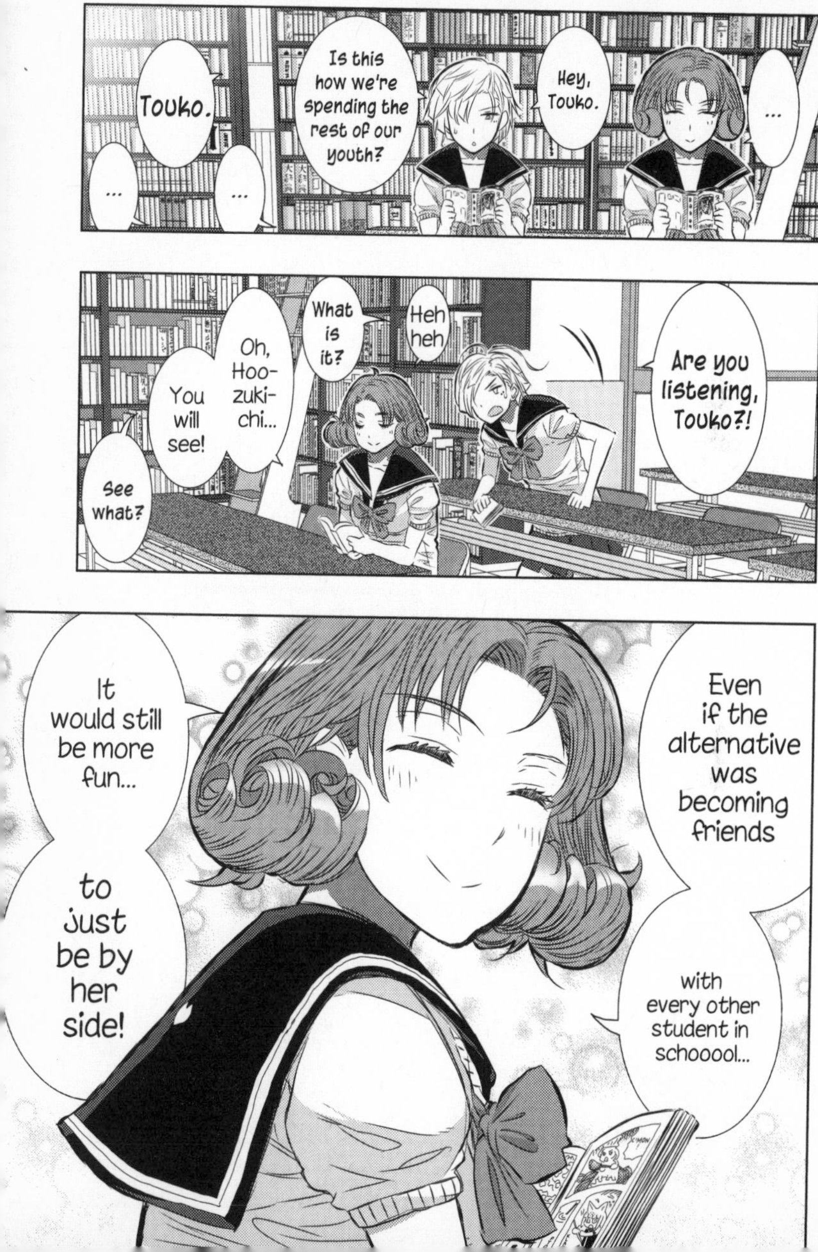
...
Hey, Touko.
Is this how we're spending the rest of our youth?
Touko.
...
...
Are you listening, Touko?!
Heh heh
What is it?
Oh, Hoo-zuki-chi...
You will see!
See what?
Even if the alternative was becoming friends
with every other student in schooool...
It would still be more fun...
to just be by her side!

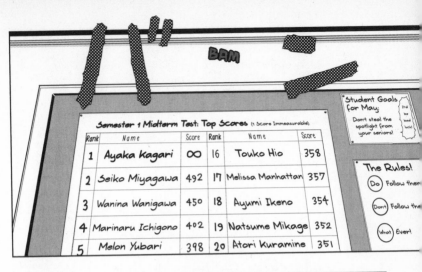

Rank	Name	Score	Rank	Name	Score
1	**Ayaka Kagari**	∞	16	Touko Hio	358
2	Seiko Miyagawa	492	17	Melissa Manhattan	357
3	Wanina Wanigawa	450	18	Ayumi Ikeno	354
4	Marinaru Ichigono	402	19	Natsume Mikage	352
5	Melon Yubari	398	20	Atori Kuramine	351

Semester 1 Midterm Test: Top Scores (∞ Score Immeasurable)

Student Goals for May:
Don't steal the spotlight from your seniors!

The Rules!
Do   Follow them
Don't   Follow the
What!   Ever!

BAM

Ooh!

I'm up there, tooo!

...You really are amazing.

You must be Kagari.

ZAKK

AV Room

!

60

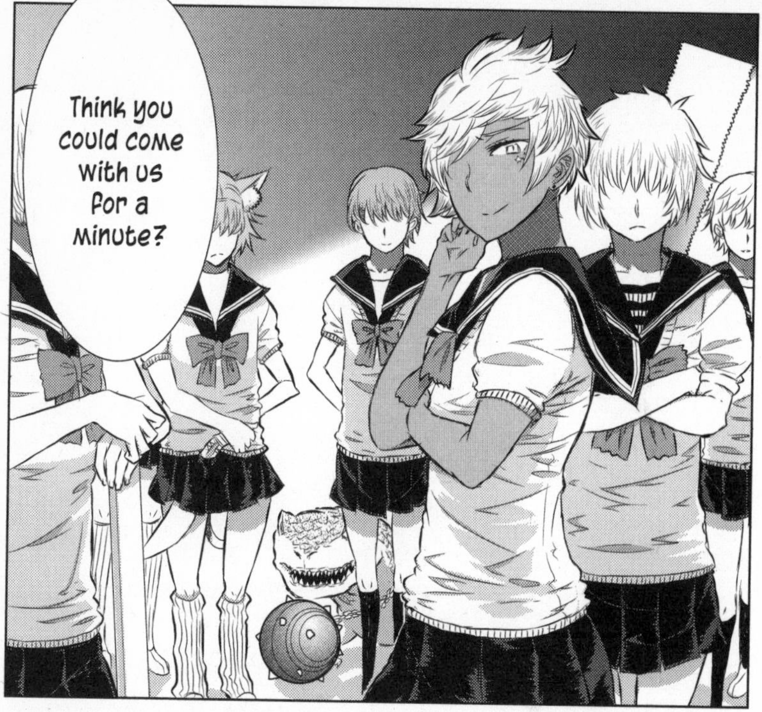
Think you could come with us for a minute?

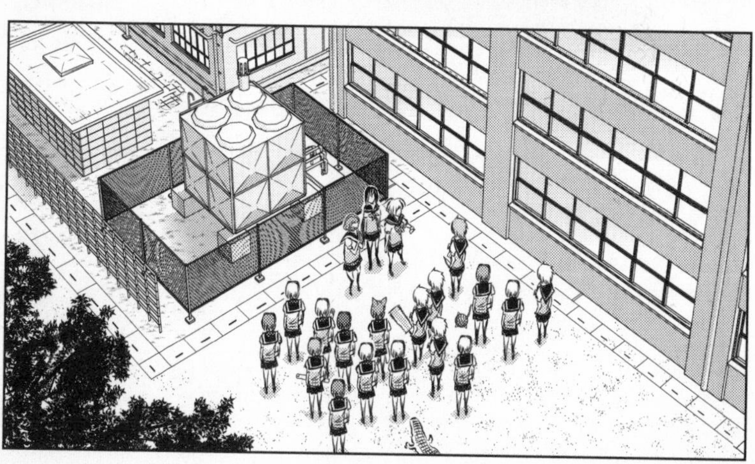

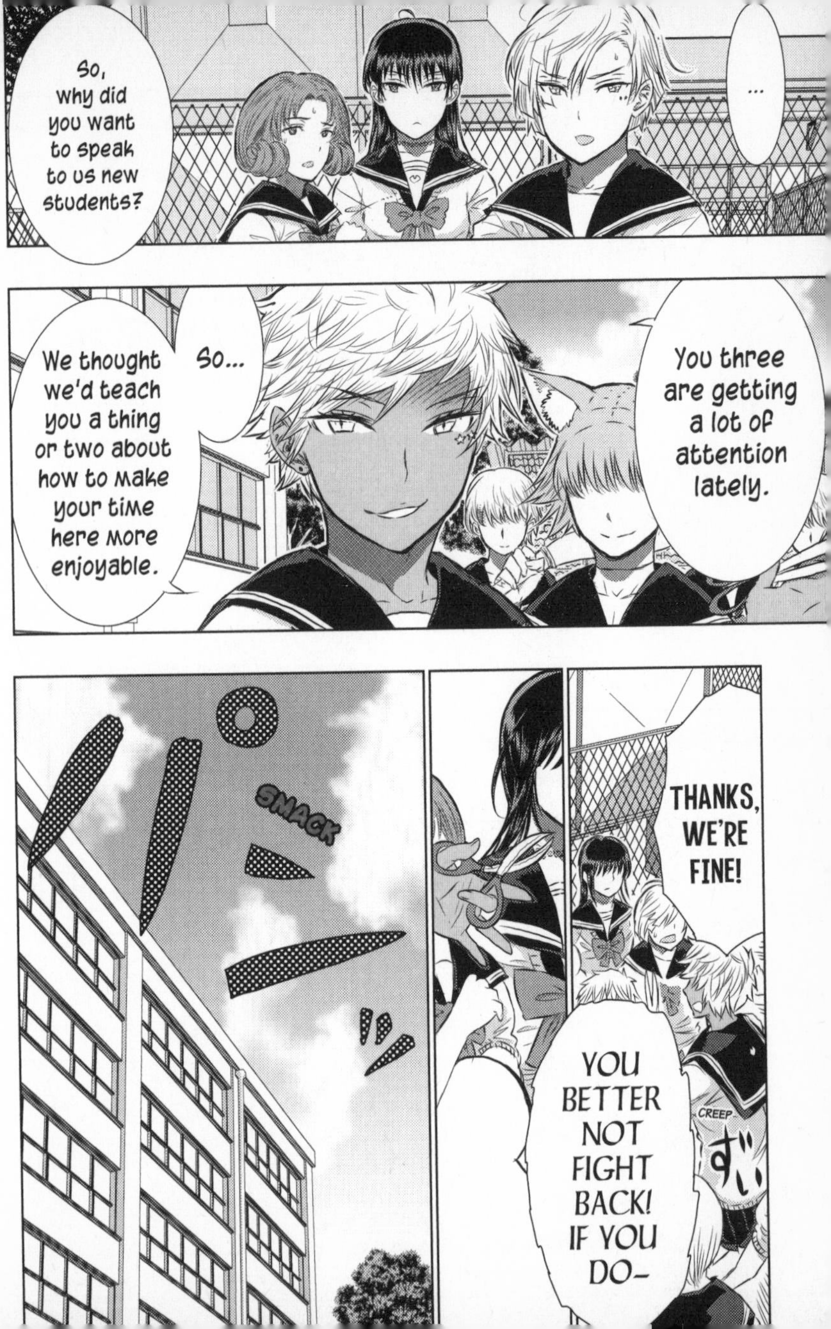
...
So, why did you want to speak to us new students?
You three are getting a lot of attention lately.
So...
We thought we'd teach you a thing or two about how to make your time here more enjoyable.
THANKS, WE'RE FINE!
CREEP
すい
YOU BETTER NOT FIGHT BACK! IF YOU DO-
SMACK

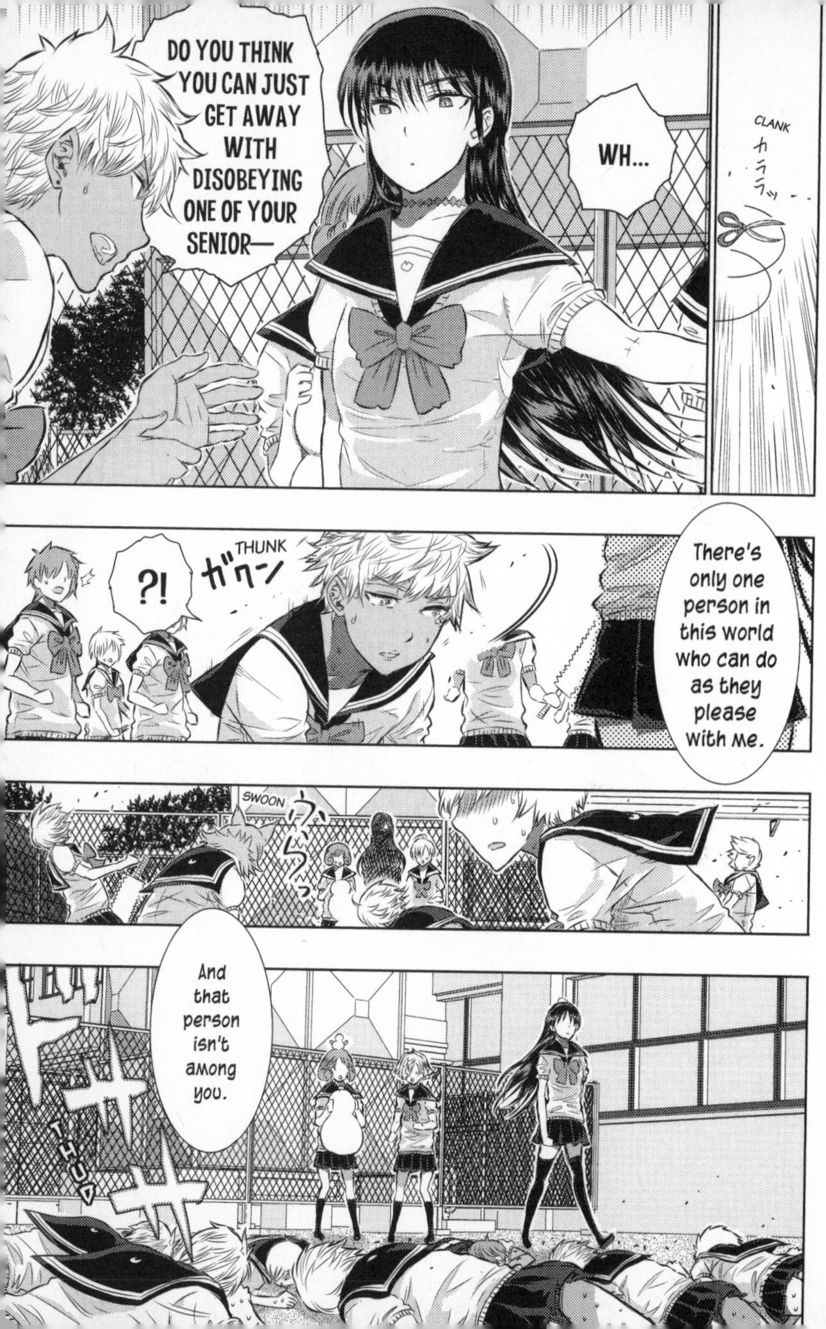
CLANK
WH...
DO YOU THINK YOU CAN JUST GET AWAY WITH DISOBEYING ONE OF YOUR SENIOR—
There's only one person in this world who can do as they please with me.
THUNK
?!
SWOON
And that person isn't among you.
THUD

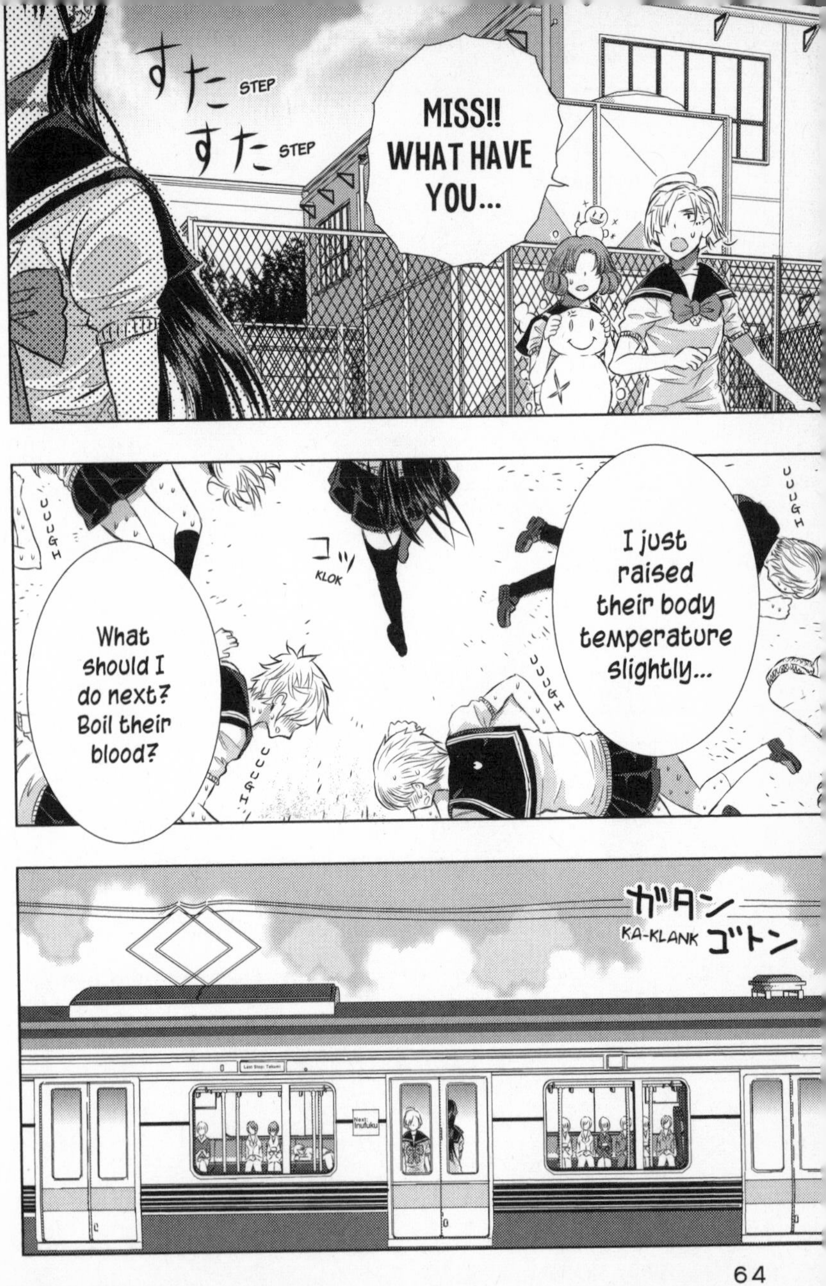
MISS!! WHAT HAVE YOU...
すた STEP
すた STEP
UUUGH
I just raised their body temperature slightly...
UUUGH
コッ KLOK
UUUGH
UUUGH
What should I do next? Boil their blood?
ガタンゴトン KA-KLANK
Last Stop: Takumi
Next: Inufuku

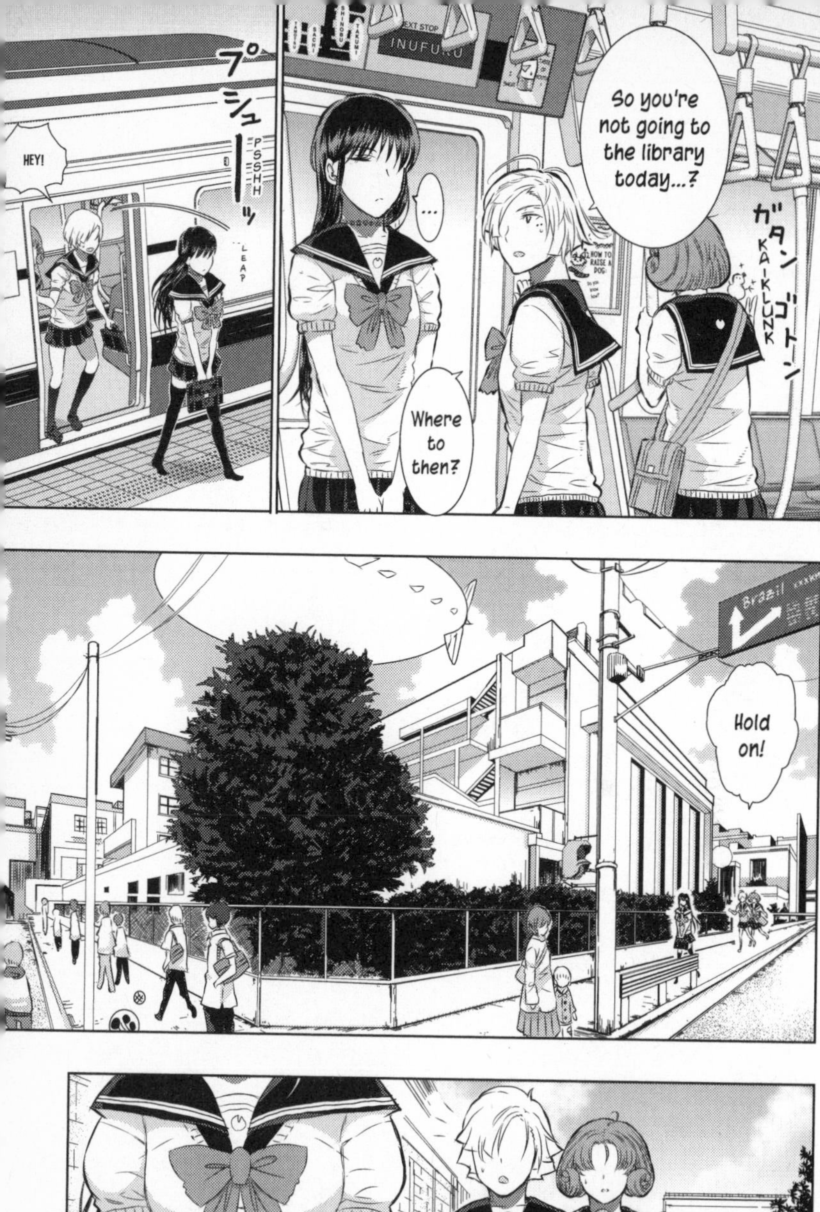
TAMOTSU
SACHI
SHINOBU
TAKUMI
NEXT STOP
INUFURU
So you're not going to the library today...?
ガタンゴトーン
KA-KLUNK
HOW TO RAISE A DOG:
Do you know how?
...
Where to then?
プシューッ
PSSHH
HEY!
LEAP
Brazil
Hold on!

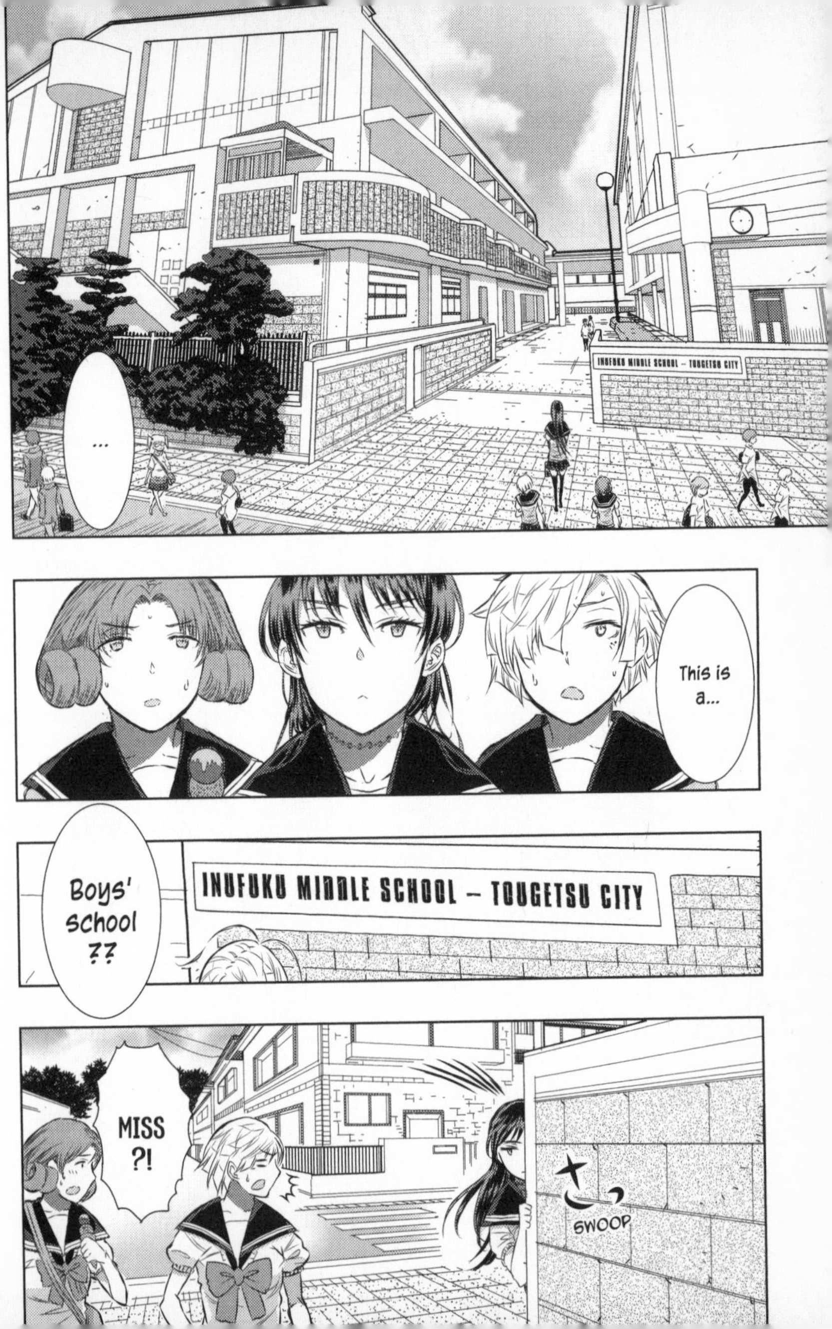
INUFUKU MIDDLE SCHOOL – TOUGETSU CITY
...
This is a...
INUFUKU MIDDLE SCHOOL – TOUGETSU CITY
Boys' school ??
SWOOP
MISS ?!

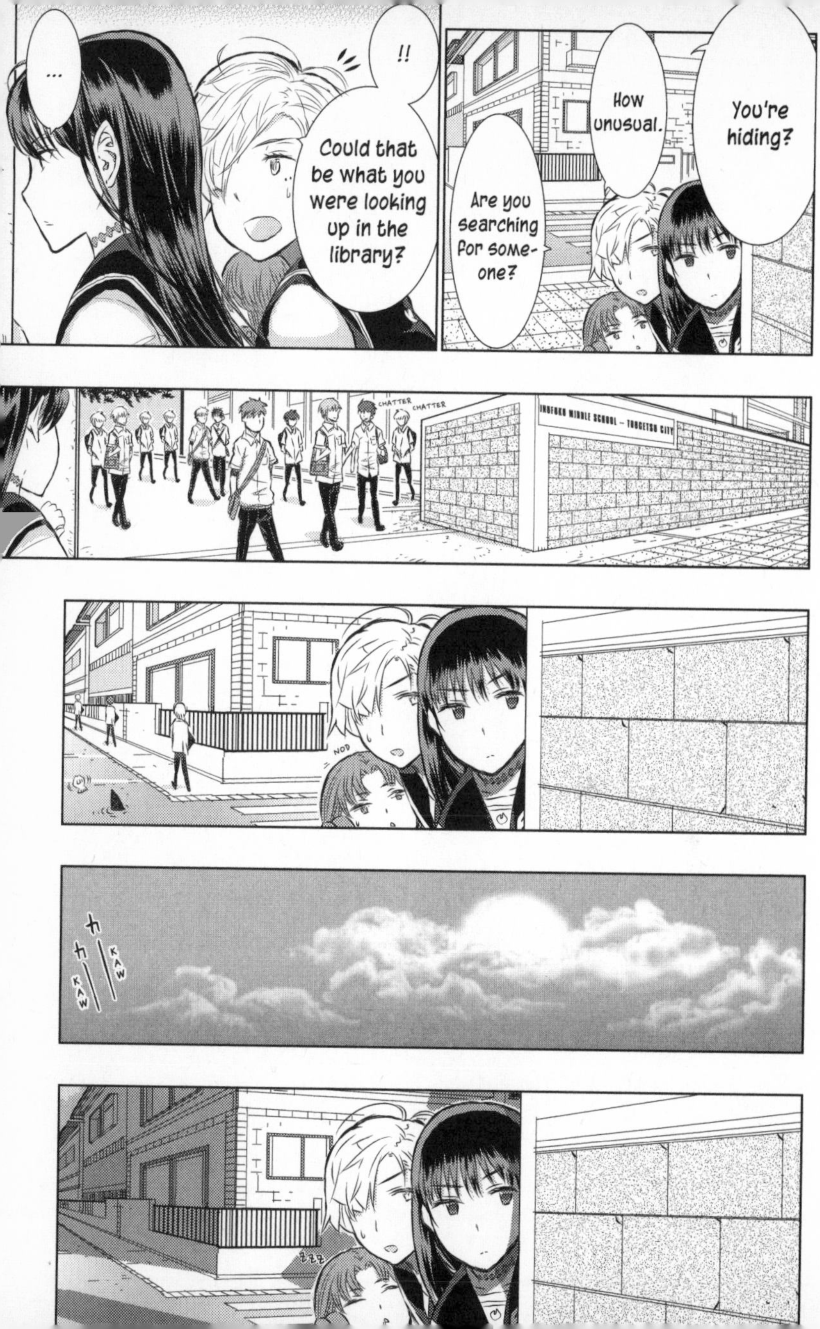

You're hiding?
How unusual.
Are you searching for some-one?
!!
Could that be what you were looking up in the library?
...
CHATTER
CHATTER
INUFUKU MIDDLE SCHOOL – TOUGETSU CITY
NOD
カー
カー
KAW
KAW
ZZZ

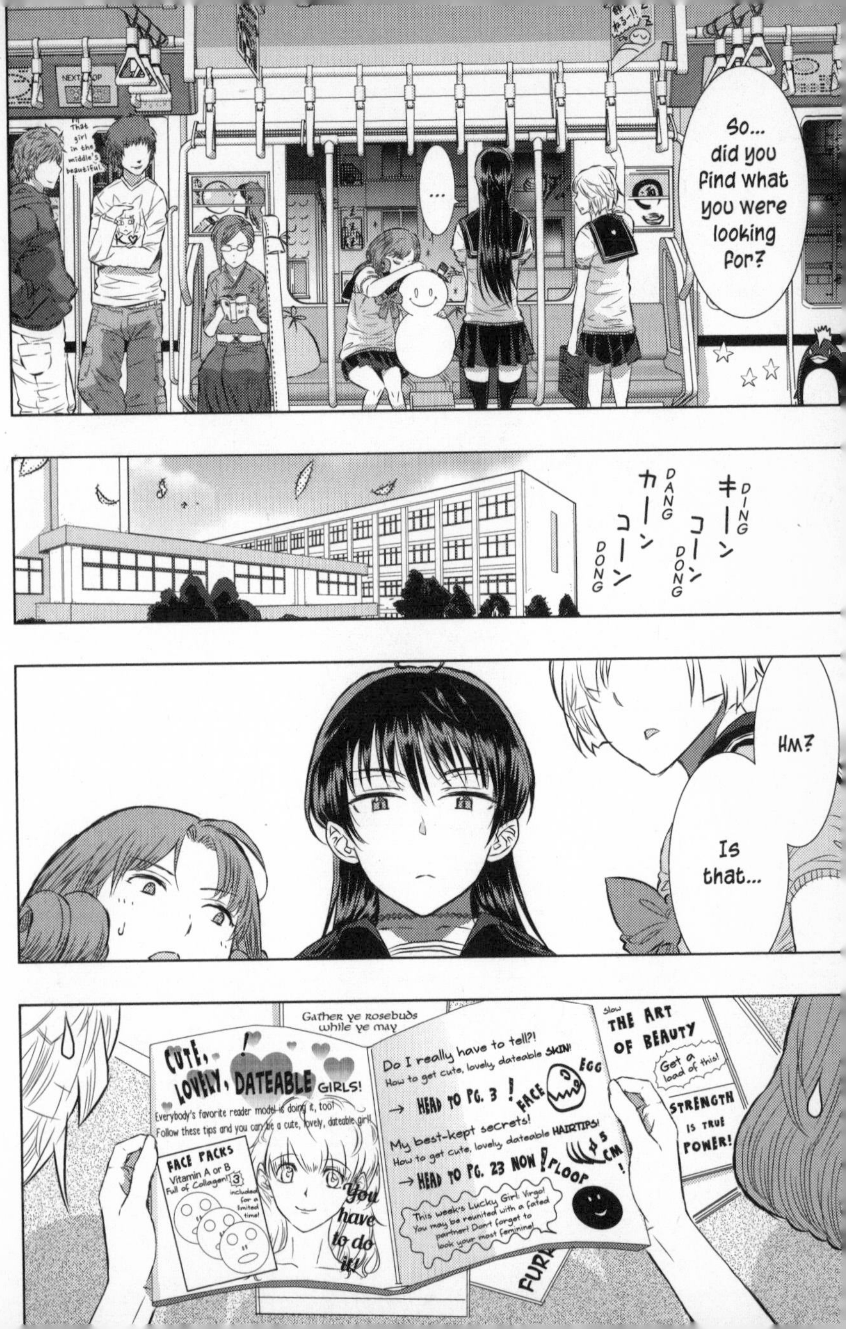
So... did you find what you were looking for?
...
That girl in the middle's beautiful.
キーン DING
コーン DONG
カーン DANG
コーン DONG
HM?
Is that...
Gather ye rosebuds while ye may
Slow THE ART OF BEAUTY
Get a load of this!
STRENGTH IS TRUE POWER!
Do I really have to tell?!
How to get cute, lovely, dateable SKIN!
→ HEAD TO PG. 3 !
FACE EGG
My best-kept secrets!
How to get cute, lovely, dateable HAIRTIPS!
→ HEAD TO PG. 23 NOW!
FLOOP
5 CM
This week's Lucky Girl: Virgo! You may be reunited with a fated partner! Don't forget to look your most feminine!
CUTE, LOVELY, DATEABLE GIRLS!
Everybody's favorite reader model is doing it, too!
Follow these tips and you can be a cute, lovely, dateable girl!
FACE PACKS
Vitamin A or B
Full of Collagen!
3 included for a limited time!
You have to do it!
FURA

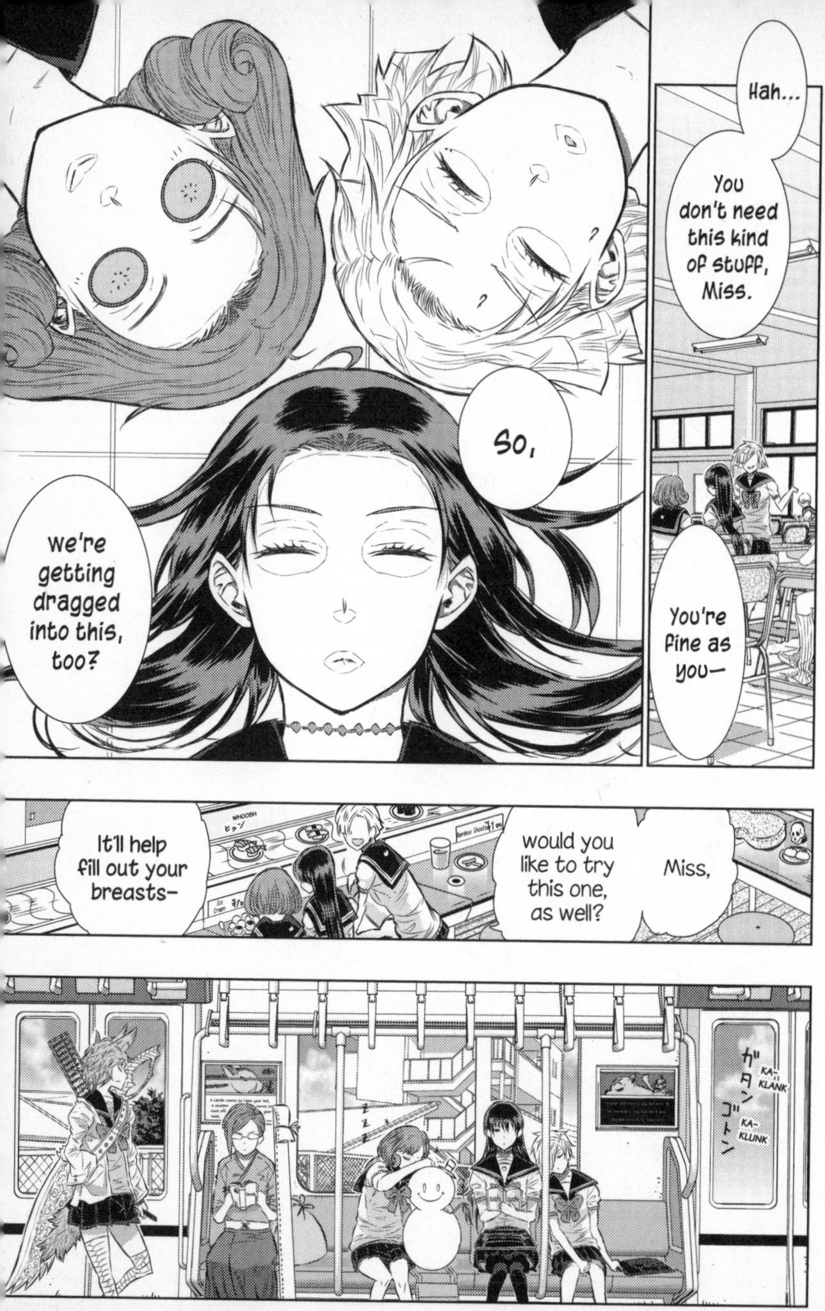
Hah...
You don't need this kind of stuff, Miss.
You're fine as you—
So,
we're getting dragged into this, too?
Miss,
would you like to try this one, as well?
WHOOSH
It'll help fill out your breasts-
KA-KLANK
KA-KLUNK

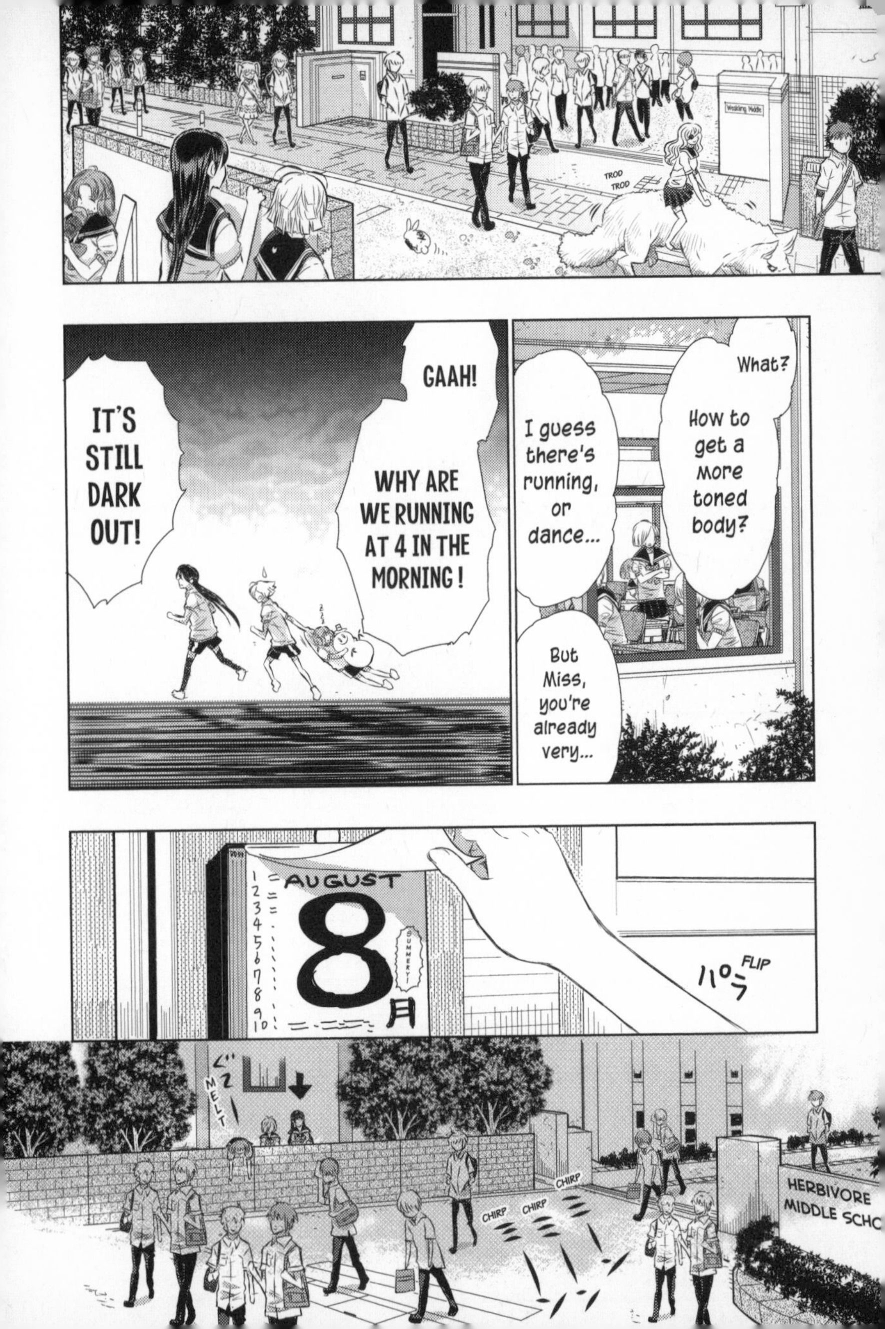
Weakling Middle
TROD TROD
What?
How to get a more toned body?
I guess there's running, or dance...
But Miss, you're already very...
GAAH!
WHY ARE WE RUNNING AT 4 IN THE MORNING !
IT'S STILL DARK OUT!
パラ FLIP
SUMMERY!
AUGUST
8
月
HERBIVORE MIDDLE SCHO
CHIRP
CHIRP CHIRP
ぐ〜 MELT

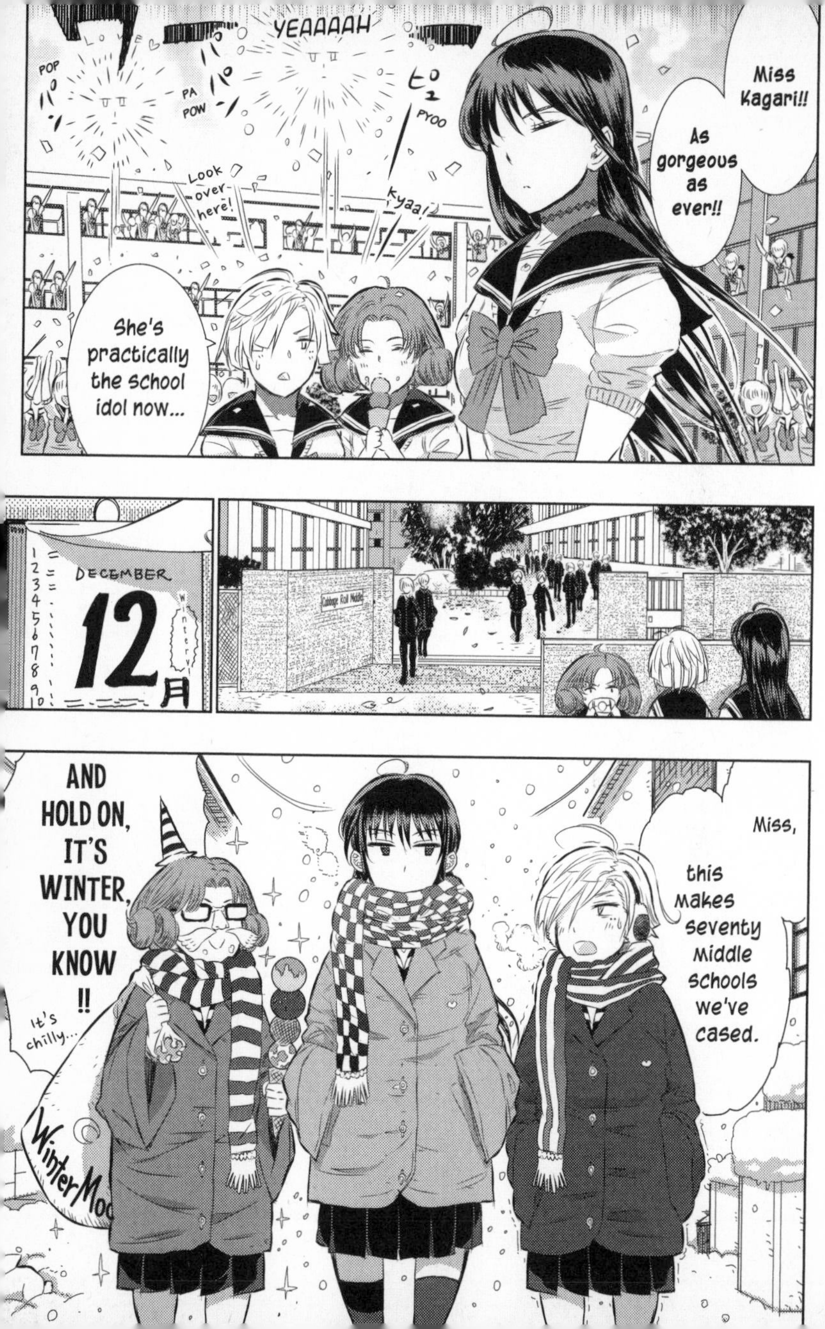

Miss Kagari!!
As gorgeous as ever!!
YEAAAAH
PYOO
Kyaa!
Look over here!
PA POW
POP
She's practically the school idol now...
Cabbage Roll Middle
DECEMBER
12月
wintery
Miss, this makes seventy middle schools we've cased.
AND HOLD ON, IT'S WINTER, YOU KNOW!!
It's chilly...

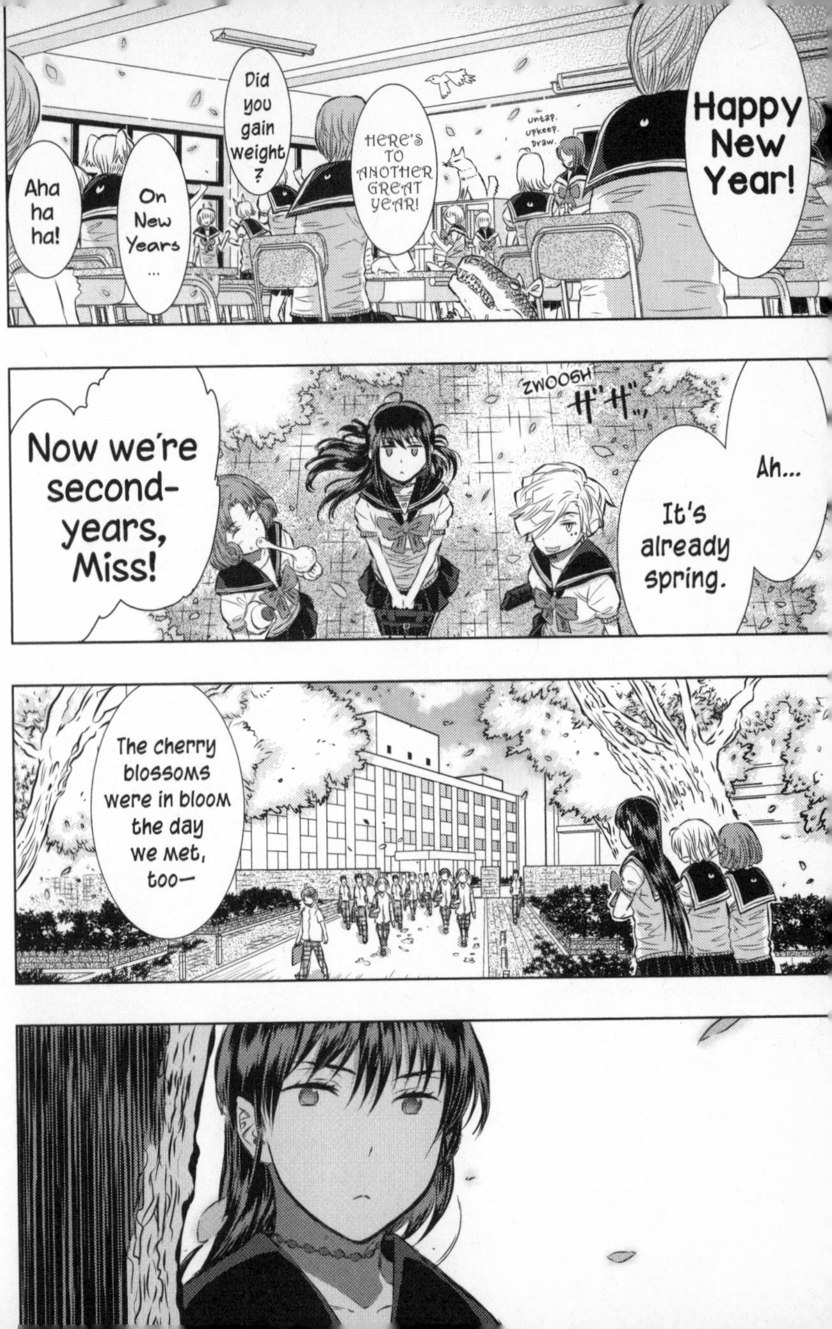
Happy New Year!
untap. upkeep. Draw.
HERE'S TO ANOTHER GREAT YEAR!
Did you gain weight?
On New Years ...
Aha ha ha!
Ah...
It's already spring.
ZWOOSH
ザザッ
Now we're second-years, Miss!
The cherry blossoms were in bloom the day we met, too—

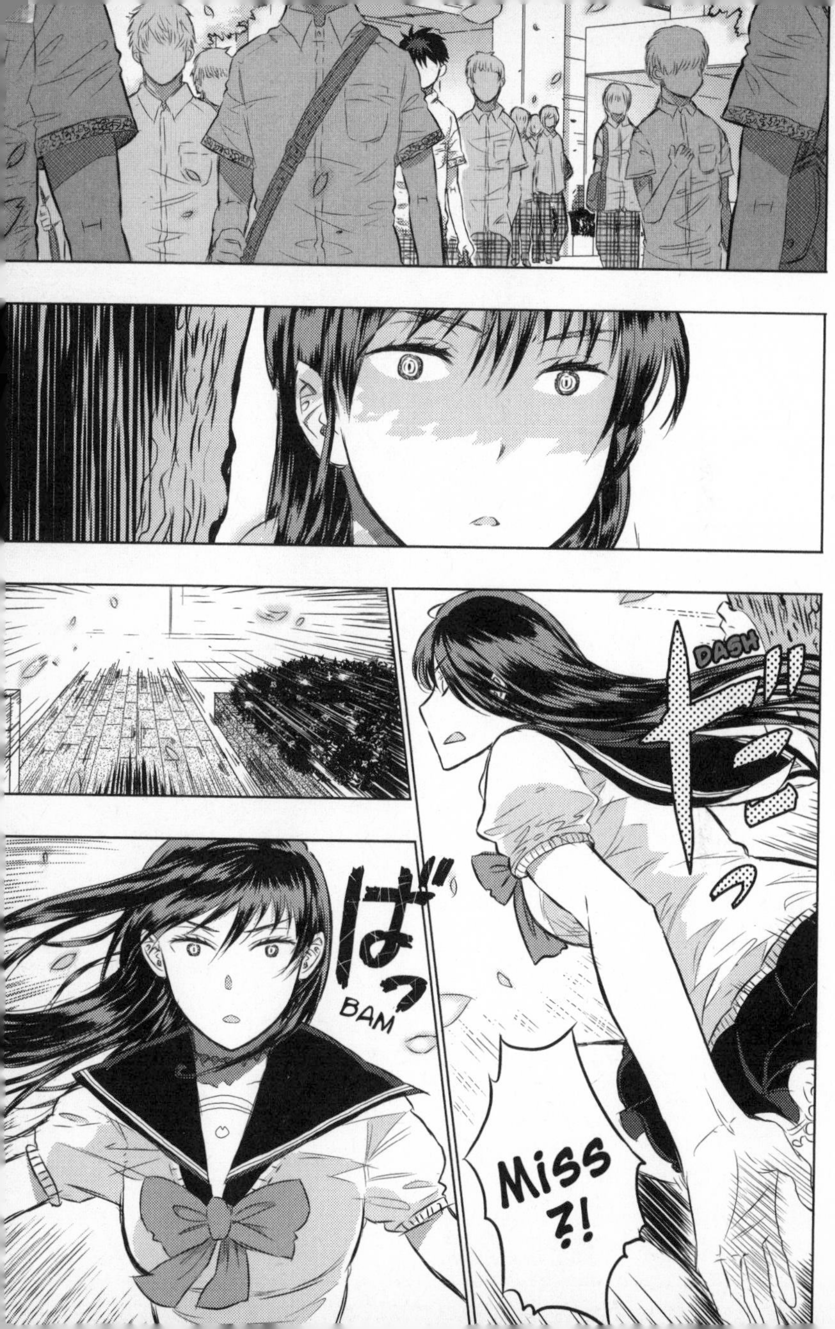
DASH
ザッ
Miss ?!
ばっ
BAM

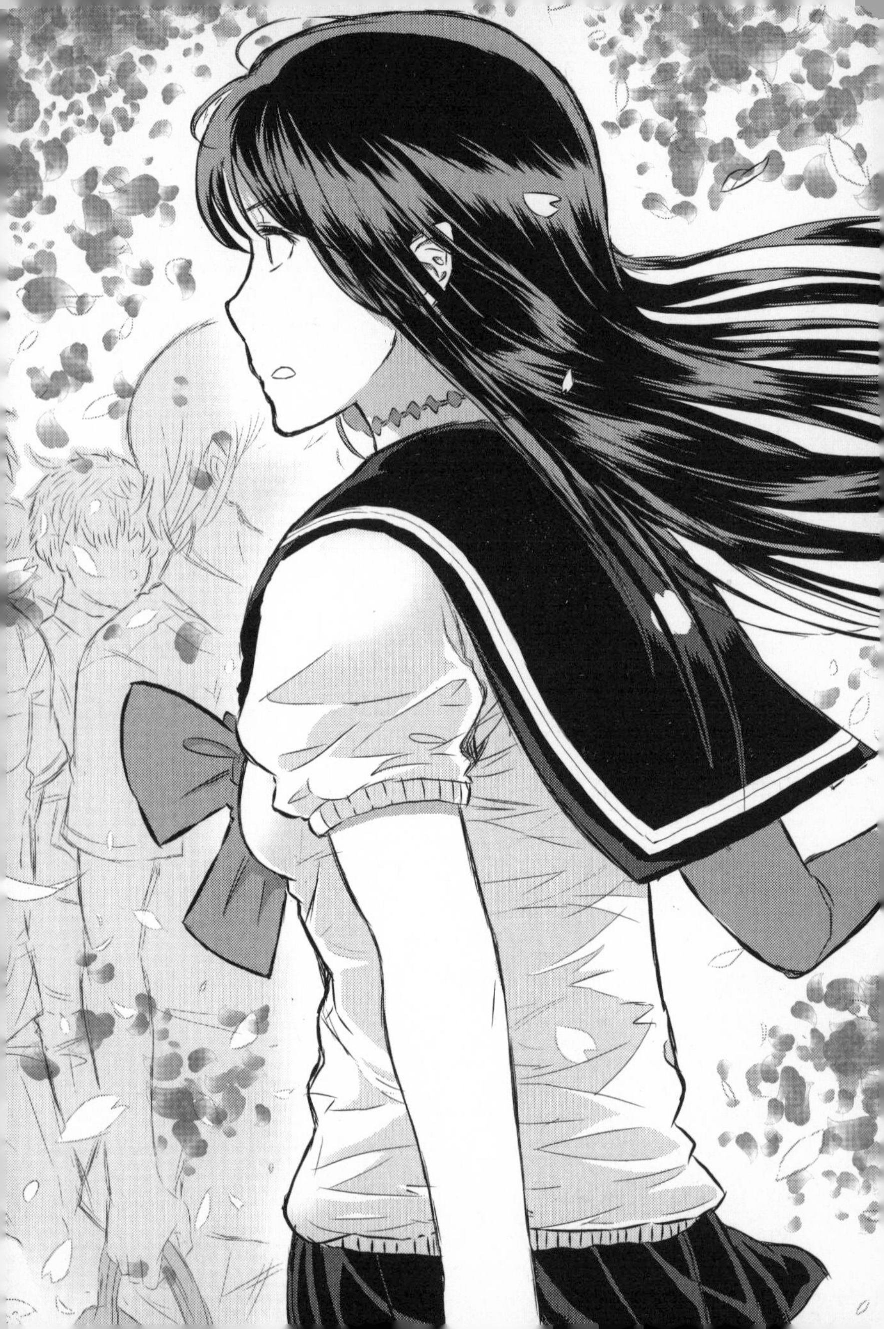

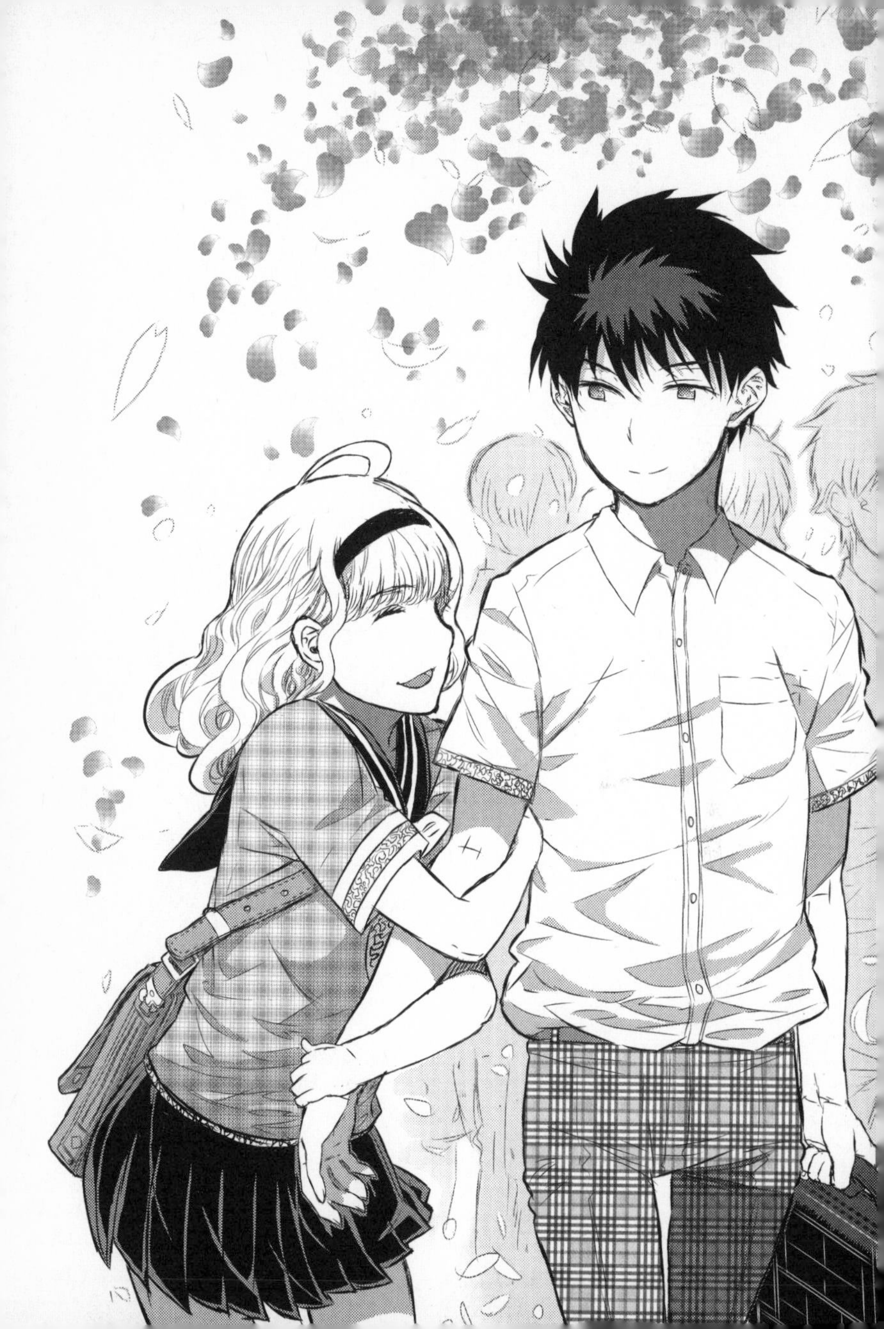

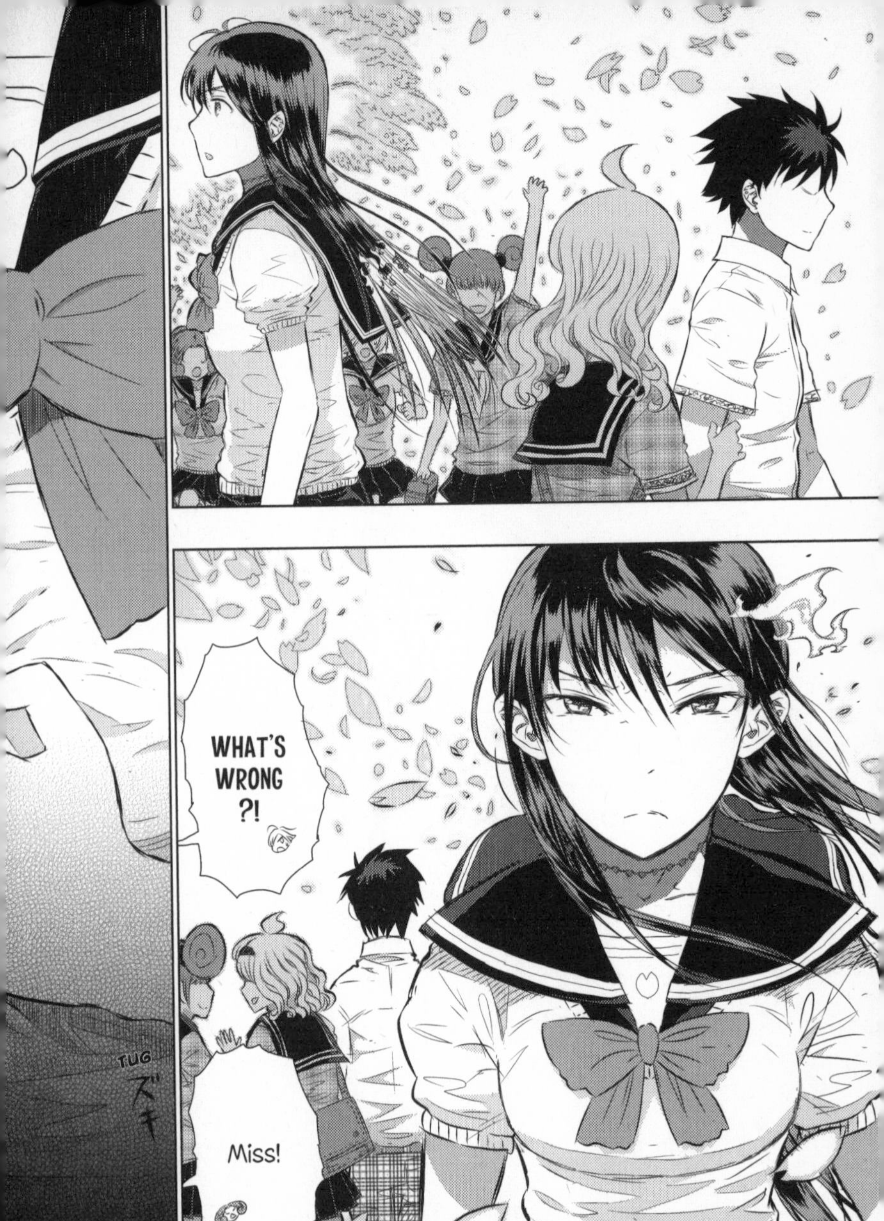
WHAT'S WRONG ?!
Miss!
TUG
ズキ

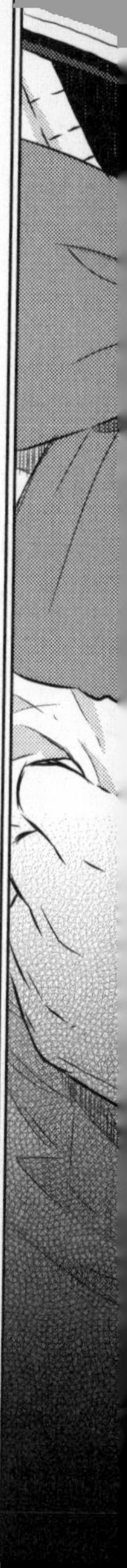

...I found him!

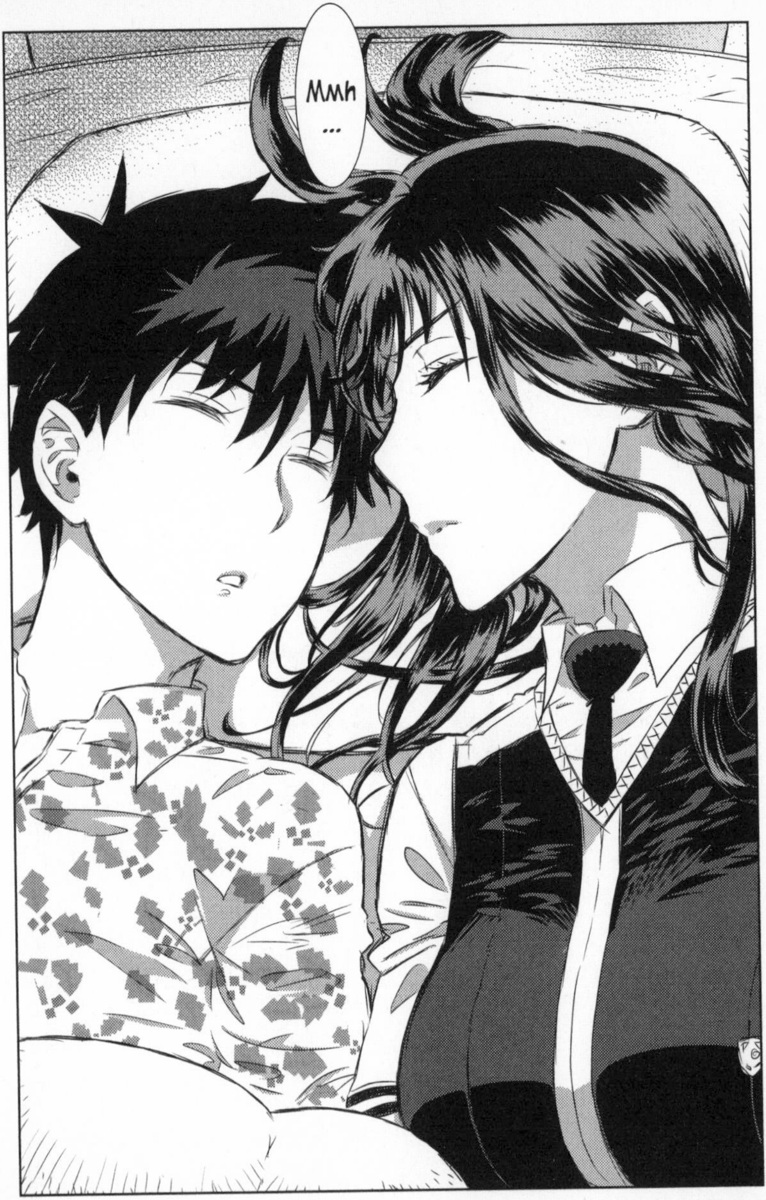
Mmh
...

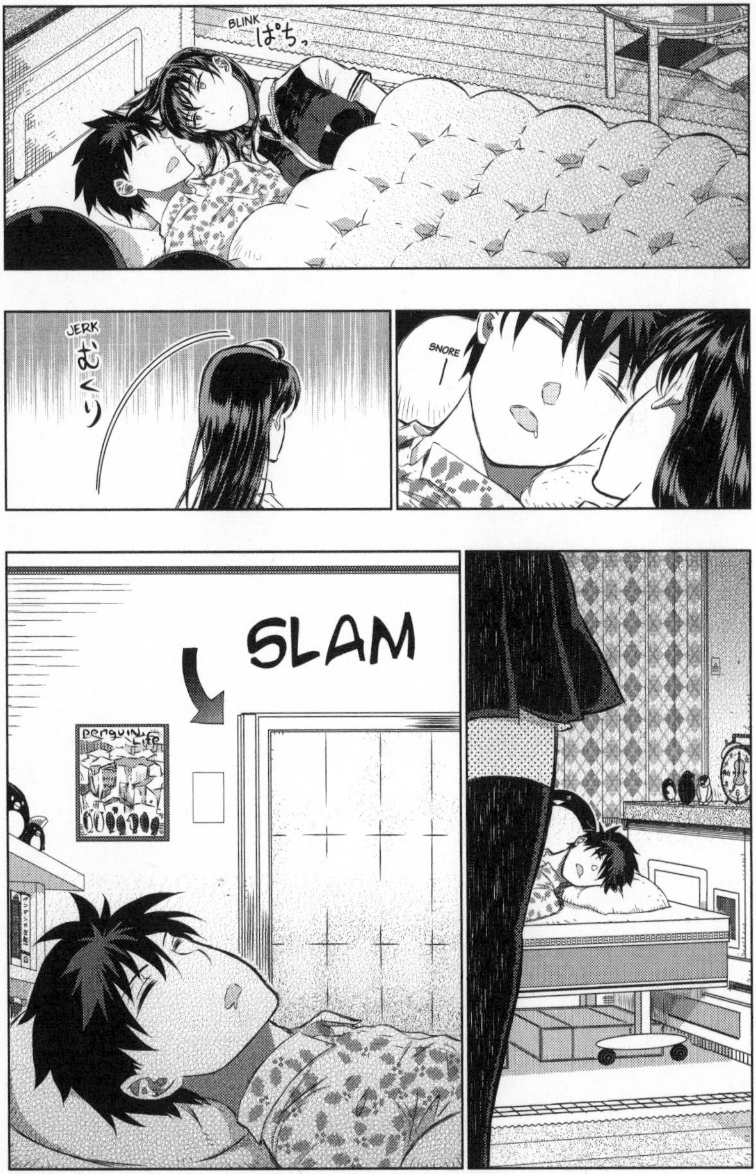
BLINK
ぱちっ
SNORE
JERK
むくり
SLAM
penguin Life

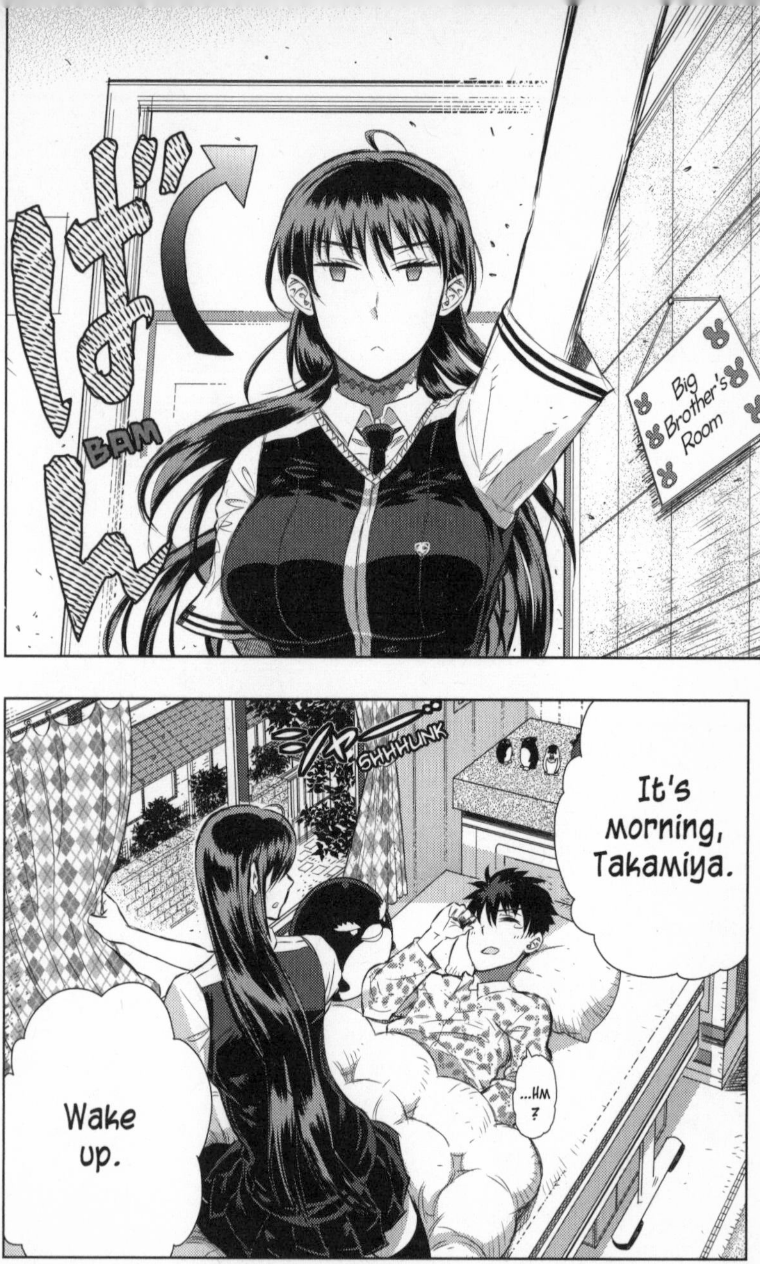
Big Brother's Room
ばん
BAM
It's morning, Takamiya.
SHHHUNK
...Hm?
Wake up.

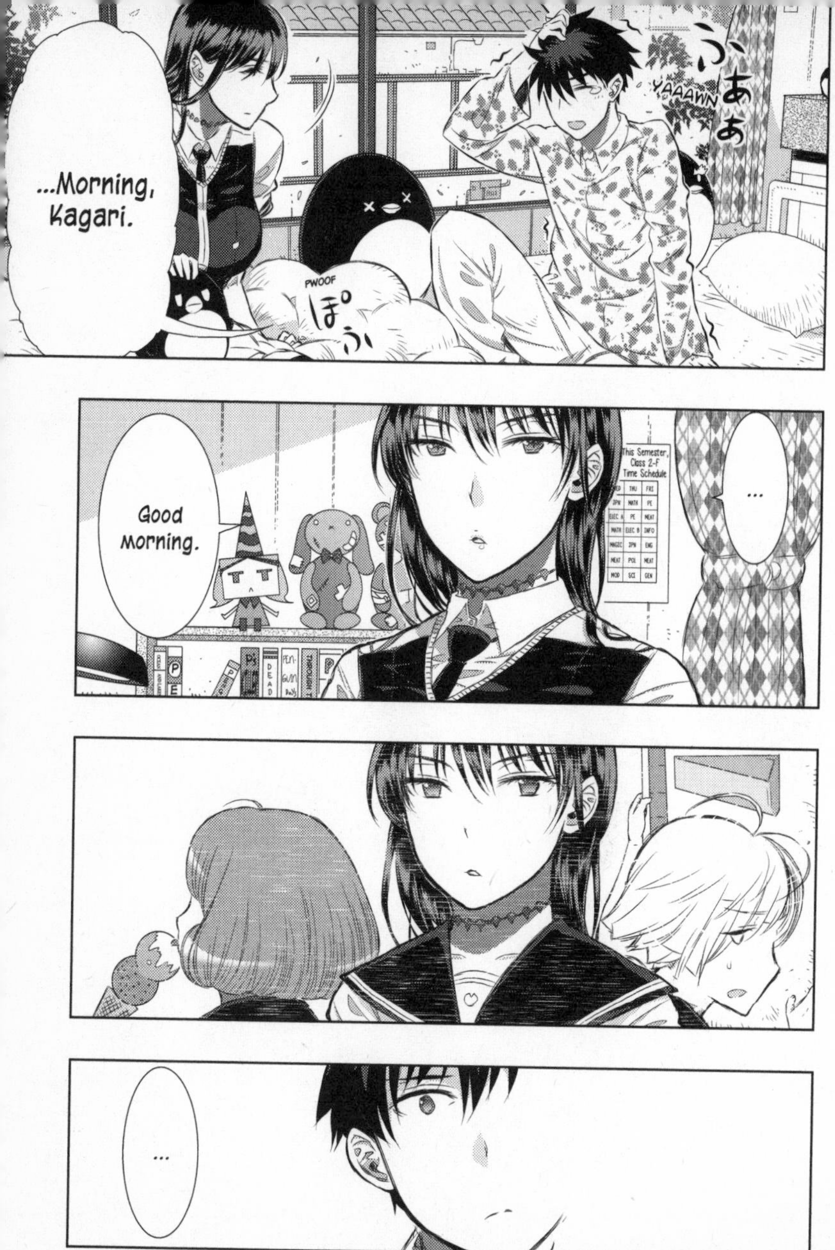
ふあぁ
YAAAWN
...Morning, Kagari.
PWOOF
ぽふ
...
This Semester, Class 2-F Time Schedule
Good morning.
...

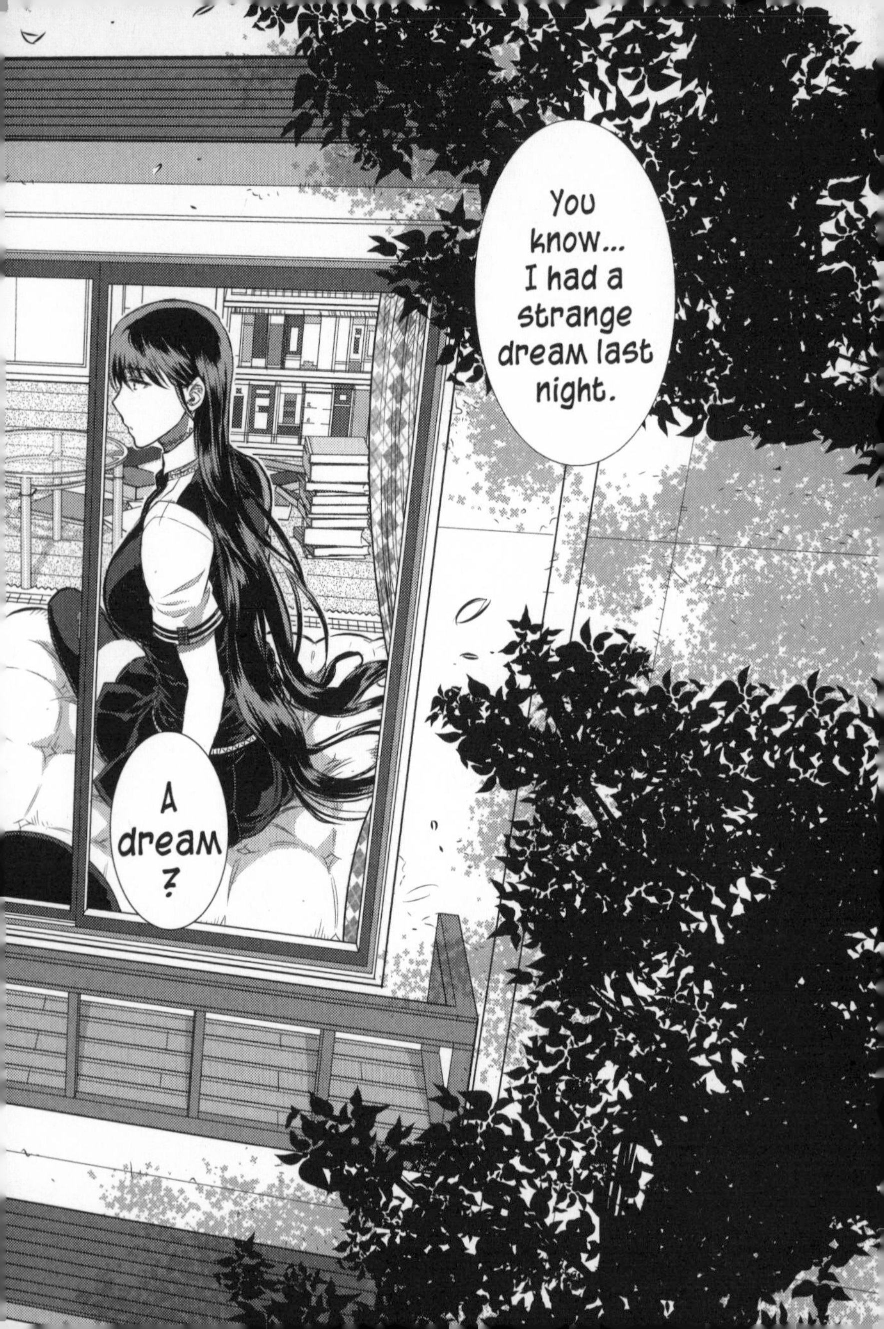
You know... I had a strange dream last night.
A dream?

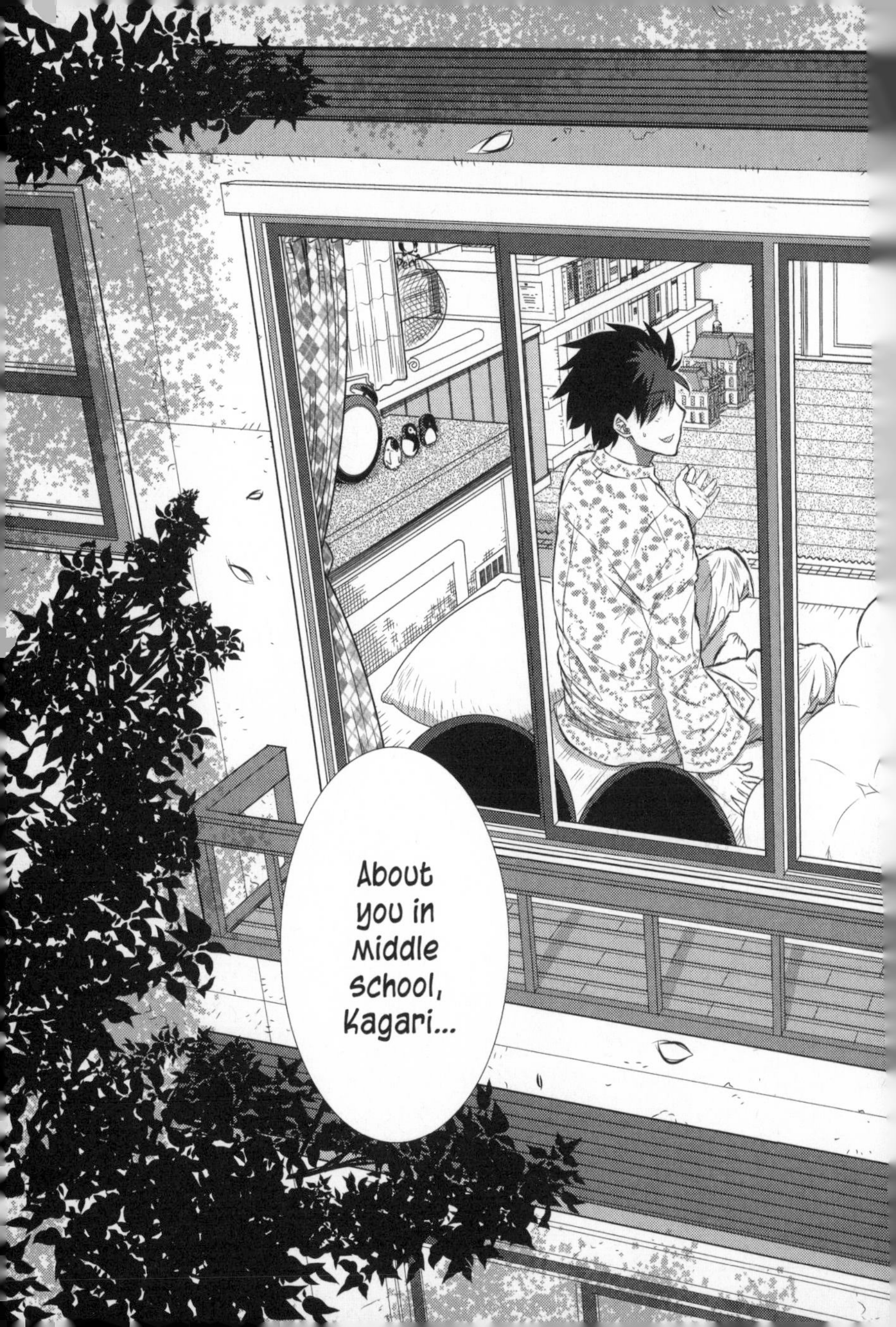
About you in middle school, Kagari...

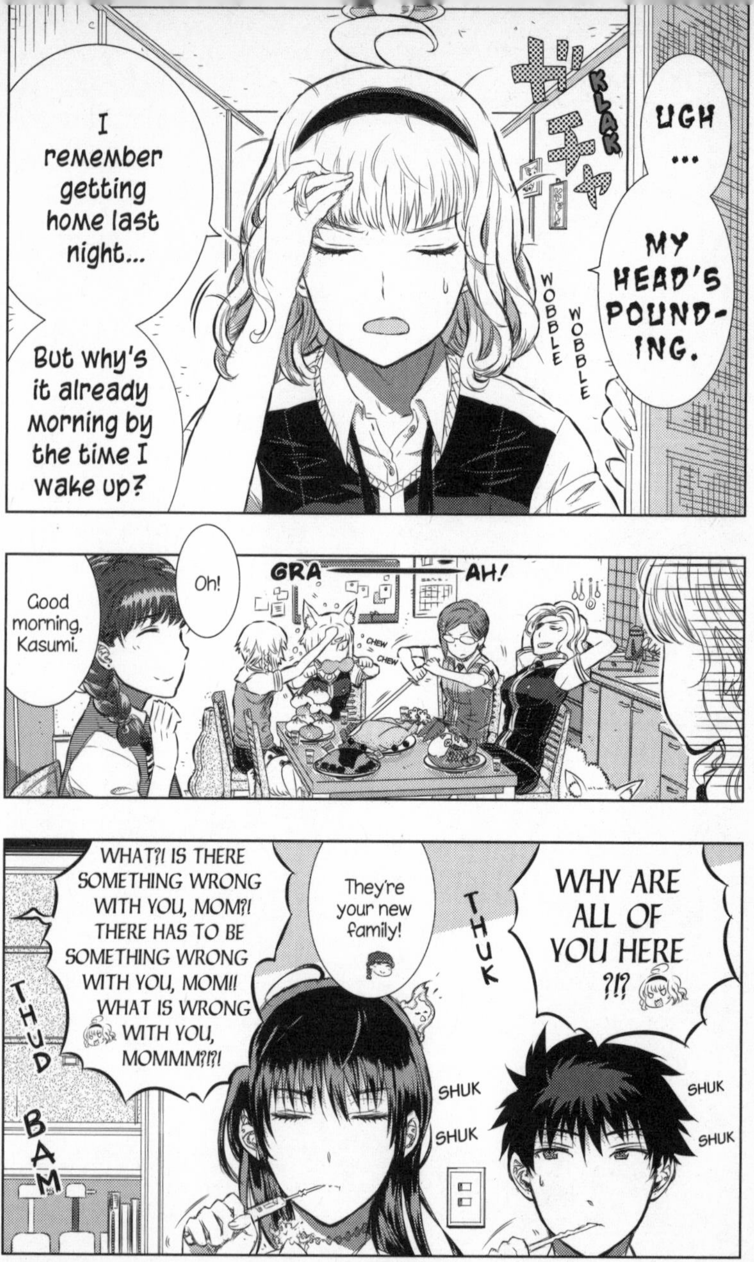
KLAK
UGH... MY HEAD'S POUNDING.
WOBBLE WOBBLE
I remember getting home last night...
But why's it already morning by the time I wake up?
GRA—AH!
CHEW CHEW
Oh!
Good morning, Kasumi.
WHY ARE ALL OF YOU HERE ?!?
THUK
They're your new family!
SHUK SHUK
SHUK SHUK
WHAT?! IS THERE SOMETHING WRONG WITH YOU, MOM?! THERE HAS TO BE SOMETHING WRONG WITH YOU, MOM!! WHAT IS WRONG WITH YOU, MOMMM?!?!
THUD BAM

CHAPTER 14: *END*

Present

Thanks for always helping me out.
...Thanks.

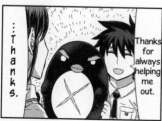

Witchcraft Works

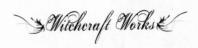

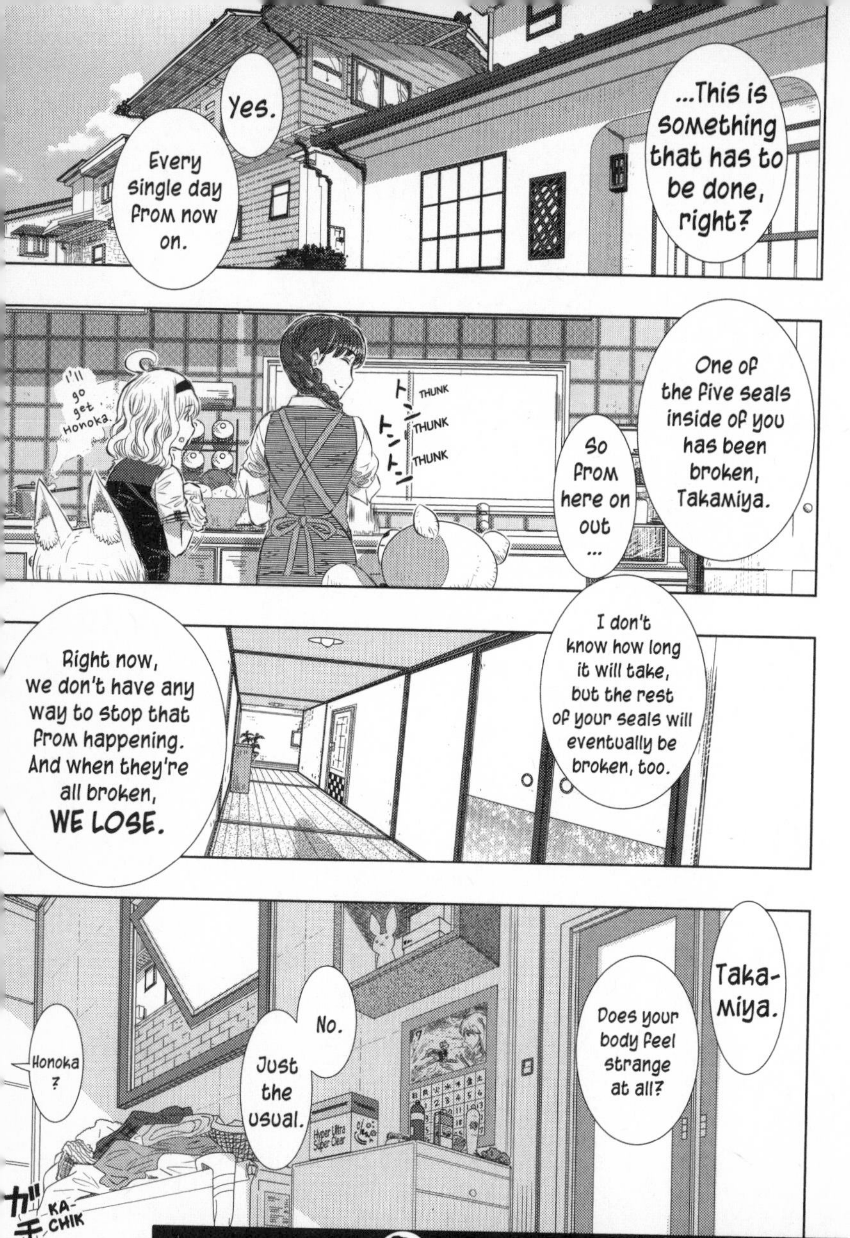
...This is something that has to be done, right?
Yes.
Every single day from now on.
One of the five seals inside of you has been broken, Takamiya.
So from here on out ...
THUNK
THUNK
THUNK
I'll go get Honoka.
I don't know how long it will take, but the rest of your seals will eventually be broken, too.
Right now, we don't have any way to stop that from happening. And when they're all broken, **WE LOSE.**
Taka-miya.
Does your body feel strange at all?
No.
Just the usual.
Hyper Ultra Super Clear
Honoka?
KA-CHIK

CHAPTER 15 Takamiya and the Strong-Armed Witch

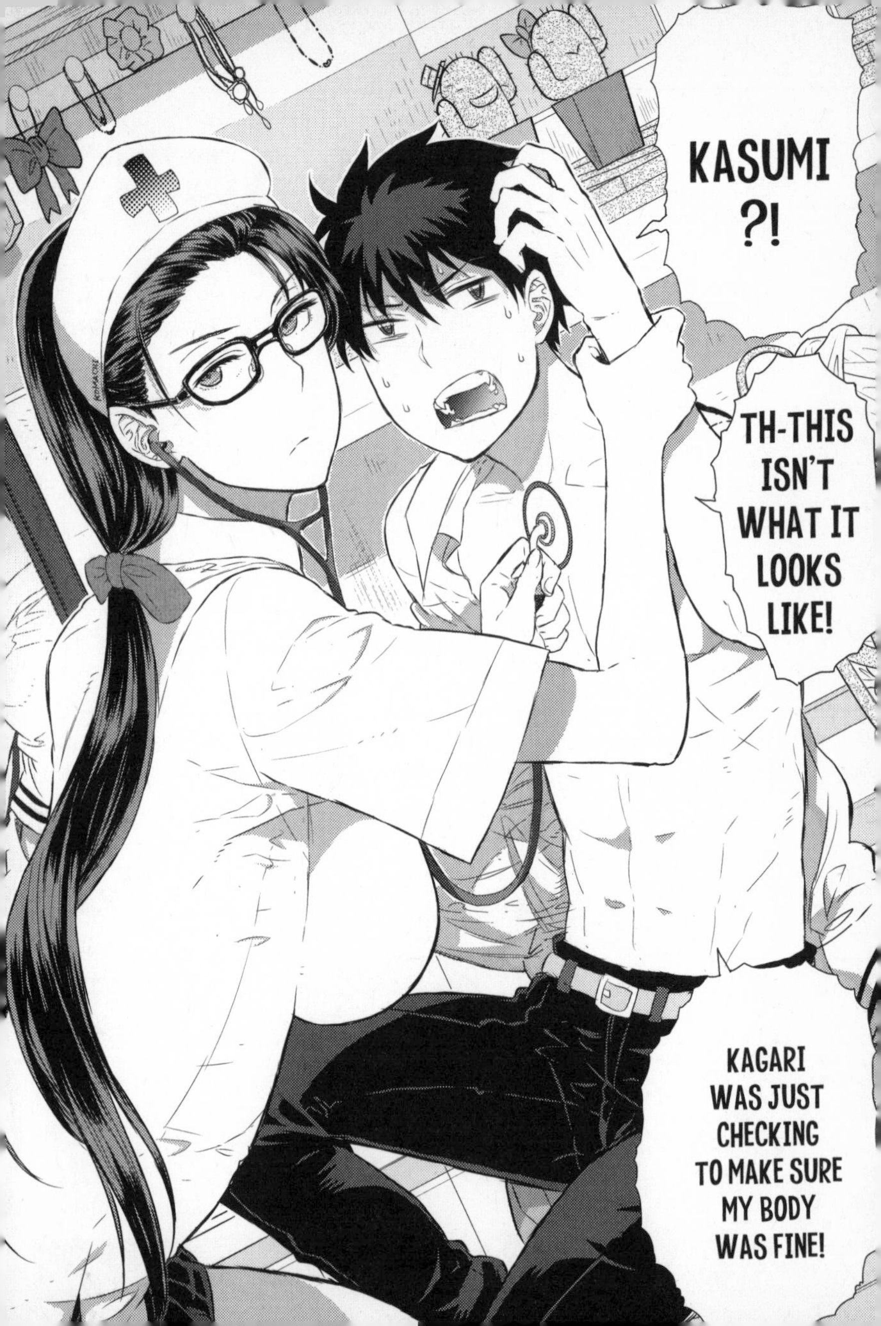
KASUMI ?!
TH-THIS ISN'T WHAT IT LOOKS LIKE!
KAGARI WAS JUST CHECKING TO MAKE SURE MY BODY WAS FINE!

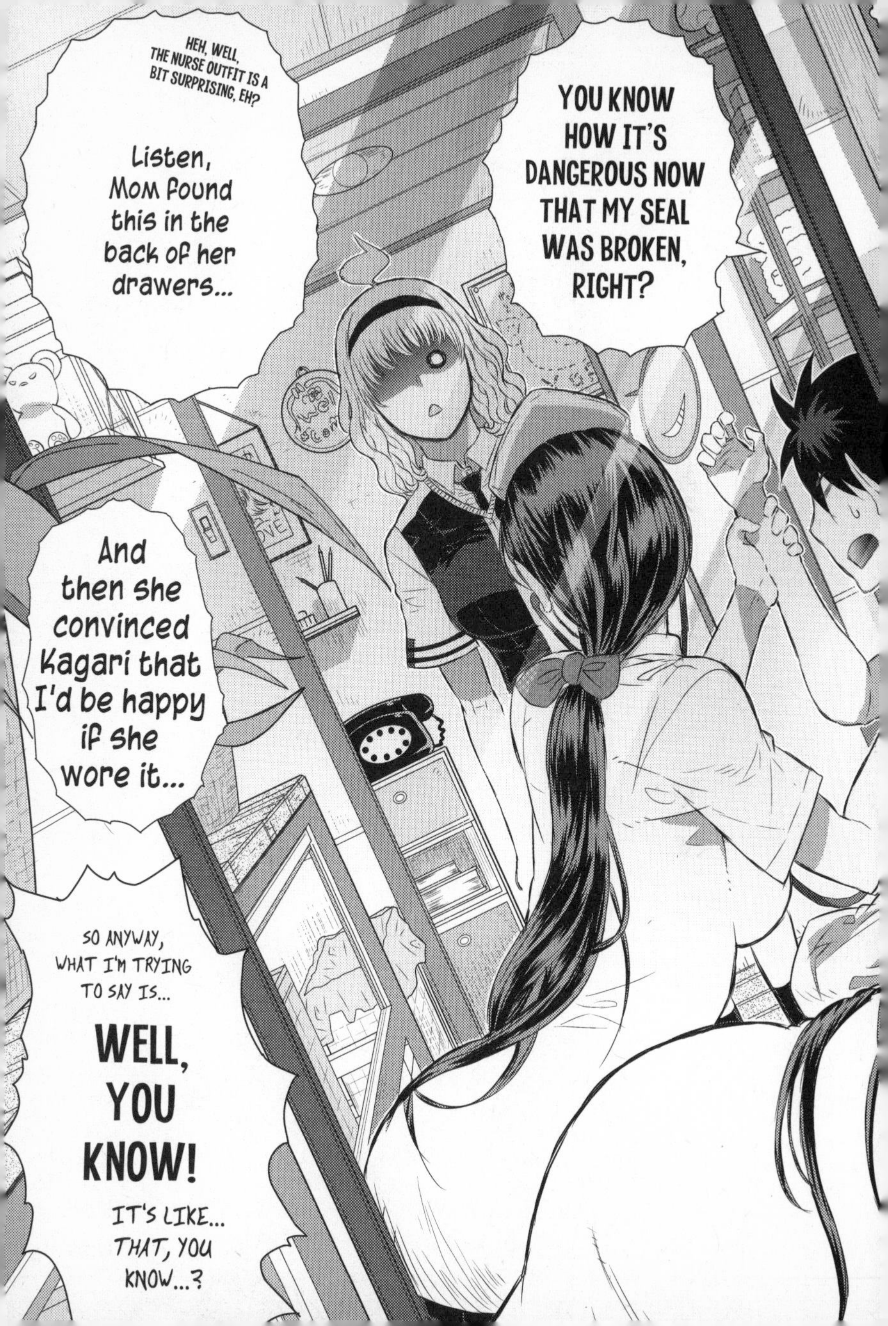
YOU KNOW HOW IT'S DANGEROUS NOW THAT MY SEAL WAS BROKEN, RIGHT?
HEH, WELL, THE NURSE OUTFIT IS A BIT SURPRISING, EH?
Listen, Mom found this in the back of her drawers...
And then she convinced Kagari that I'd be happy if she wore it...
SO ANYWAY, WHAT I'M TRYING TO SAY IS...
WELL, YOU KNOW!
IT'S LIKE... THAT, YOU KNOW...?

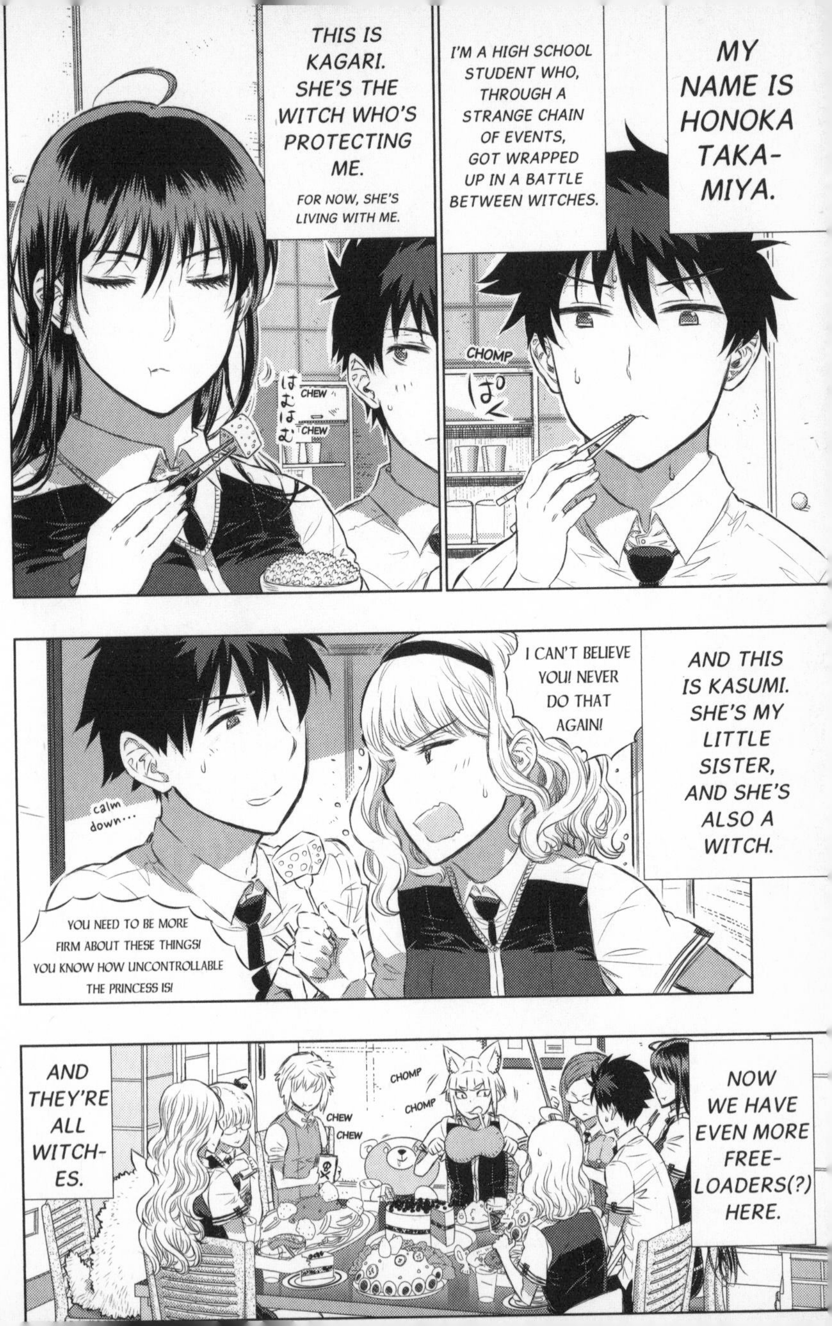
MY NAME IS HONOKA TAKA-MIYA.
I'M A HIGH SCHOOL STUDENT WHO, THROUGH A STRANGE CHAIN OF EVENTS, GOT WRAPPED UP IN A BATTLE BETWEEN WITCHES.
CHOMP
ぱく
THIS IS KAGARI. SHE'S THE WITCH WHO'S PROTECTING ME.
FOR NOW, SHE'S LIVING WITH ME.
CHEW
はむはむ
CHEW
AND THIS IS KASUMI. SHE'S MY LITTLE SISTER, AND SHE'S ALSO A WITCH.
I CAN'T BELIEVE YOU! NEVER DO THAT AGAIN!
YOU NEED TO BE MORE FIRM ABOUT THESE THINGS! YOU KNOW HOW UNCONTROLLABLE THE PRINCESS IS!
calm down...
NOW WE HAVE EVEN MORE FREE-LOADERS(?) HERE.
CHOMP
CHOMP
CHEW
CHEW
AND THEY'RE ALL WITCH-ES.

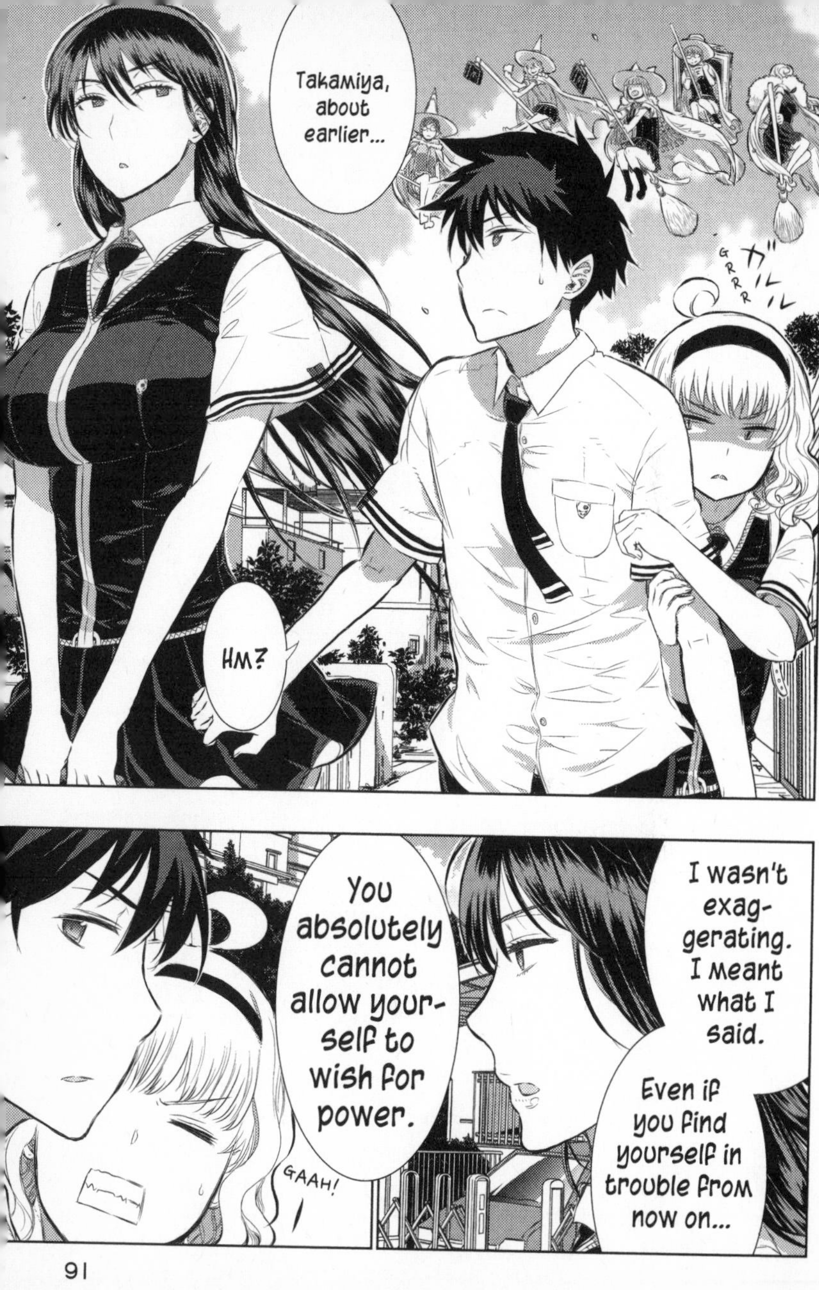

Takamiya, about earlier...
GRRR
ガルル
HM?
I wasn't exag-gerating. I meant what I said.
Even if you find yourself in trouble from now on...
You absolutely cannot allow your-self to wish for power.
GAAH!

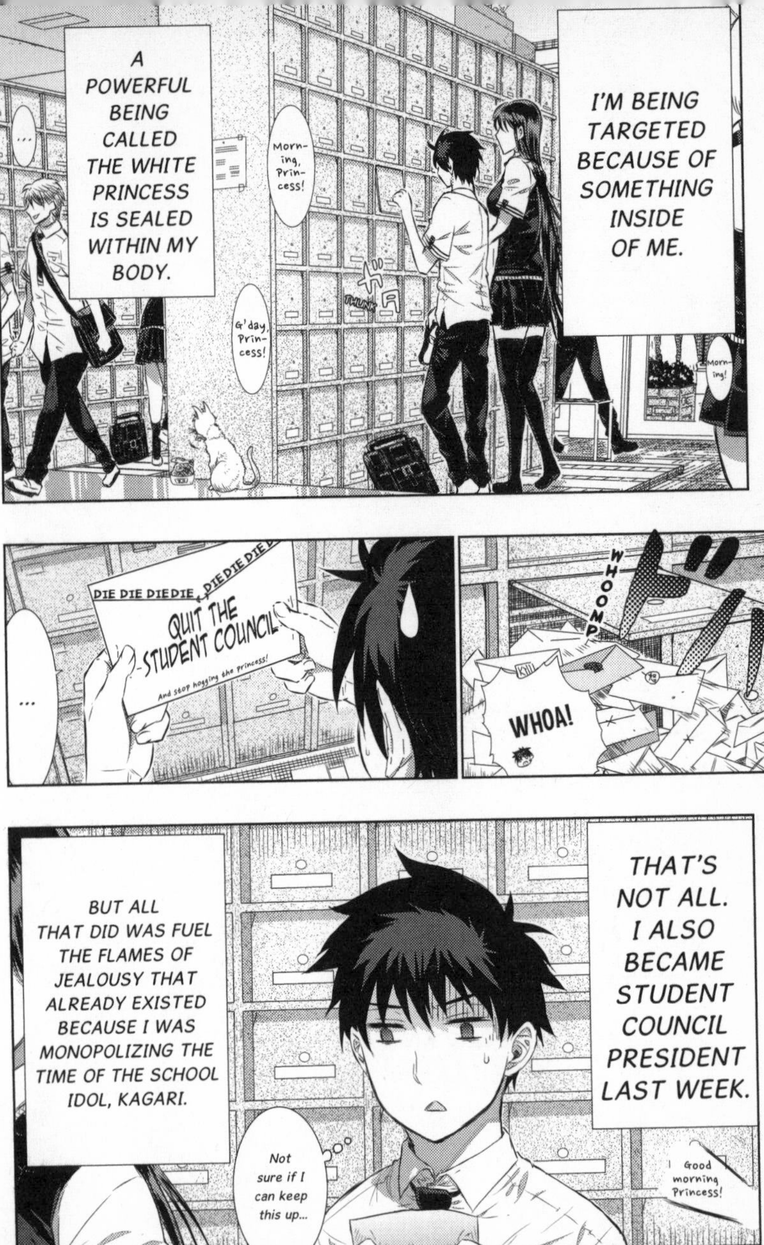
I'M BEING TARGETED BECAUSE OF SOMETHING INSIDE OF ME.
Morn-ing!
Morn-ing, Prin-cess!
THUNK
G'day, Prin-cess!
A POWERFUL BEING CALLED THE WHITE PRINCESS IS SEALED WITHIN MY BODY.
...
WHOOMP
WHOA!
DIE DIE DIEDIE DIEDIE DIE
QUIT THE STUDENT COUNCIL
And stop hogging the princess!
...
THAT'S NOT ALL. I ALSO BECAME STUDENT COUNCIL PRESIDENT LAST WEEK.
Good morning Princess!
BUT ALL THAT DID WAS FUEL THE FLAMES OF JEALOUSY THAT ALREADY EXISTED BECAUSE I WAS MONOPOLIZING THE TIME OF THE SCHOOL IDOL, KAGARI.
Not sure if I can keep this up...

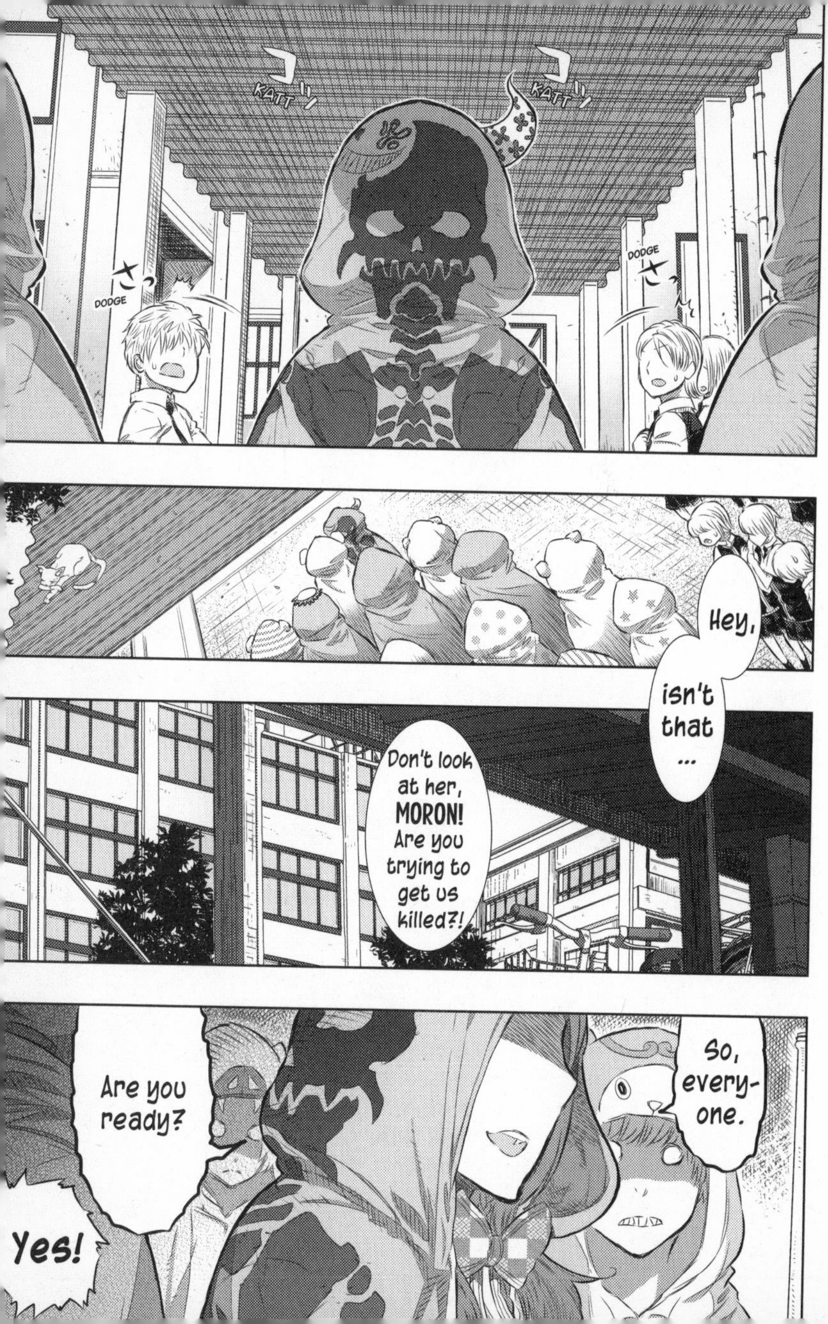
KATT
KATT
DODGE
DODGE
Hey, isn't that ...
Don't look at her, MORON! Are you trying to get us killed?!
So, every-one.
Are you ready?
Yes!

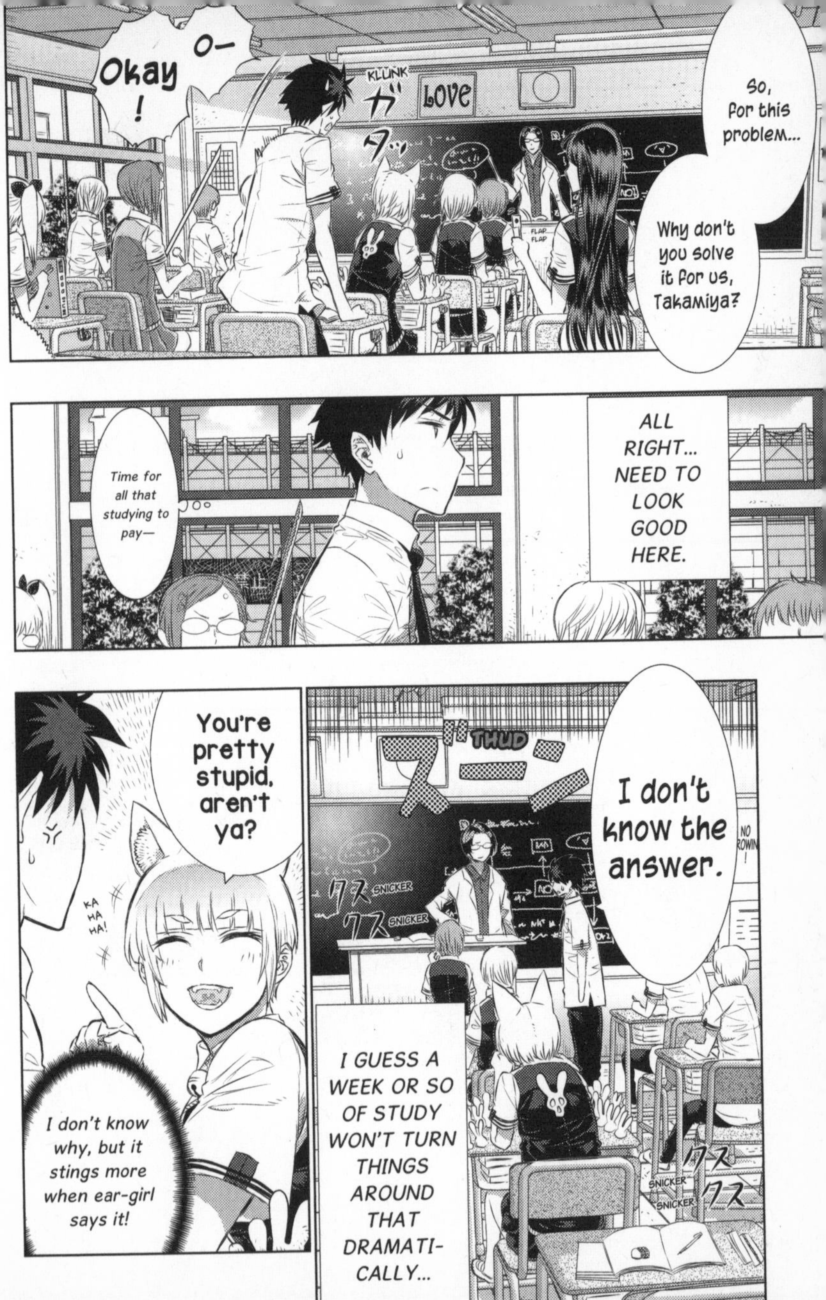
So, for this problem...
Why don't you solve it for us, Takamiya?
LOVE
KLUNK
O— Okay!
FLAP FLAP
ALL RIGHT... NEED TO LOOK GOOD HERE.
Time for all that studying to pay—
I don't know the answer.
THUD
SNICKER
SNICKER
I GUESS A WEEK OR SO OF STUDY WON'T TURN THINGS AROUND THAT DRAMATI-CALLY...
SNICKER
SNICKER
You're pretty stupid, aren't ya?
KA HA HA!
I don't know why, but it stings more when ear-girl says it!

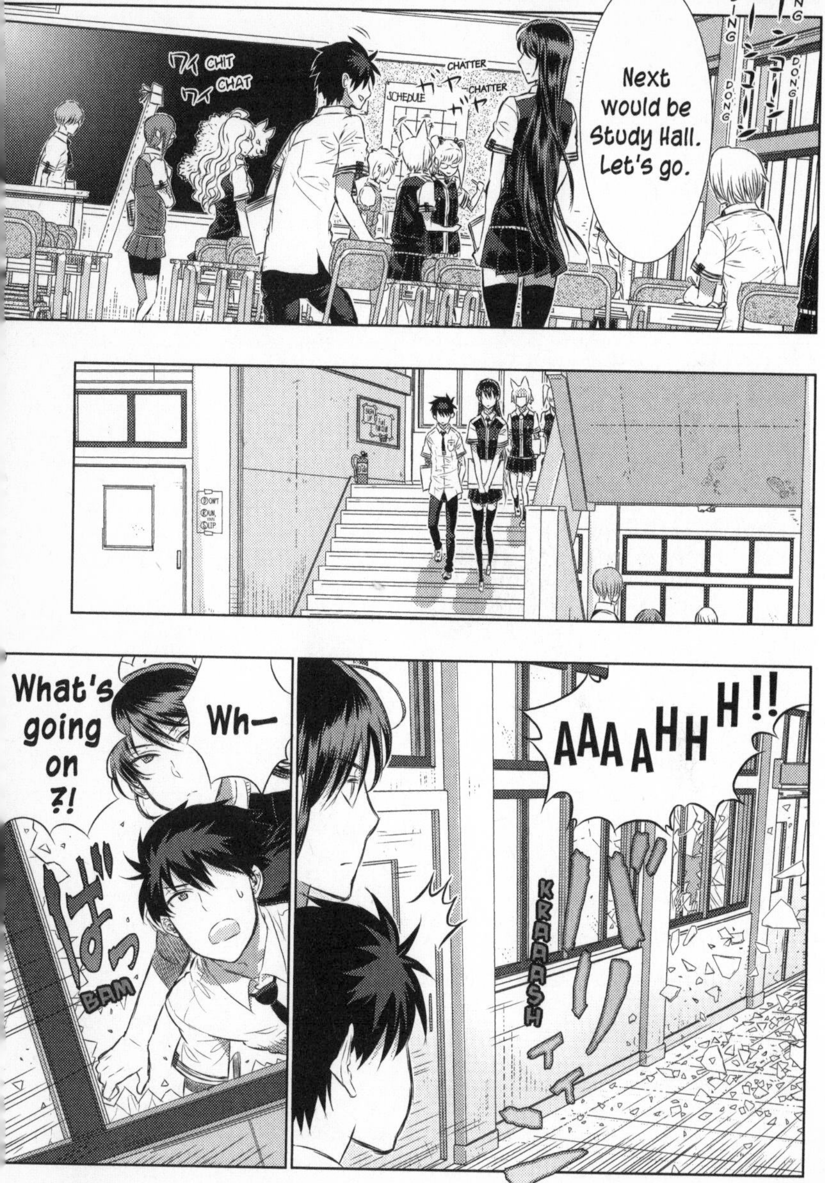
DING DONG DING DONG
Next would be Study Hall. Let's go.
CHATTER
ガヤ
CHATTER
ガヤ
SCHEDULE
ワイ CHIT
ワイ CHAT
AAAAHHHH!!
KRAAAASH
Wh—
What's going on?!
BAM

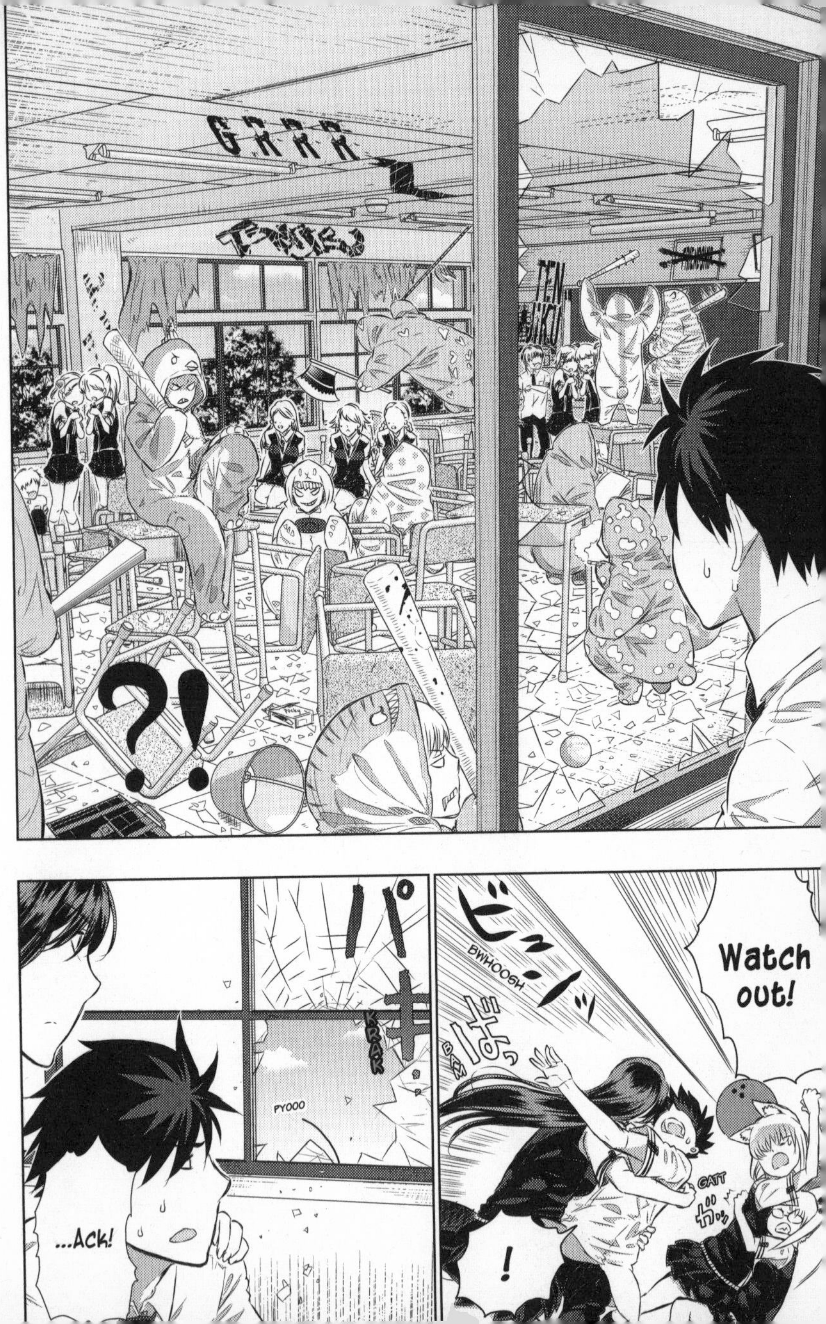
?!
Watch out!
BWHOOSH
ビュ-ッ
BAM
ばっ
GATT
ガッ
!
パキ
KRAK
PYOOO
...Ack!

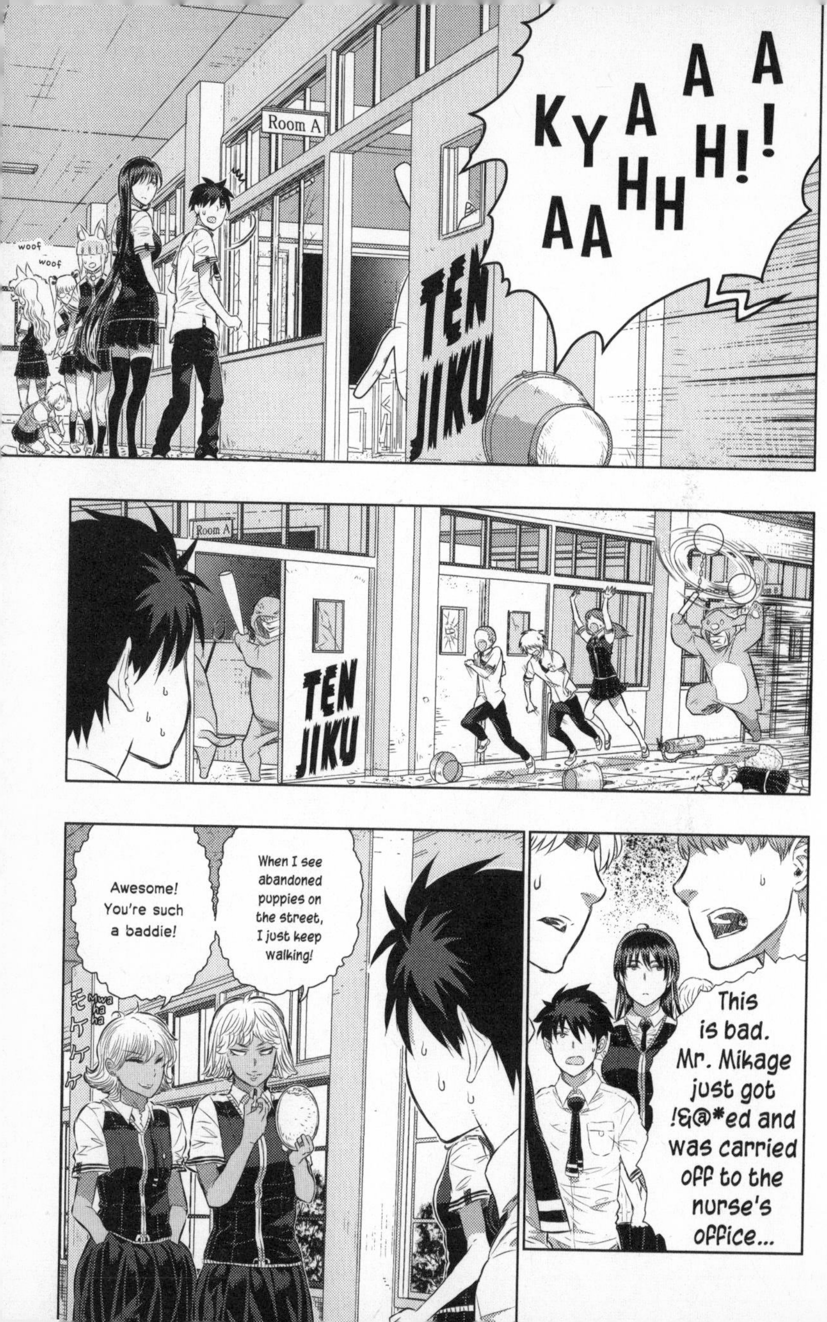
KYAAAAAHHH!!
Room A
woof
woof
TEN JIKU
Room A
TEN JIKU
This is bad. Mr. Mikage just got !&@*ed and was carried off to the nurse's office...
When I see abandoned puppies on the street, I just keep walking!
Awesome! You're such a baddie!
Mwa ha ha

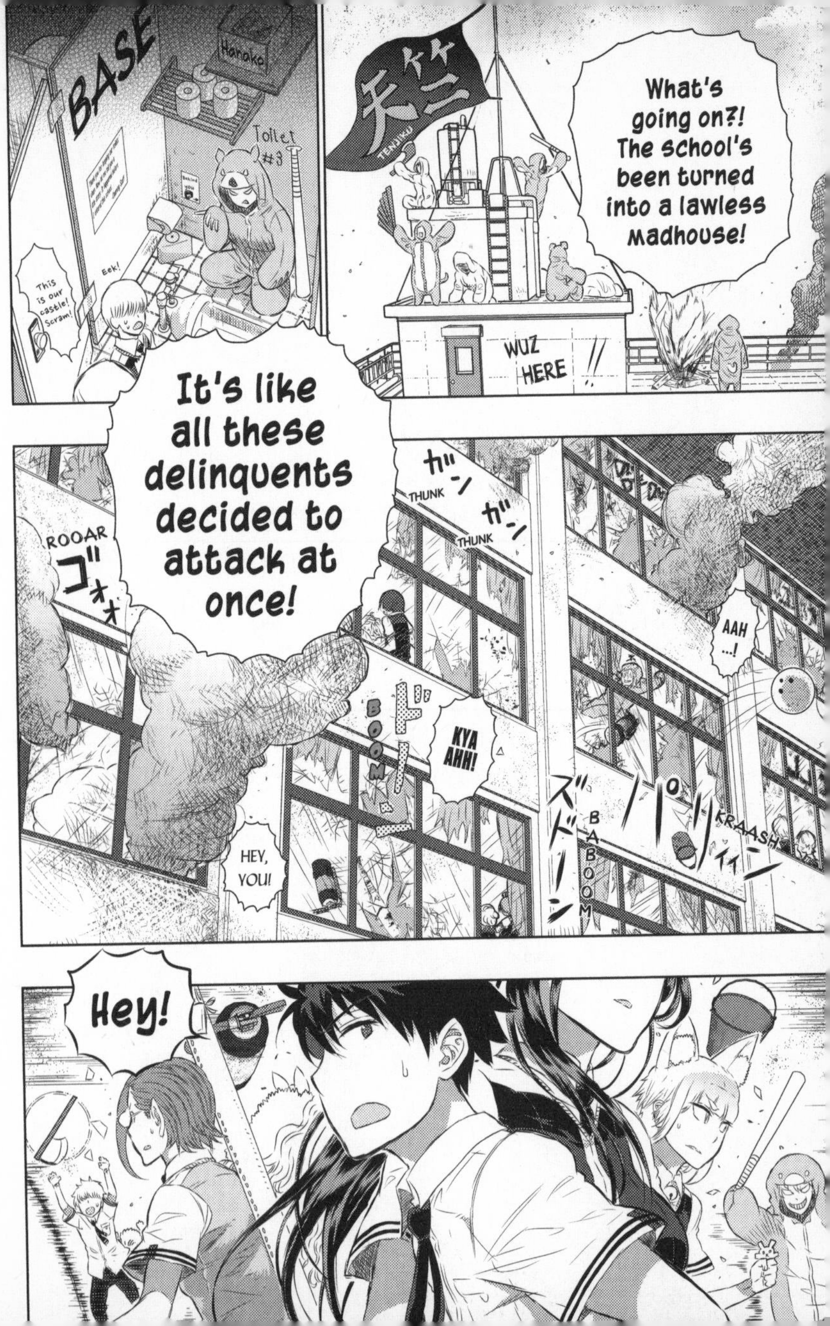
天竺
TENJIKU
What's going on?! The school's been turned into a lawless madhouse!
WUZ HERE
BASE
Hanako
Toilet #3
Behind you
Eek!
This is our castle! Scram!
It's like all these delinquents decided to attack at once!
ガン THUNK
ガン THUNK
AAH ...!
KRAASH
ズドーン BABOOM
ド BOOM
KYA AHH!
HEY, YOU!
ゴォォ ROOAR
Hey!

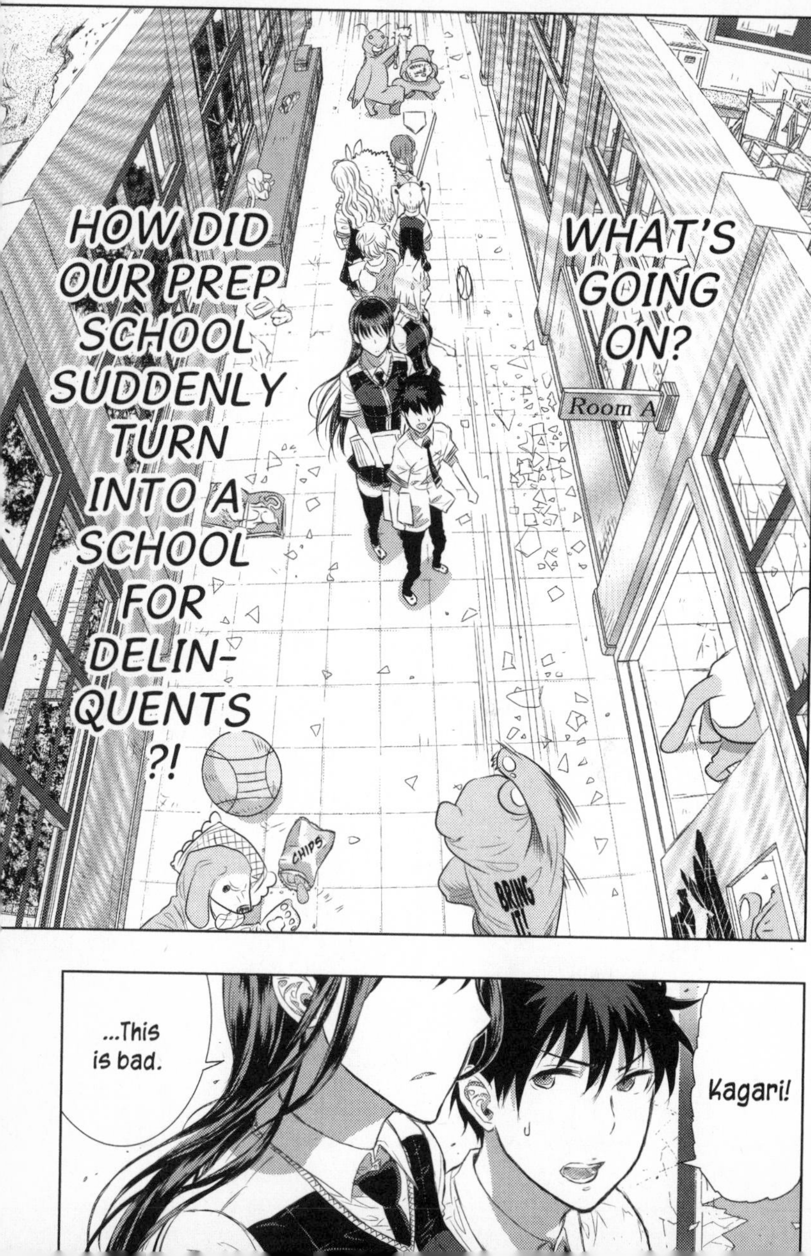
WHAT'S GOING ON?
HOW DID OUR PREP SCHOOL SUDDENLY TURN INTO A SCHOOL FOR DELIN-QUENTS ?!
Room A
BRING IT!
CHIPS
Kagari!
...This is bad.

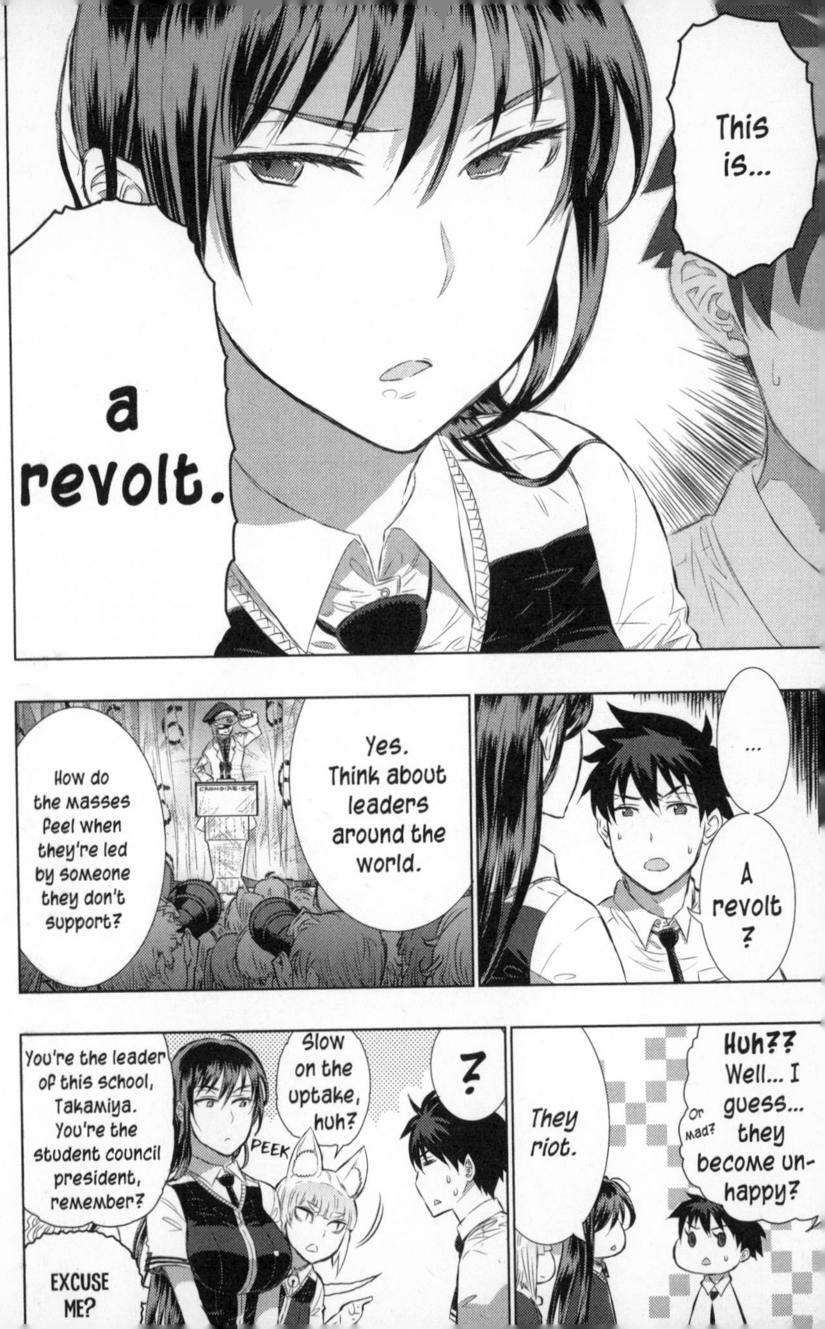
This is...
a revolt.
...
A revolt?
Yes. Think about leaders around the world.
How do the masses feel when they're led by someone they don't support?
Huh?? Well... I guess... they become un-happy?
Or mad?
They riot.
?
Slow on the uptake, huh?
PEEK
You're the leader of this school, Takamiya. You're the student council president, remember?
EXCUSE ME?

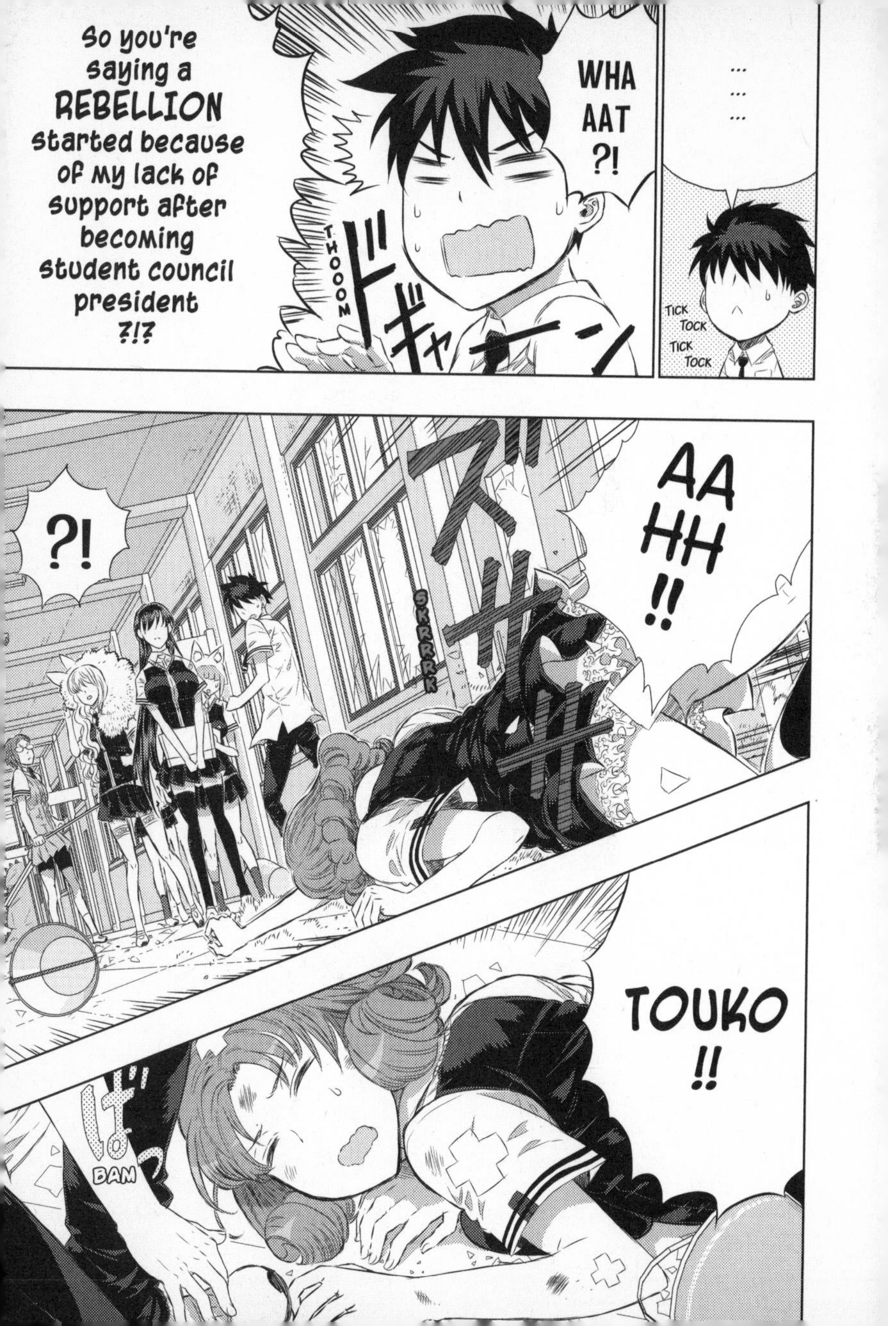

...
...
...
TICK
TOCK
TICK
TOCK
WHA AAT ?!
So you're saying a REBELLION started because of my lack of support after becoming student council president ?!?
THOOOOM
AA HH !!
SKRRRK
?!
TOUKO !!
BAM

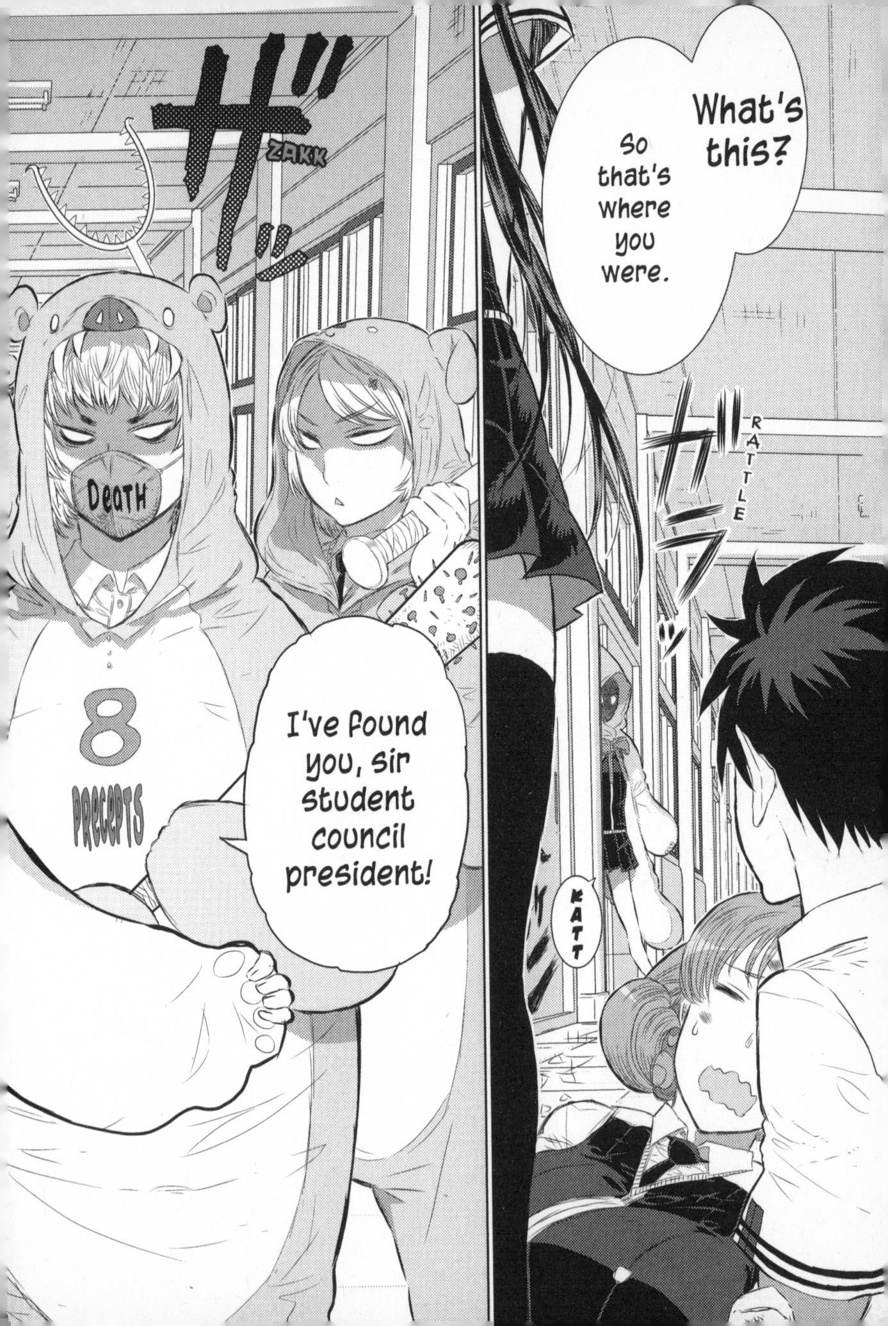
What's this?
So that's where you were.
RATTLE
KATT
ZAKK
Death
8
PRECEPTS
I've found you, sir student council president!

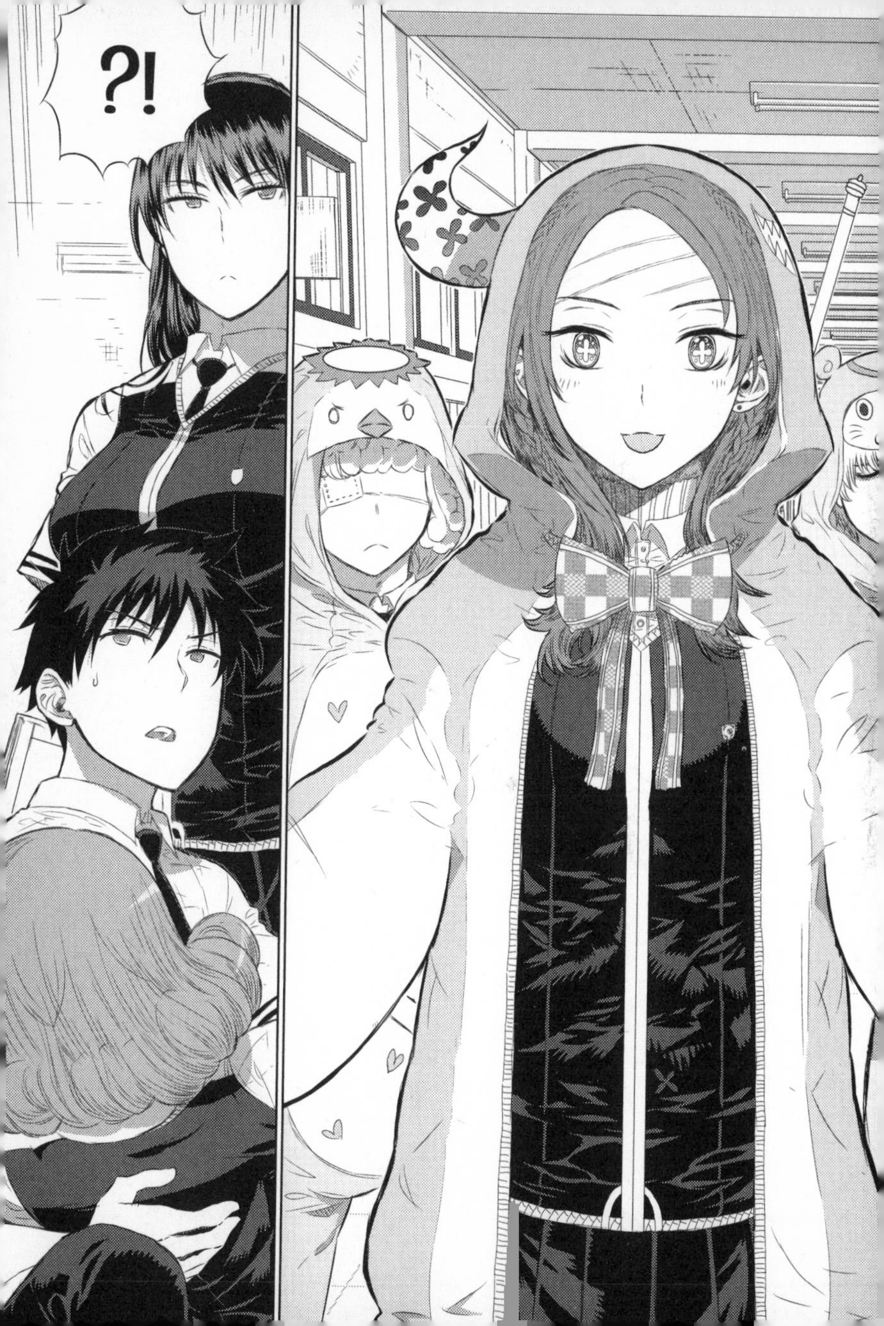
?!

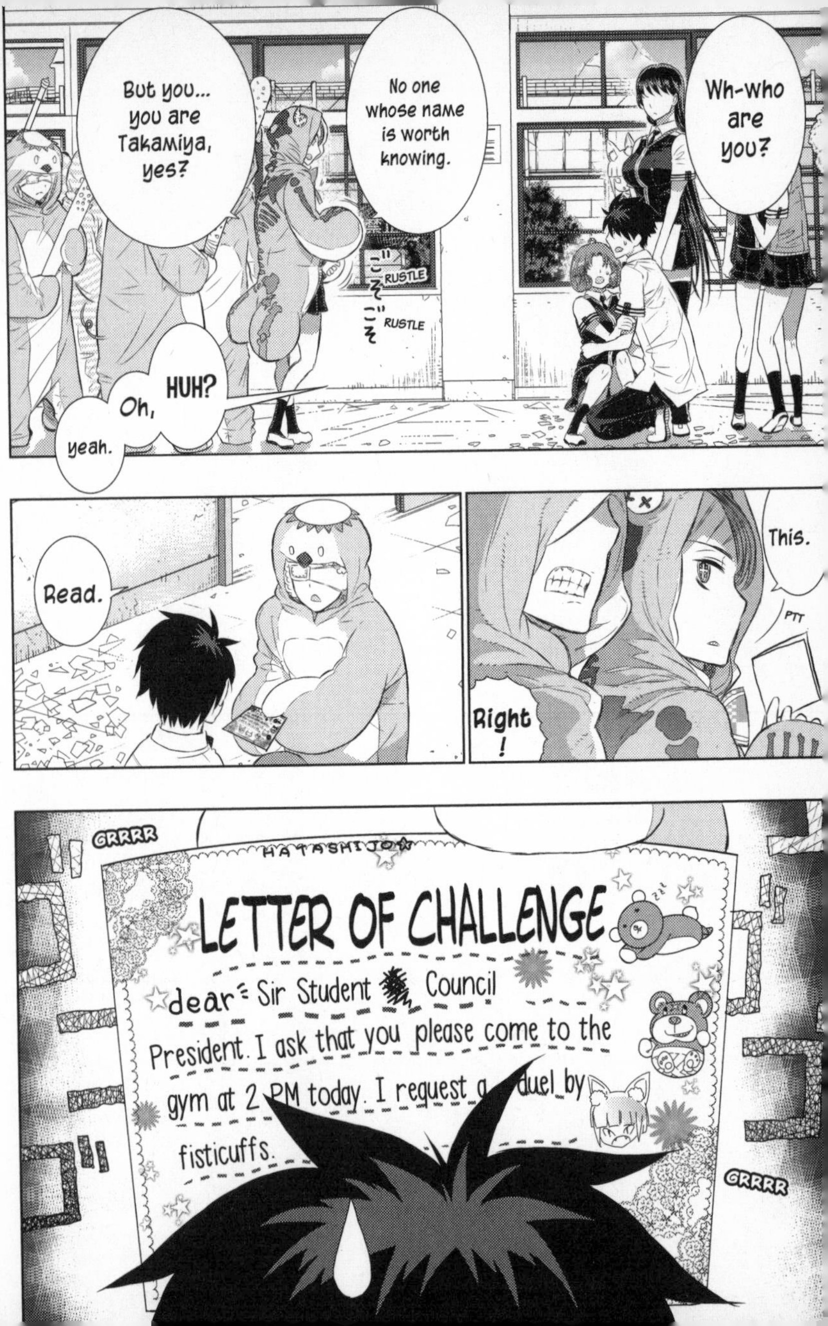
Wh-who are you?
No one whose name is worth knowing.
ごそ RUSTLE
ごそ RUSTLE
But you... you are Takamiya, yes?
HUH?
Oh,
yeah.
This.
PTT
Right!
Read.
GRRRR
HATASHIJO☆
LETTER OF CHALLENGE
dear: Sir Student Council
President. I ask that you please come to the
gym at 2 PM today. I request a duel by
fisticuffs.
GRRRR

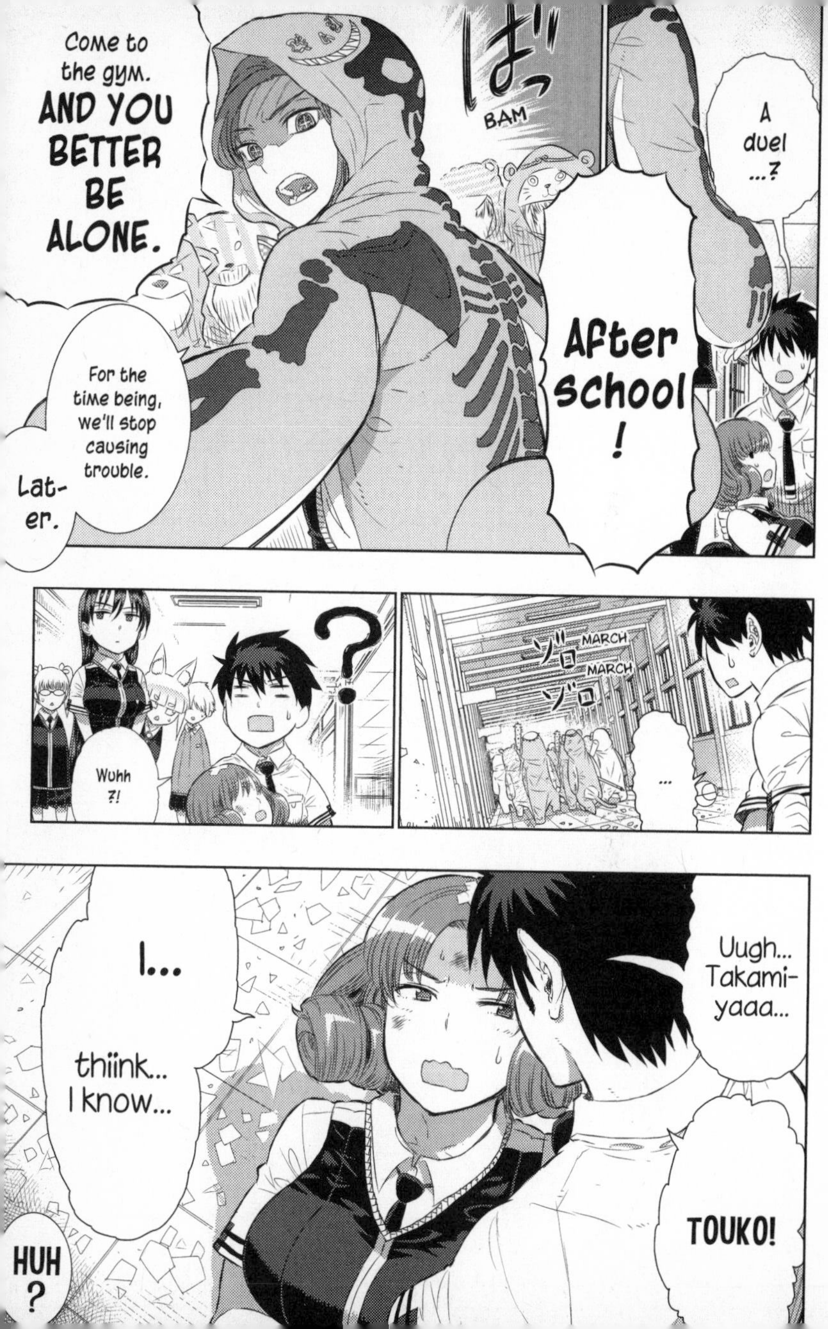
A duel ...?
ぱっ
BAM
After school !
Come to the gym.
AND YOU BETTER BE ALONE.
For the time being, we'll stop causing trouble.
Lat-er.
ゾロゾロ
MARCH MARCH
...
Wuhh ?!
Uugh... Takami-yaaa...
TOUKO!
I...
thiiink... I know...
HUH ?

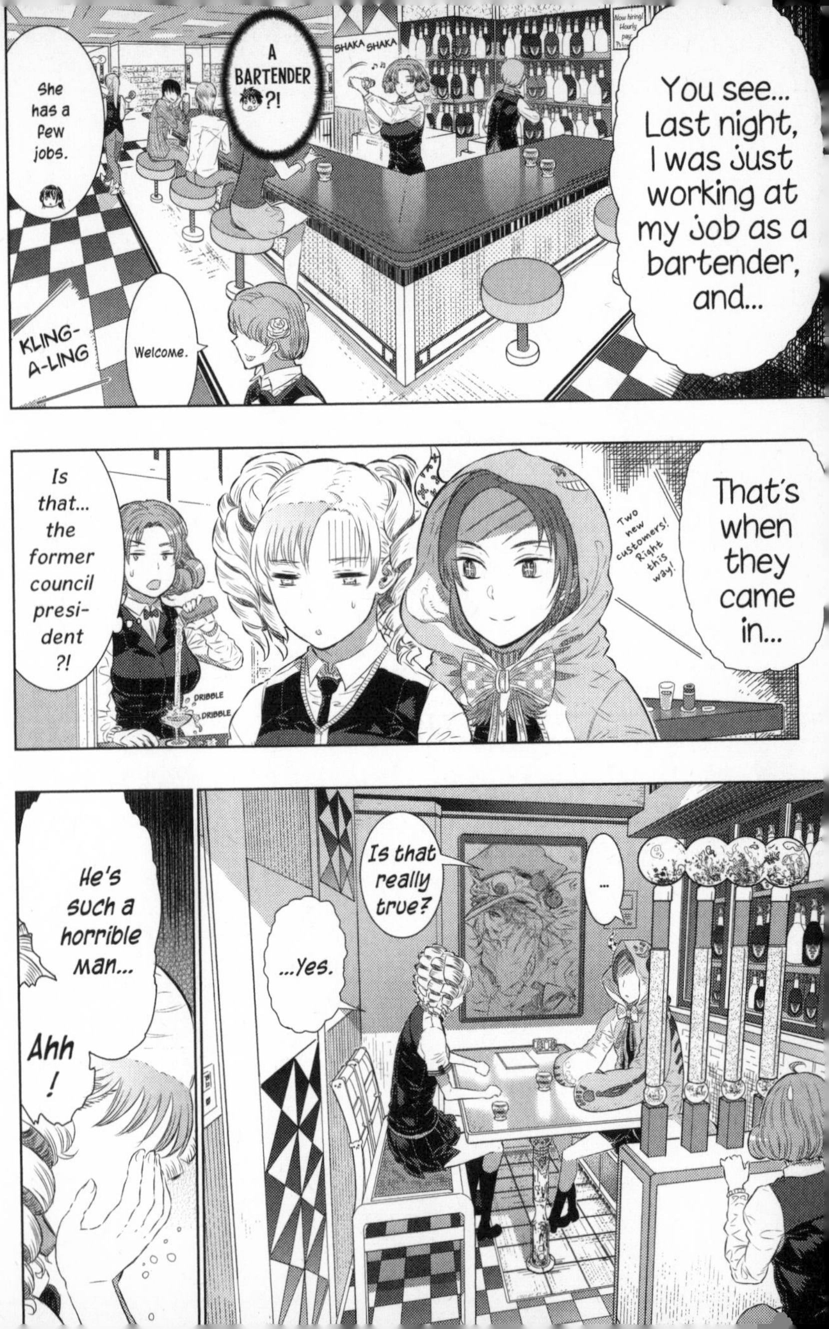
You see... Last night, I was just working at my job as a bartender, and...
Now hiring! Hourly pay
SHAKA SHAKA
A BARTENDER ?!
She has a few jobs.
Welcome.
KLING-A-LING
That's when they came in...
Two new customers! Right this way!
Is that... the former council president?!
DRIBBLE DRIBBLE
...
Is that really true?
...Yes.
He's such a horrible man...
Ahh!

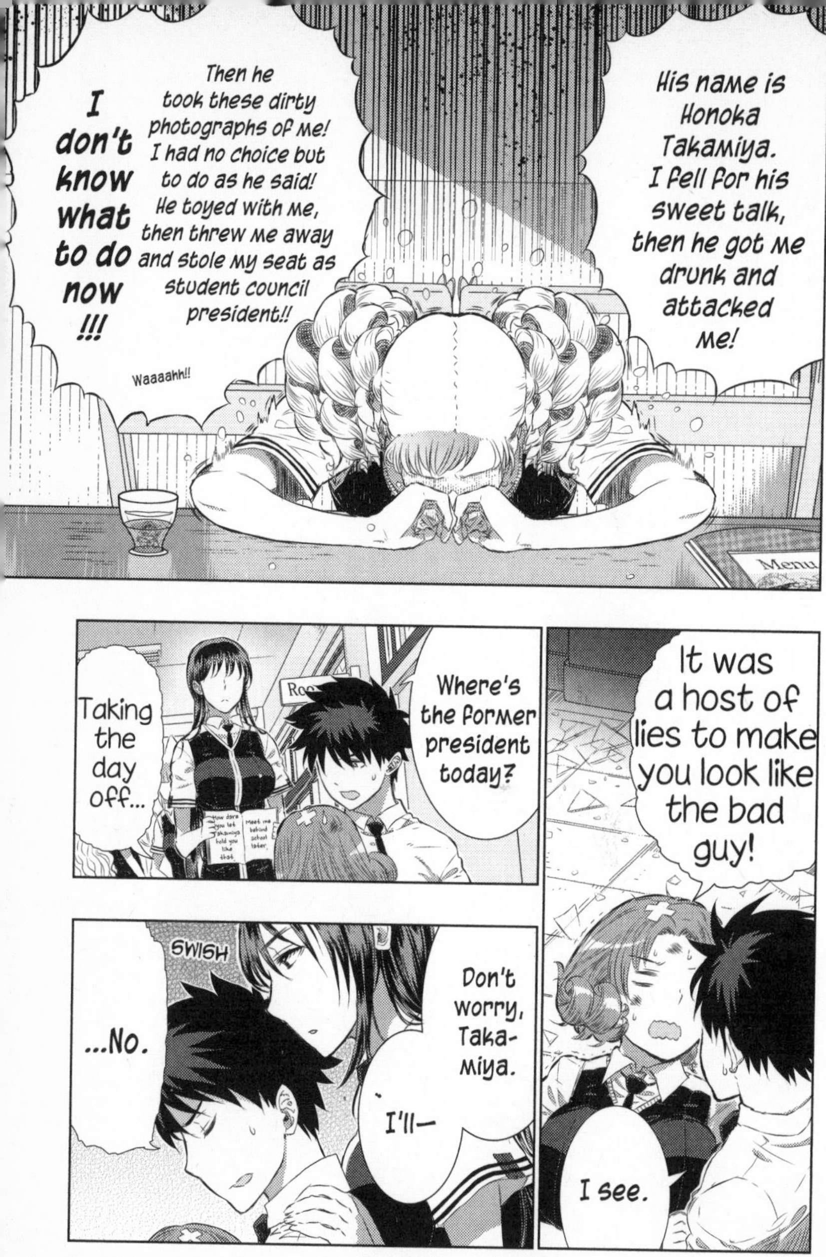
His name is Honoka Takamiya. I fell for his sweet talk, then he got me drunk and attacked me!
Then he took these dirty photographs of me! I had no choice but to do as he said! He toyed with me, then threw me away and stole my seat as student council president!!
I don't know what to do now!!!
Waaaahh!!
Menu
It was a host of lies to make you look like the bad guy!
Where's the former president today?
Taking the day off...
How dare you let Takamiya hold you like that.
Meet me behind school later.
I see.
Don't worry, Takamiya.
I'll—
SWISH
...No.

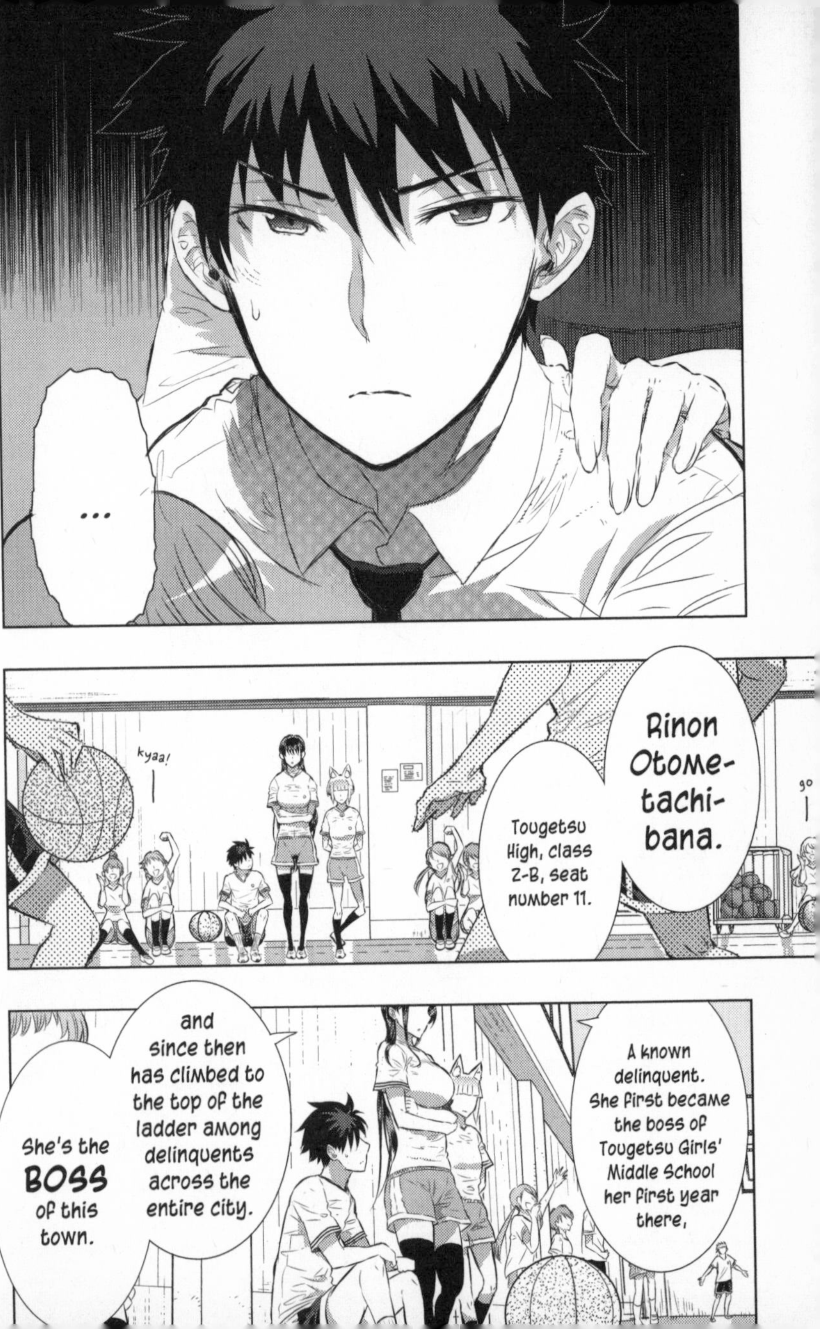
...
go
Rinon Otome-tachibana.
Tougetsu High, class 2-B, seat number 11.
kyaa!
A known delinquent. She first became the boss of Tougetsu Girls' Middle School her first year there,
and since then has climbed to the top of the ladder among delinquents across the entire city.
She's the BOSS of this town.

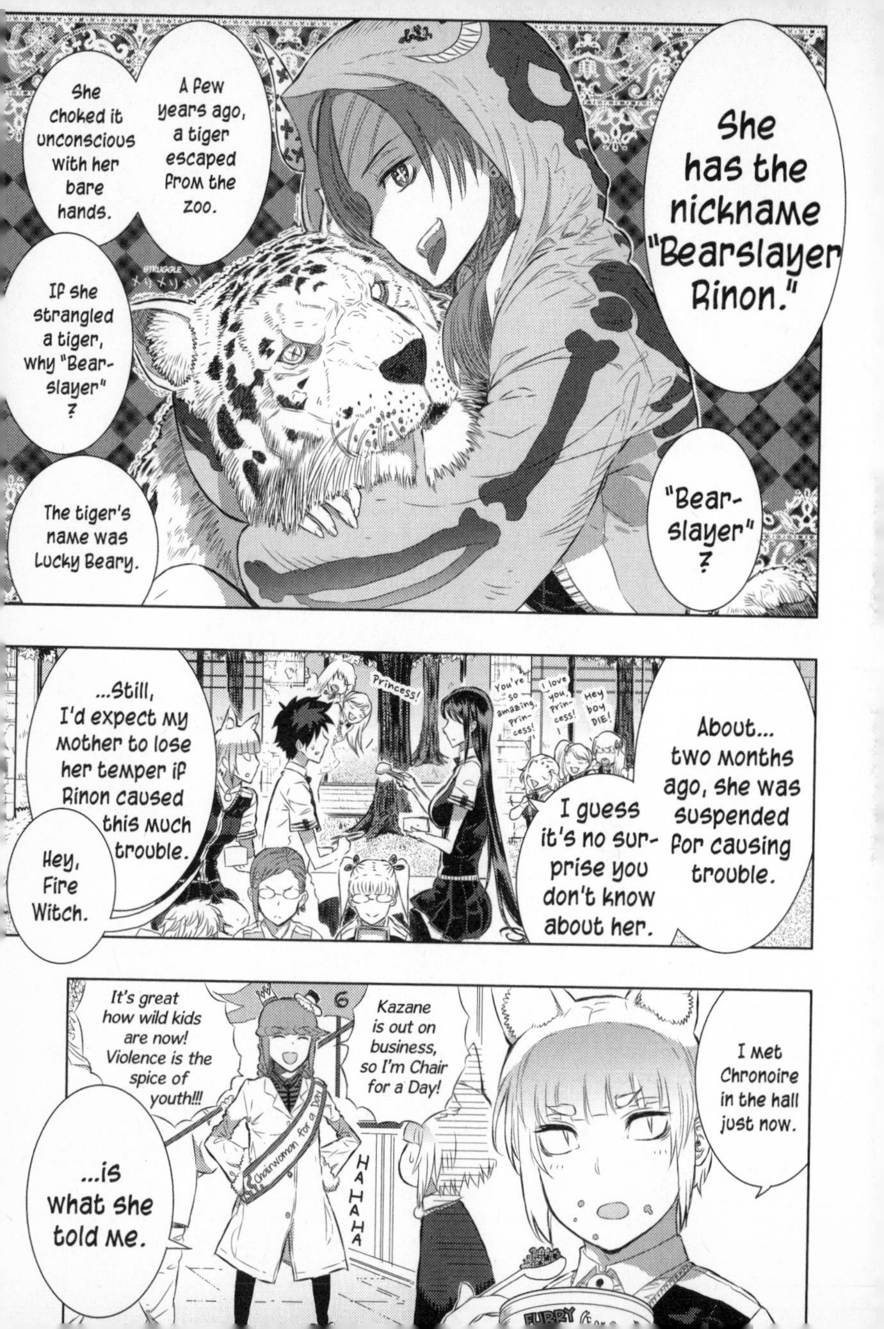
She has the nickname "Bearslayer Rinon."
A few years ago, a tiger escaped from the zoo.
She choked it unconscious with her bare hands.
"Bear-slayer"?
If she strangled a tiger, why "Bear-slayer"?
The tiger's name was Lucky Beary.
About... two months ago, she was suspended for causing trouble.
I guess it's no surprise you don't know about her.
Hey boy DIE!
I love you, Prin-cess!
You're so amazing, prin-cess!
Princess!
...Still, I'd expect my mother to lose her temper if Rinon caused this much trouble.
Hey, Fire Witch.
I met Chronoire in the hall just now.
Kazane is out on business, so I'm Chair for a Day!
It's great how wild kids are now! Violence is the spice of youth!!!
Chairwoman for a Day
HAHAHAHA
...is what she told me.

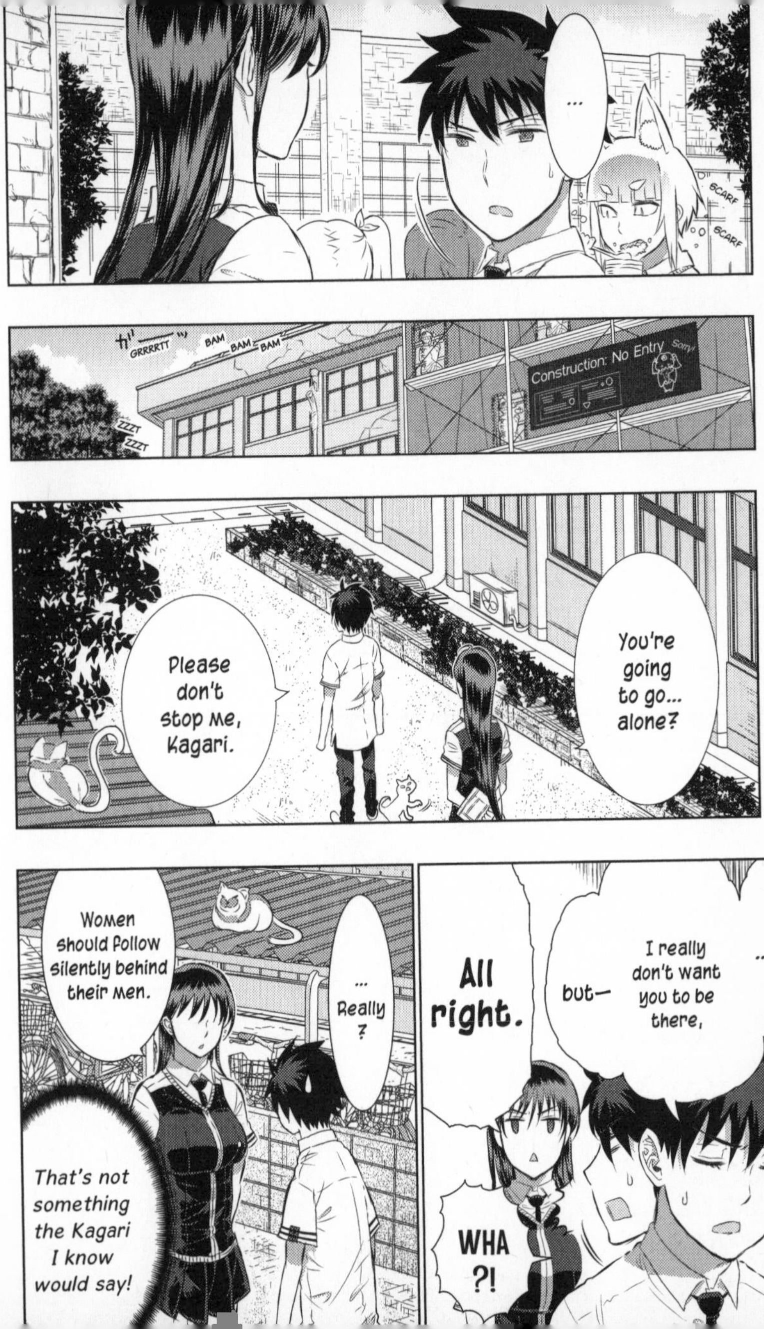
...
SCARF
SCARF
GRRRRTT
BAM
BAM
BAM
ZZZT
ZZZT
Construction: No Entry
Sorry!
You're going to go... alone?
Please don't stop me, Kagari.
...Well,
I really don't want you to be there,
but—
All right.
WHA ?!
Women should follow silently behind their men.
... Really ?
That's not something the Kagari I know would say!

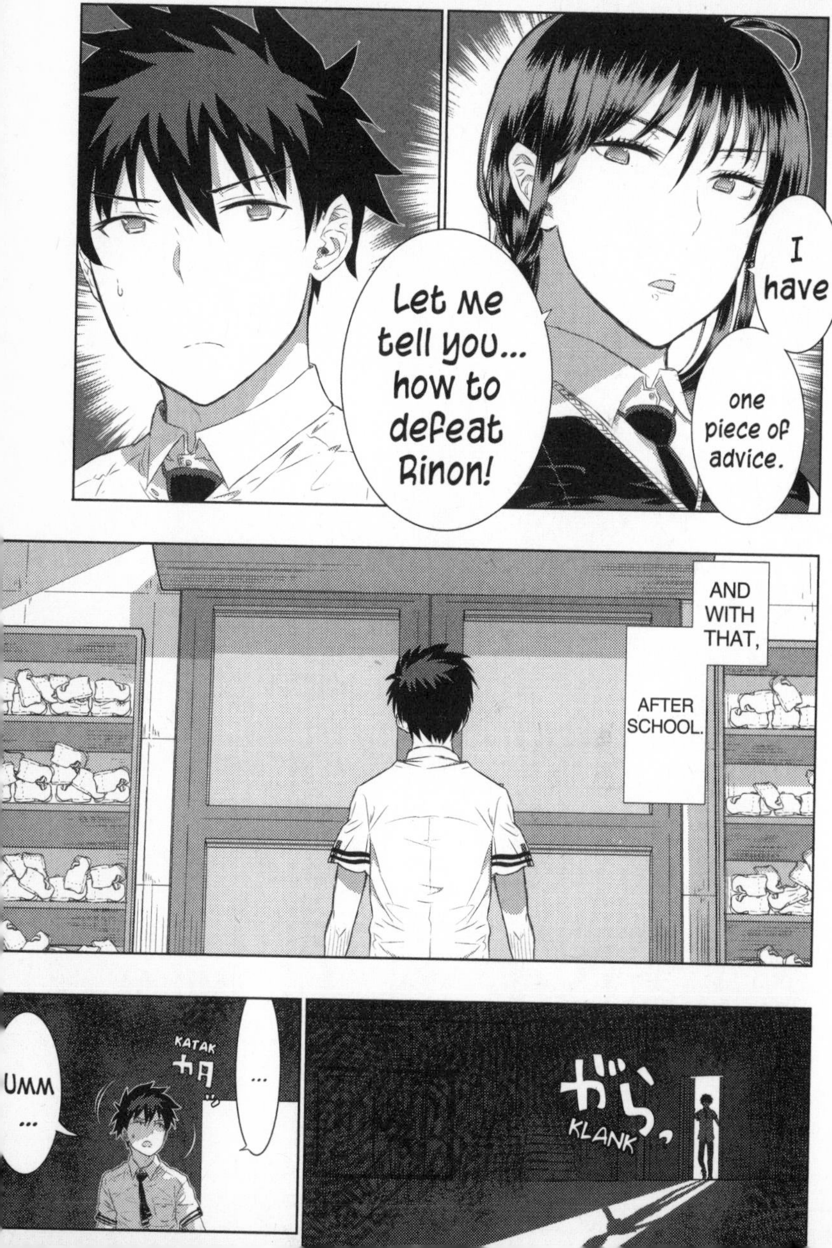
I have
one piece of advice.
Let me tell you... how to defeat Rinon!
AND WITH THAT,
AFTER SCHOOL.
がら、
KLANK
...
KATAK
カタ
UMM ...

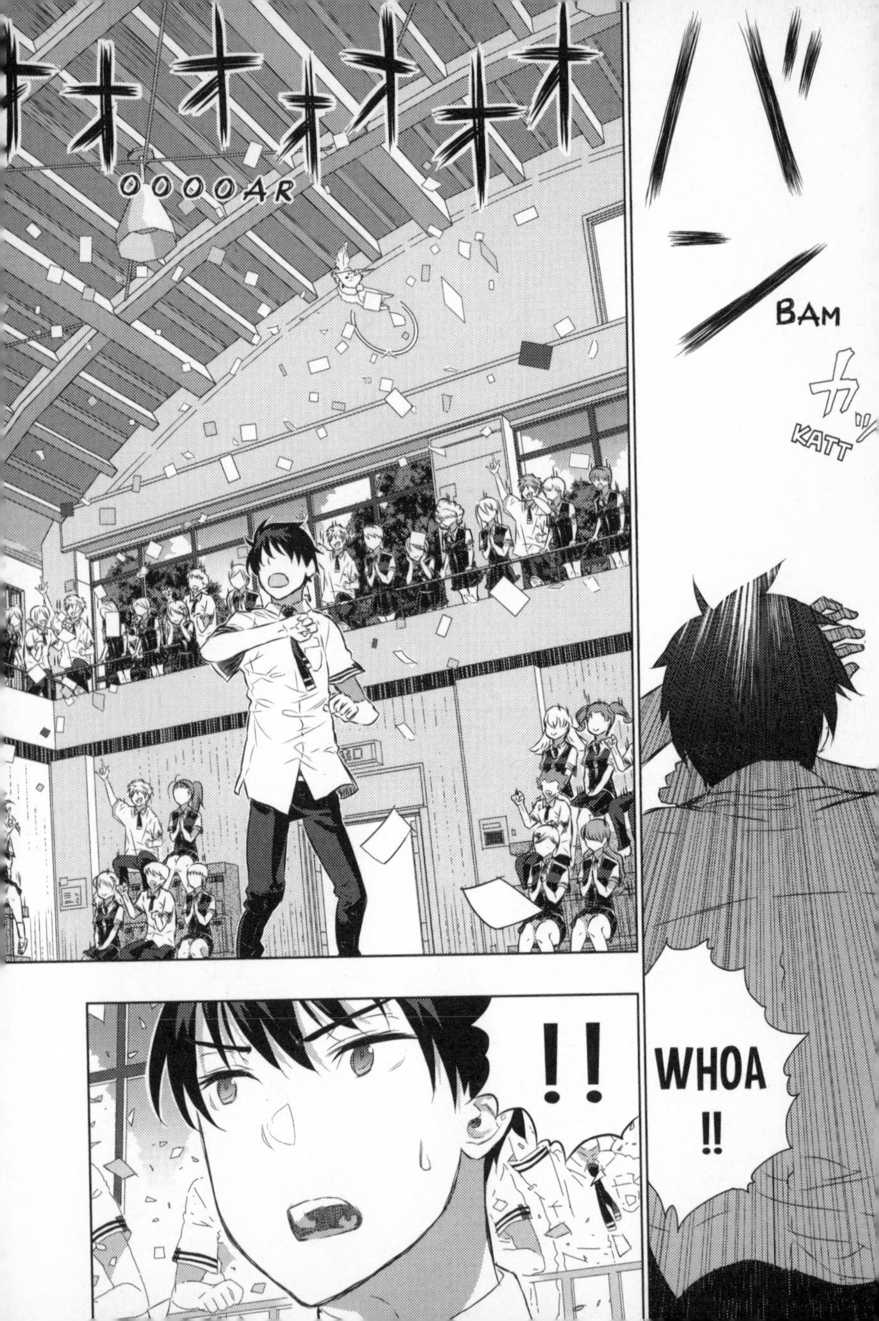
バーン
BAM
カッ
KATT
WHOA !!
オオオオオ
OOOOAR
!!

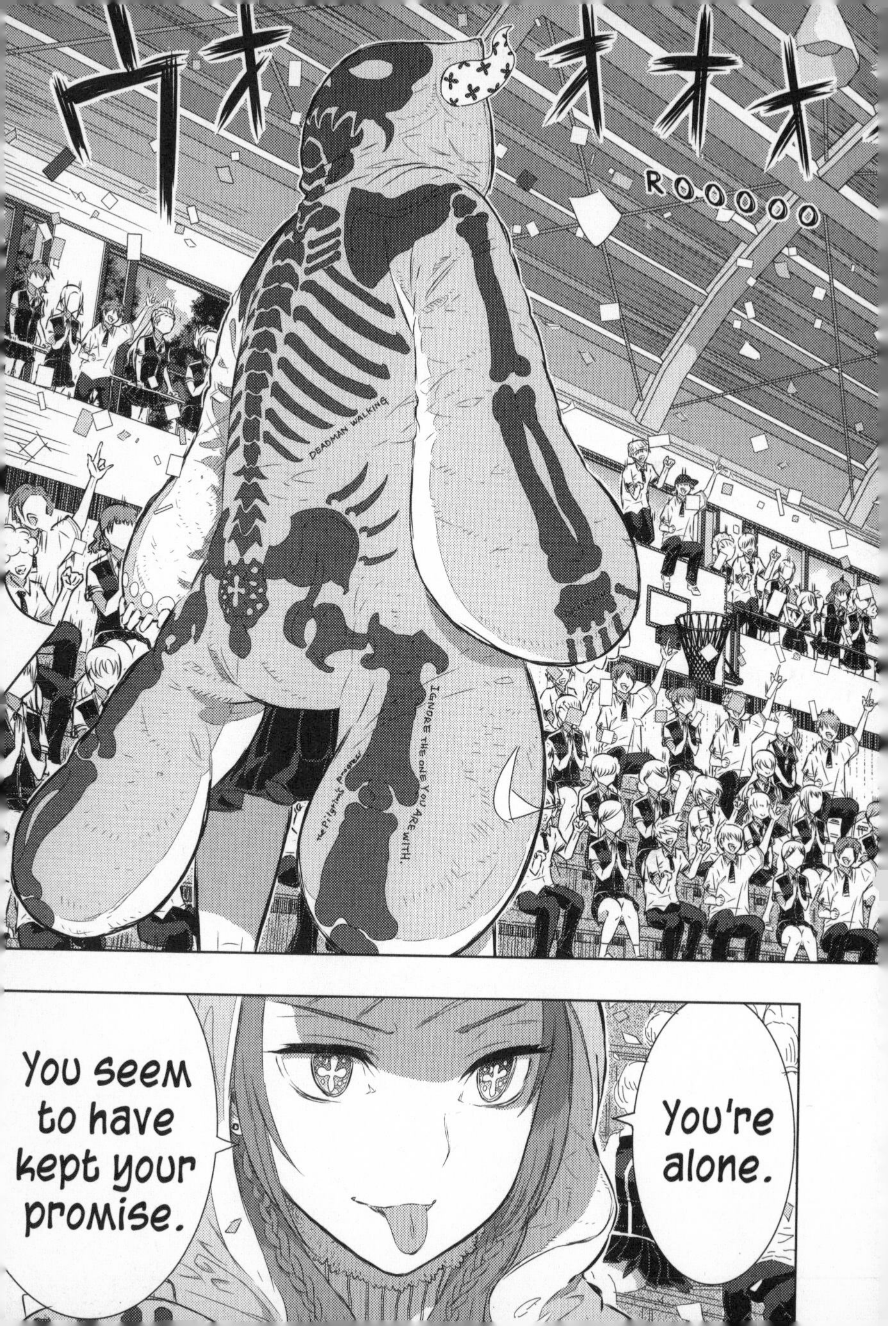
ウオオオオ
ROOOOO
DEADMAN WALKING
IGNORE THE ONE YOU ARE WITH.
The Pilgrim's Progress
You're alone.
You seem to have kept your promise.

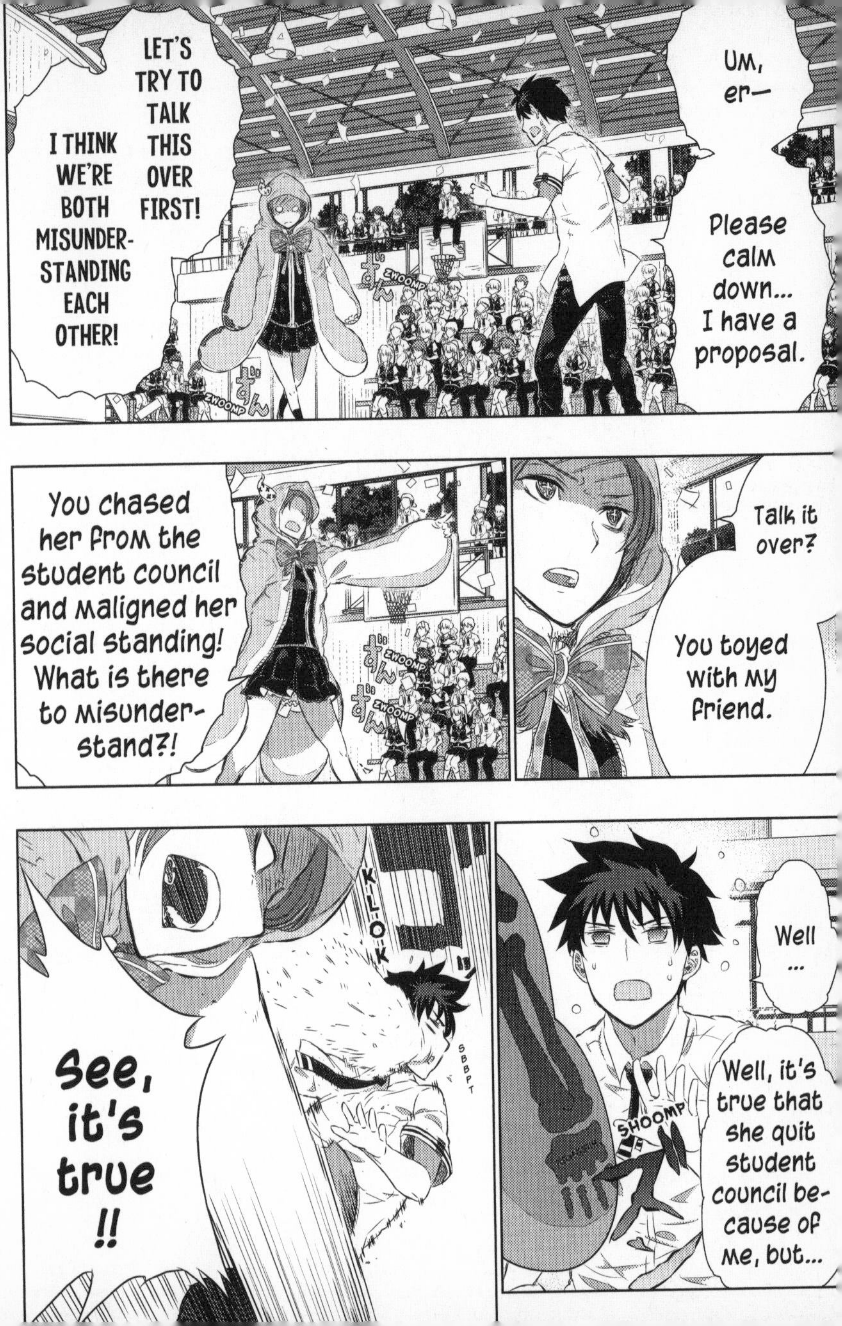
Um, er—
Please calm down... I have a proposal.
LET'S TRY TO TALK THIS OVER FIRST!
I THINK WE'RE BOTH MISUNDERSTANDING EACH OTHER!
ZWOOMP
ZWOOMP
Talk it over?
You toyed with my friend.
You chased her from the student council and maligned her social standing! What is there to misunderstand?!
ZWOOMP
ZWOOMP
Well ...
Well, it's true that she quit student council because of me, but...
SHOOMP
KLLOK
SBBPT
See, it's true !!

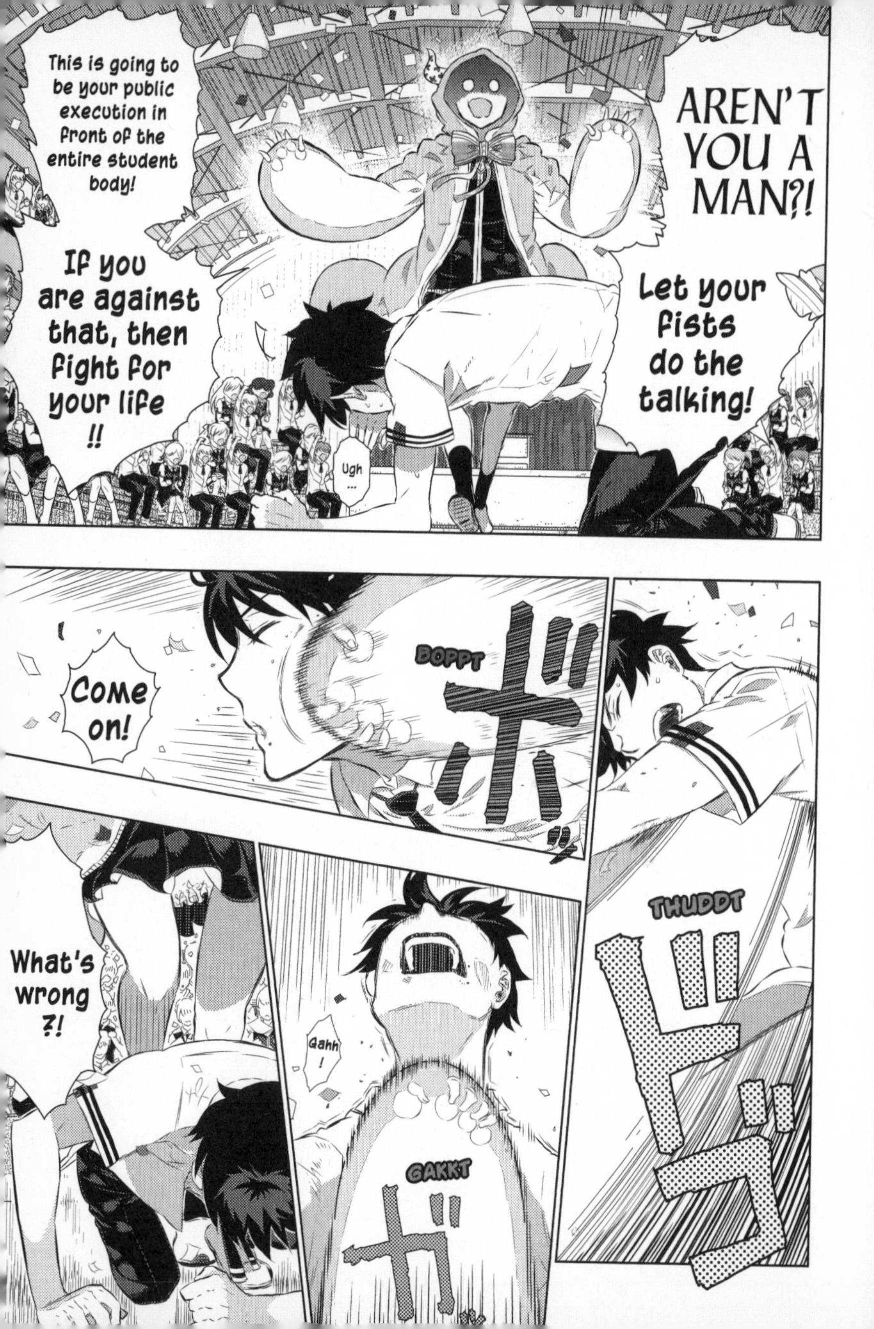
AREN'T YOU A MAN?!
This is going to be your public execution in front of the entire student body!
Let your fists do the talking!
If you are against that, then fight for your life !!
Ugh ...
BOPPT
Come on!
THUDDT
Gahh !
GAKKT
What's wrong ?!

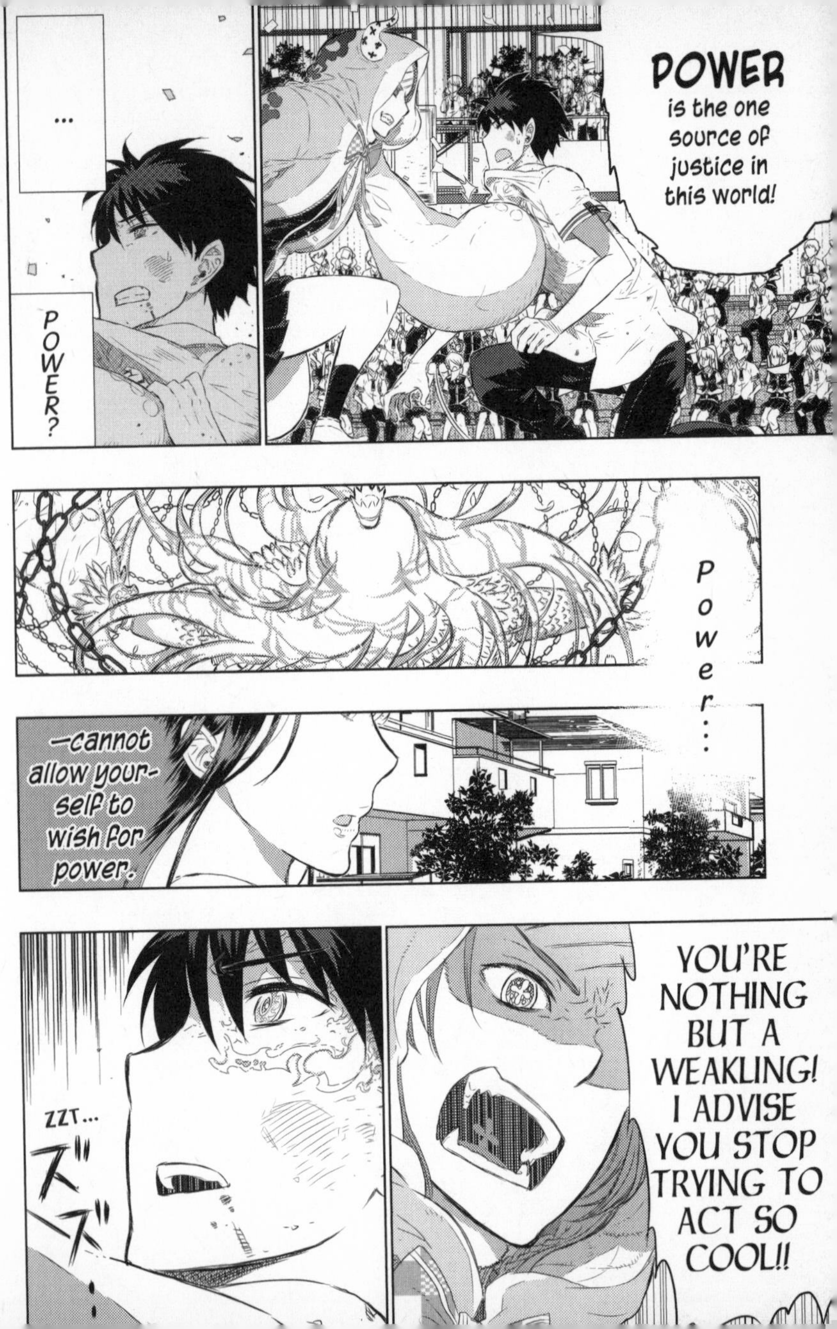
POWER is the one source of justice in this world!
...
POWER?
Power...
—cannot allow yourself to wish for power.
YOU'RE NOTHING BUT A WEAKLING! I ADVISE YOU STOP TRYING TO ACT SO COOL!!
ZZT...
ズズ

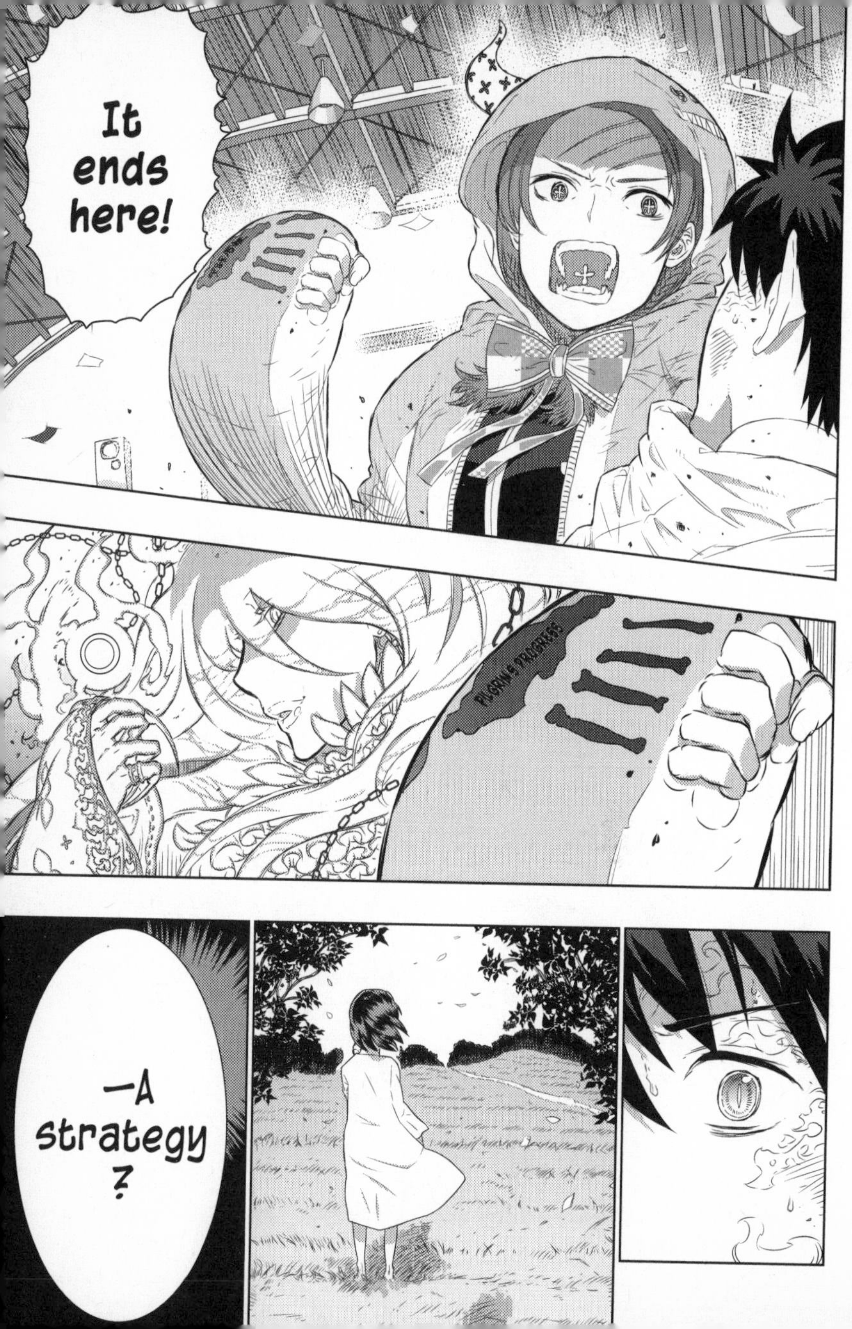
It ends here!
PILGRIM'S PROGRESS
—A strategy?

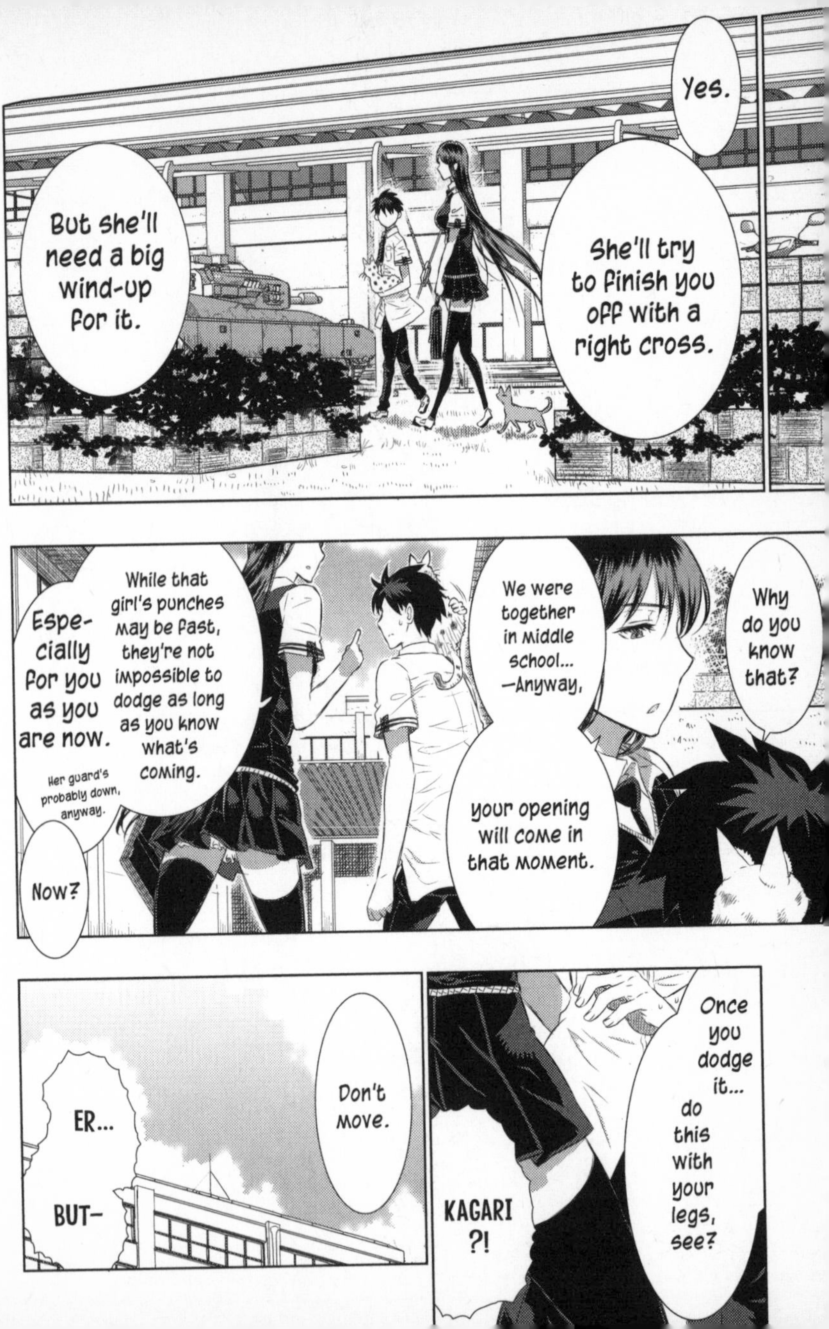
Yes.
She'll try to finish you off with a right cross.
But she'll need a big wind-up for it.
Why do you know that?
We were together in middle school... —Anyway,
your opening will come in that moment.
While that girl's punches may be fast, they're not impossible to dodge as long as you know what's coming.
Espe-cially for you as you are now.
Her guard's probably down, anyway.
Now?
Once you dodge it... do this with your legs, see?
KAGARI ?!
Don't move.
ER...
BUT–

Here it comes!
ばっ
BAM
PILGRIM'S PROGRESS
ビュン
BWOOSH
?!

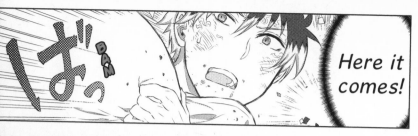

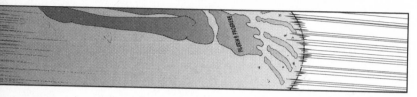

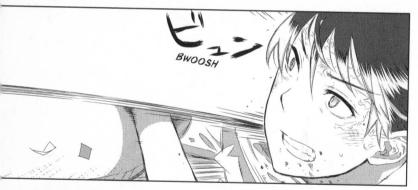

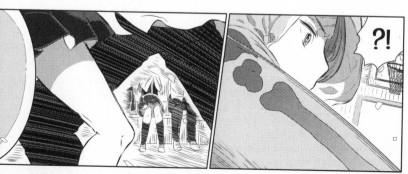

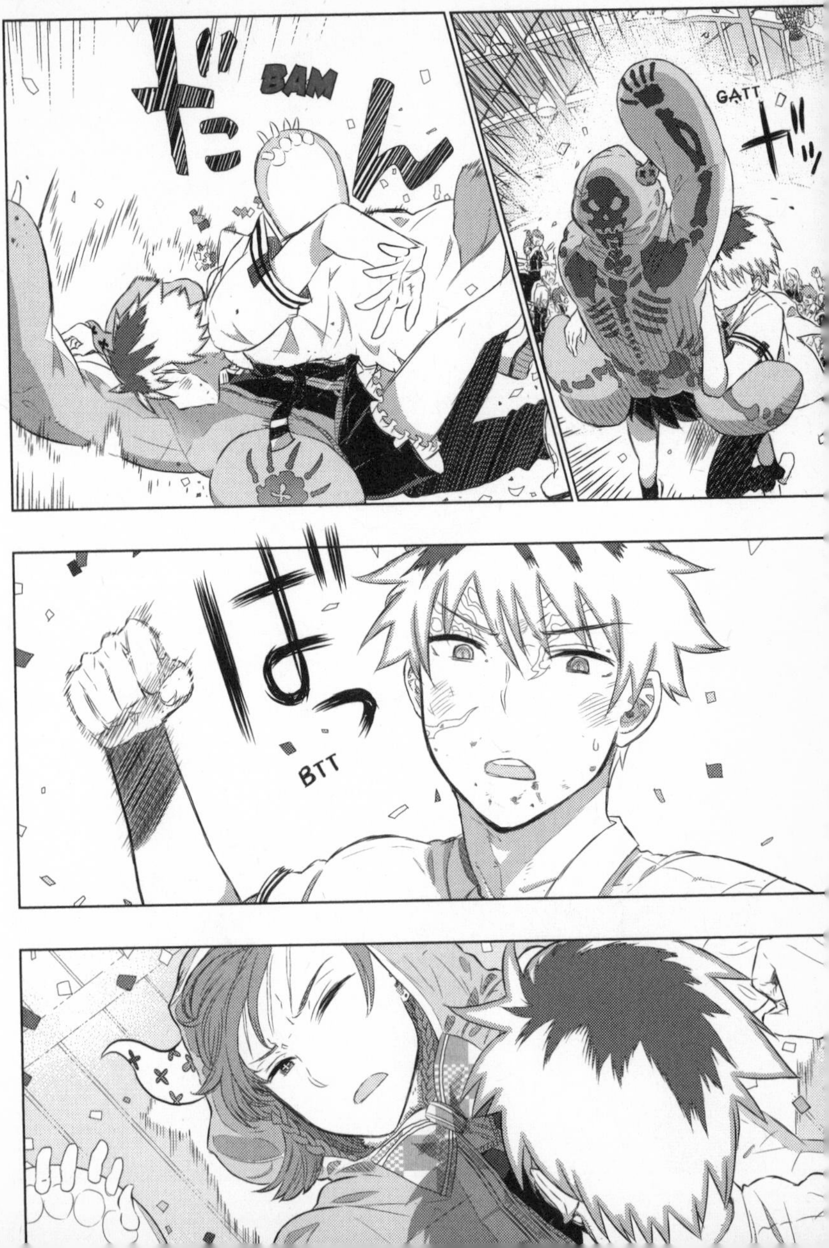
GATT
ガッ
BAM
ばっ
BTT

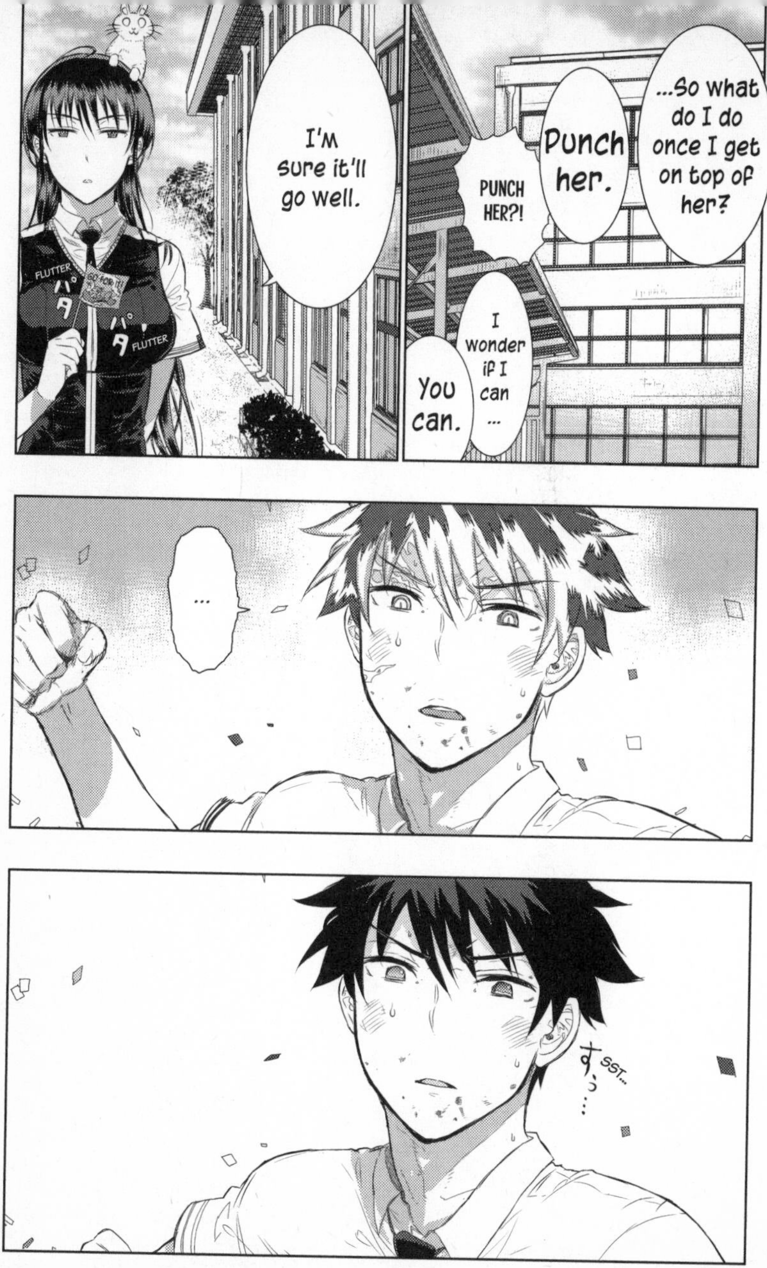
...So what do I do once I get on top of her?
Punch her.
PUNCH HER?!
I wonder if I can ...
You can.
I'M sure it'll go well.
FLUTTER
GO FOR IT!
FLUTTER
...
SST...

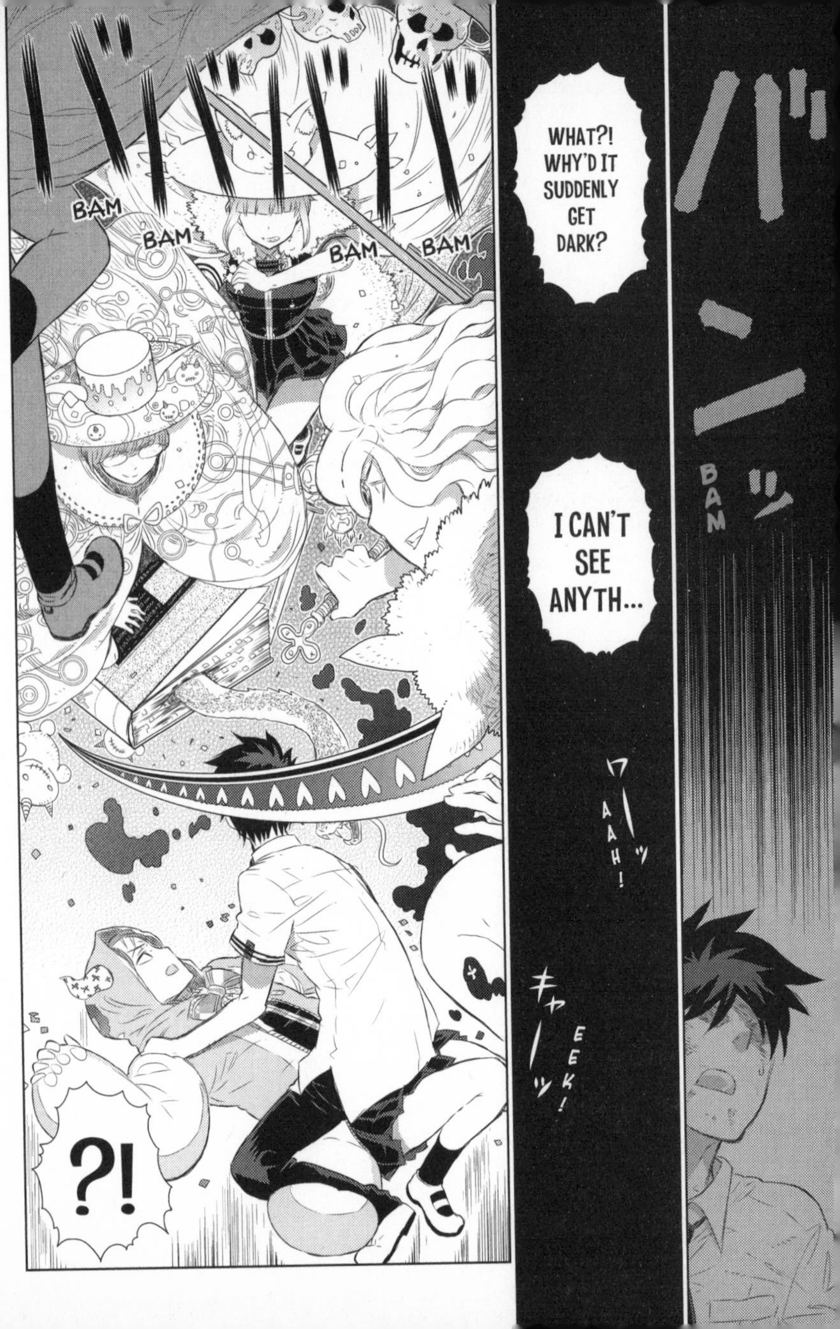
BAM
WHAT?! WHY'D IT SUDDENLY GET DARK?
I CAN'T SEE ANYTH...
AAAH!
EEEK!
BAM
BAM
BAM
BAM
?!

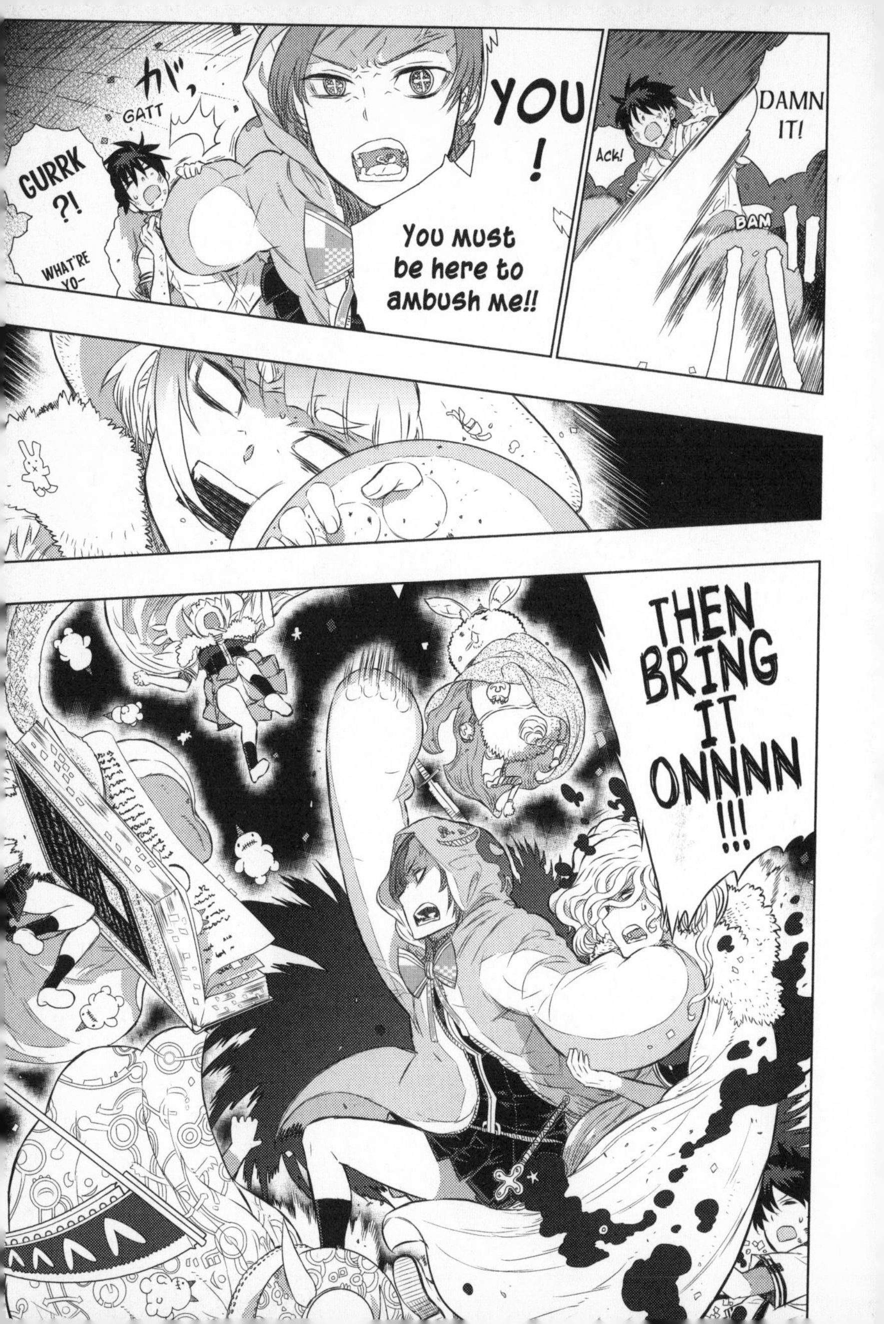
DAMN IT!
ACK!
BAM
YOU!
You must be here to ambush me!!
ガ
GATT
GURRK ?!
WHAT'RE YO-
THEN BRING IT ONNNN!!!

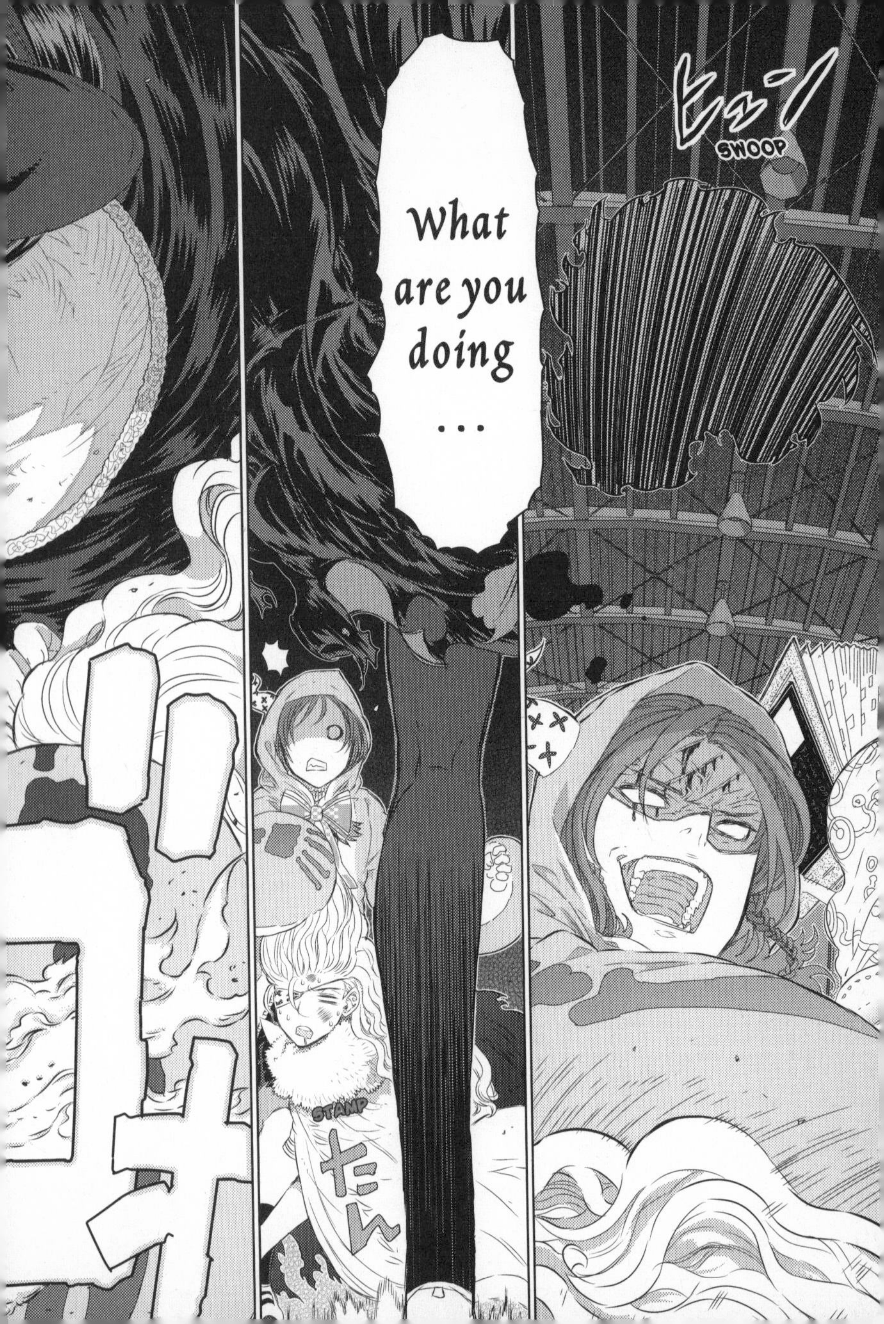
SWOOP
What are you doing ...
STAMP
たん

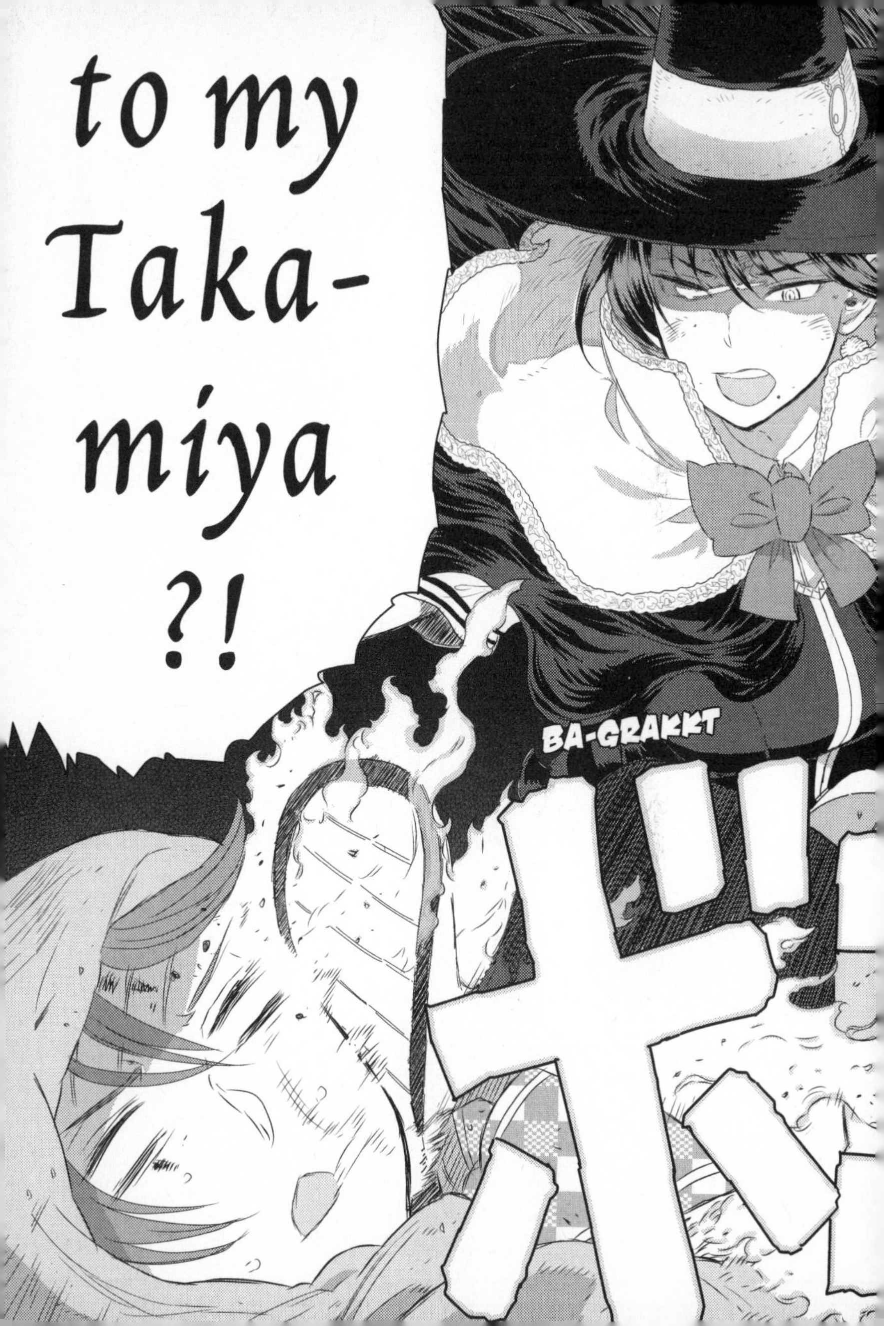
to my Taka-miya ?!
BA-GRAKKT

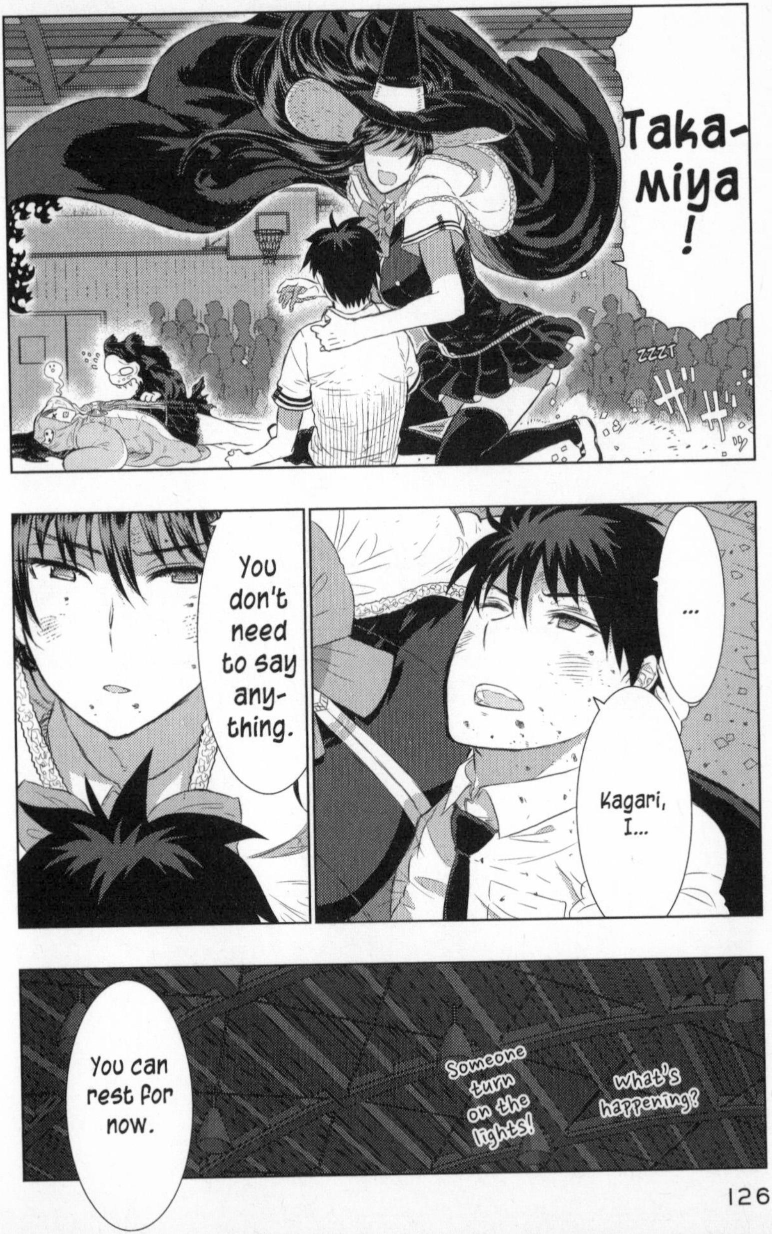
Taka-miya!
ZZZT
...
Kagari, I...
You don't need to say anything.
What's happening?
Someone turn on the lights!
You can rest for now.

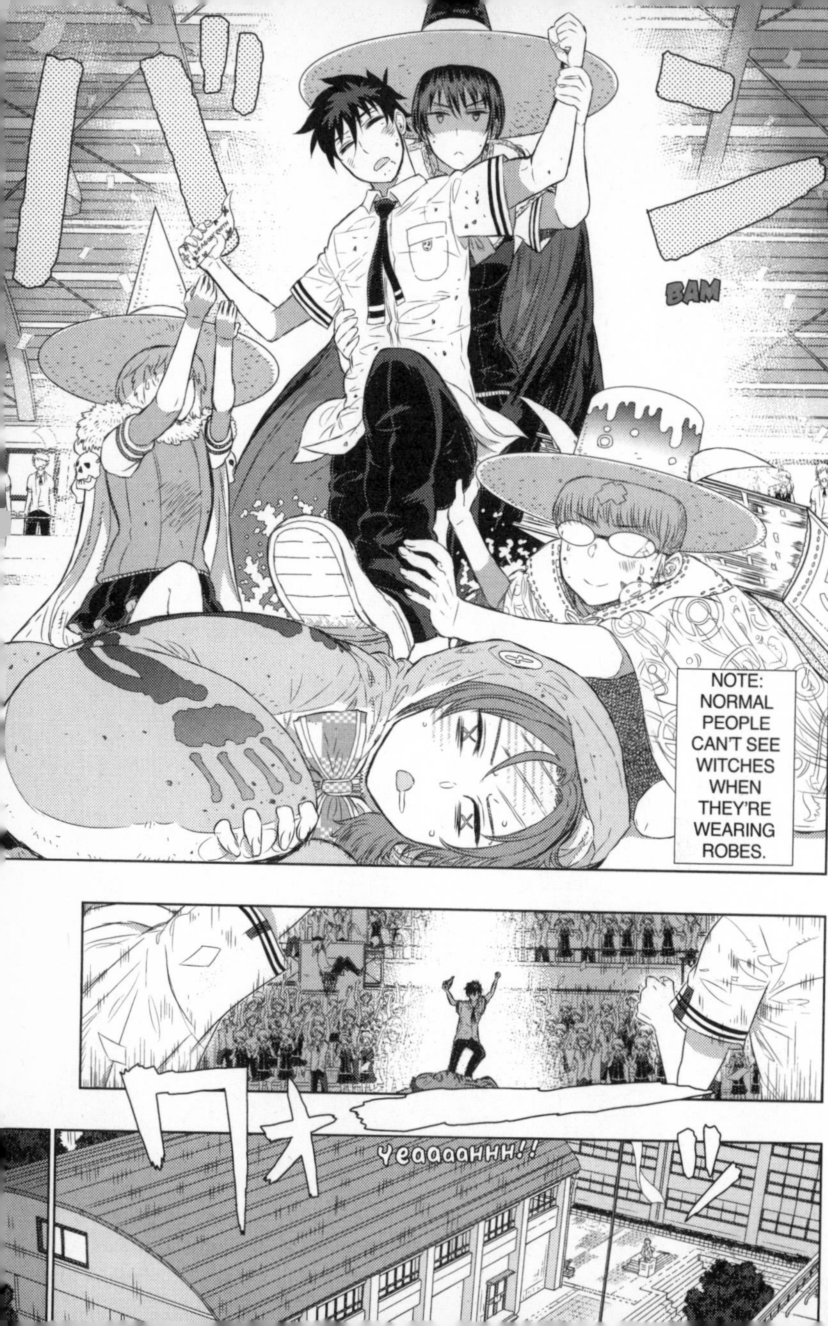
BAM
NOTE: NORMAL PEOPLE CAN'T SEE WITCHES WHEN THEY'RE WEARING ROBES.
DRAGON TOOTH
YEAAAAHHH!!

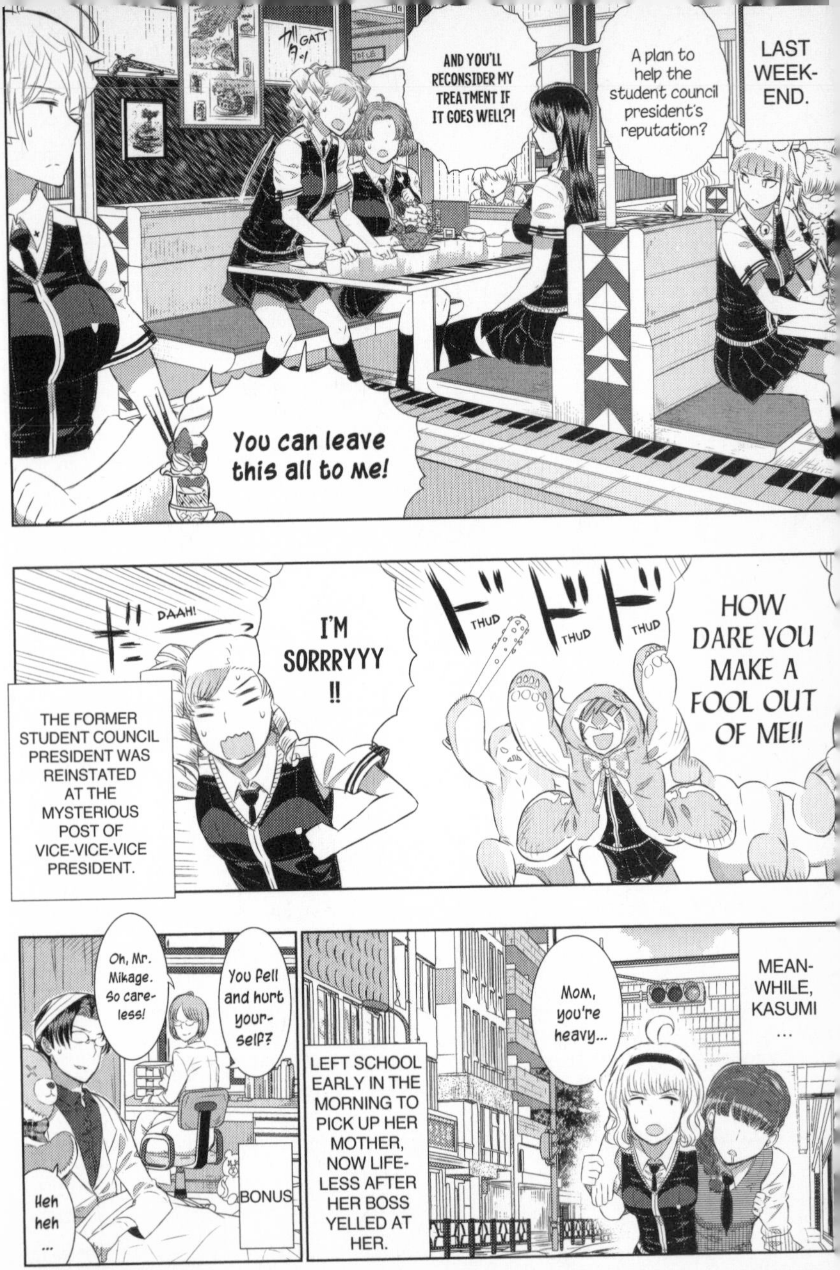
LAST WEEK-END.
A plan to help the student council president's reputation?
AND YOU'LL RECONSIDER MY TREATMENT IF IT GOES WELL?!
GATT
You can leave this all to me!
HOW DARE YOU MAKE A FOOL OUT OF ME!!
THUD
THUD
THUD
I'M SORRRYYY!!
DAAH!
THE FORMER STUDENT COUNCIL PRESIDENT WAS REINSTATED AT THE MYSTERIOUS POST OF VICE-VICE-VICE PRESIDENT.
MEAN-WHILE, KASUMI...
Mom, you're heavy...
LEFT SCHOOL EARLY IN THE MORNING TO PICK UP HER MOTHER, NOW LIFE-LESS AFTER HER BOSS YELLED AT HER.
BONUS
You fell and hurt your-self?
Oh, Mr. Mikage. So care-less!
Heh heh ...

CHAPTER 15: *END*

The Former Student Council President's Past

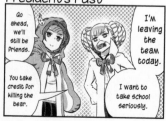

I'm leaving the team today.
FLEETING
Go ahead, we'll still be friends.
I want to take school seriously.
You take credit for killing the bear.

CHAPTER 15 BONUS

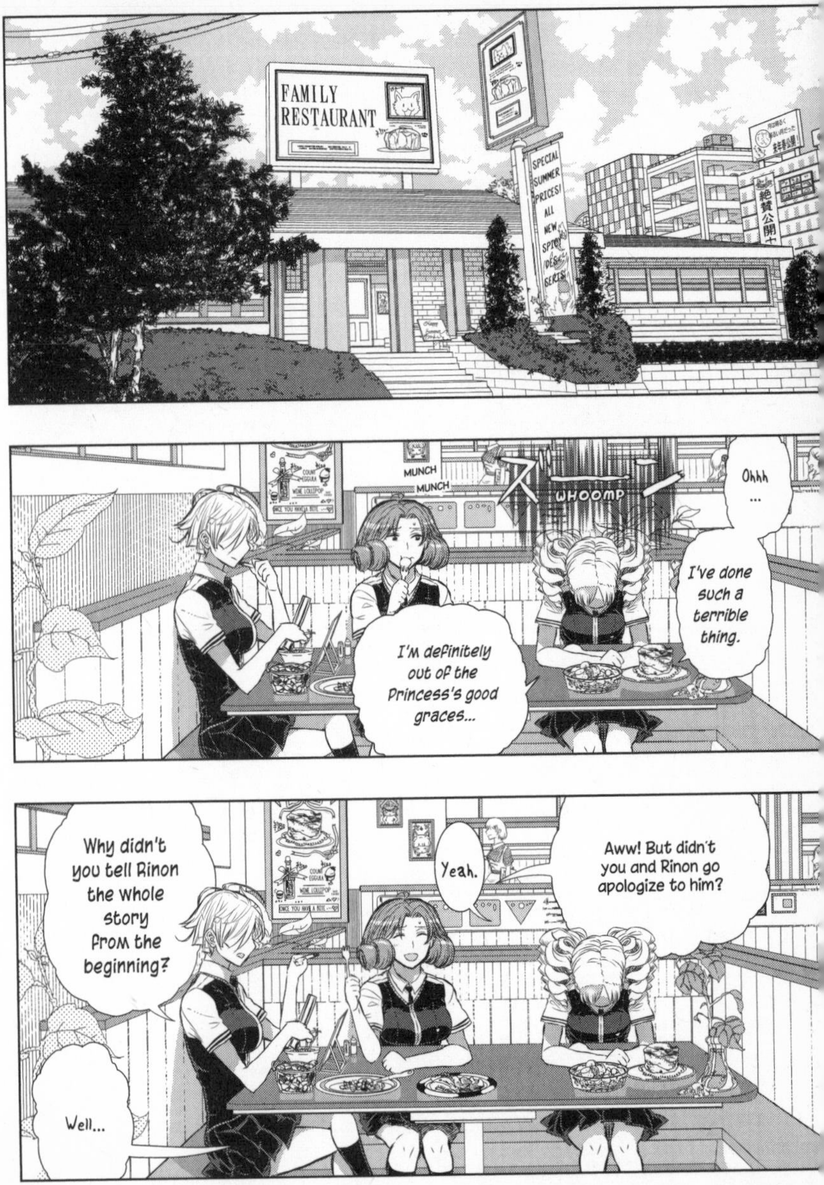
FAMILY
RESTAURANT
SPECIAL SUMMER PRICES! ALL NEW
Ohhh ...
I've done such a terrible thing.
WHOOMP
MUNCH
MUNCH
I'm definitely out of the Princess's good graces...
COUNT EGGULA
WINE LOLLIPOP
Aww! But didn't you and Rinon go apologize to him?
Yeah.
Why didn't you tell Rinon the whole story from the beginning?
Well...

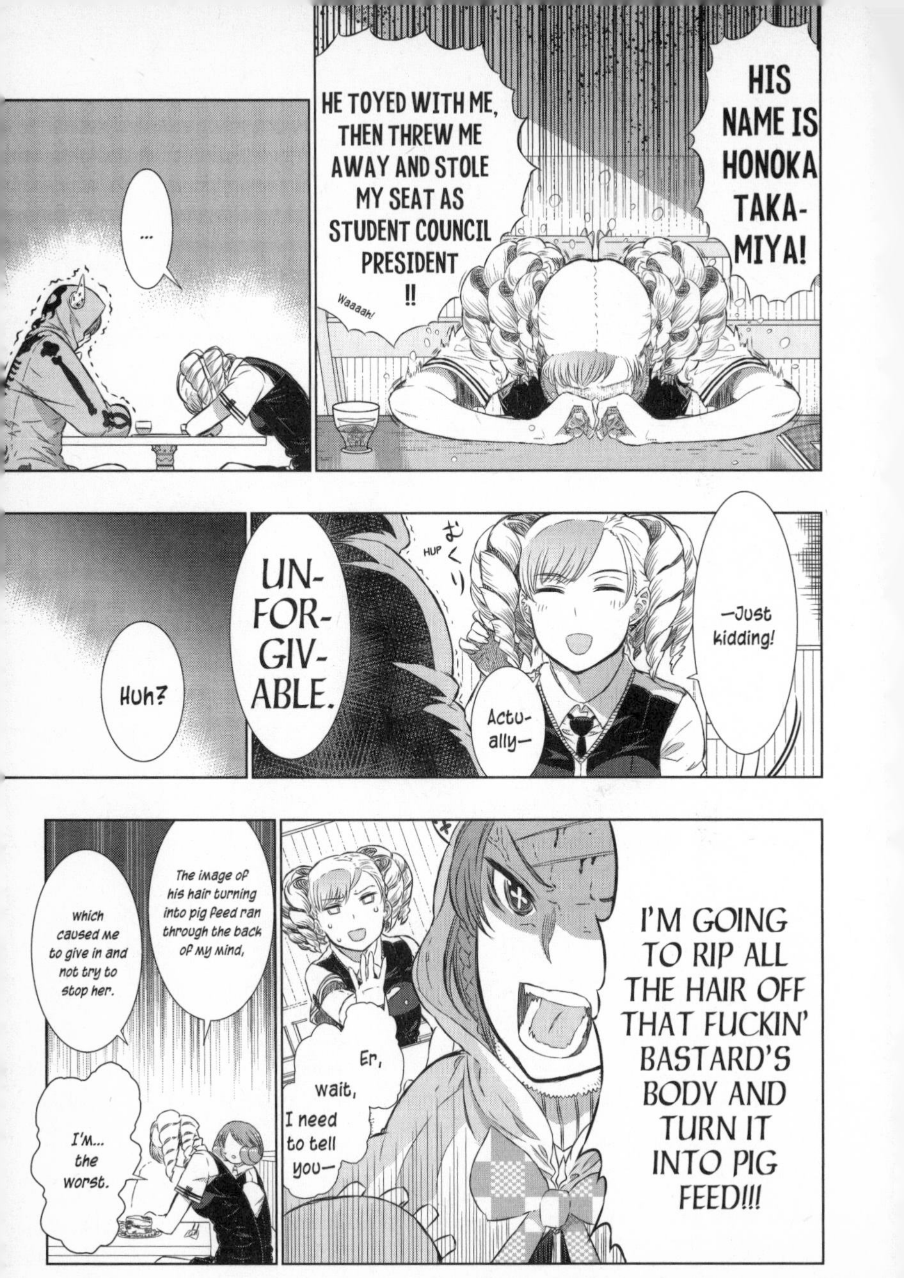
HIS NAME IS HONOKA TAKAMIYA!
HE TOYED WITH ME, THEN THREW ME AWAY AND STOLE MY SEAT AS STUDENT COUNCIL PRESIDENT !!
Waaaah!
...
—Just kidding!
Actu-ally—
むくり
HUP
UN-FOR-GIV-ABLE.
Huh?
I'M GOING TO RIP ALL THE HAIR OFF THAT FUCKIN' BASTARD'S BODY AND TURN IT INTO PIG FEED!!!
Er, wait, I need to tell you—
The image of his hair turning into pig feed ran through the back of my mind,
which caused me to give in and not try to stop her.
I'm... the worst.

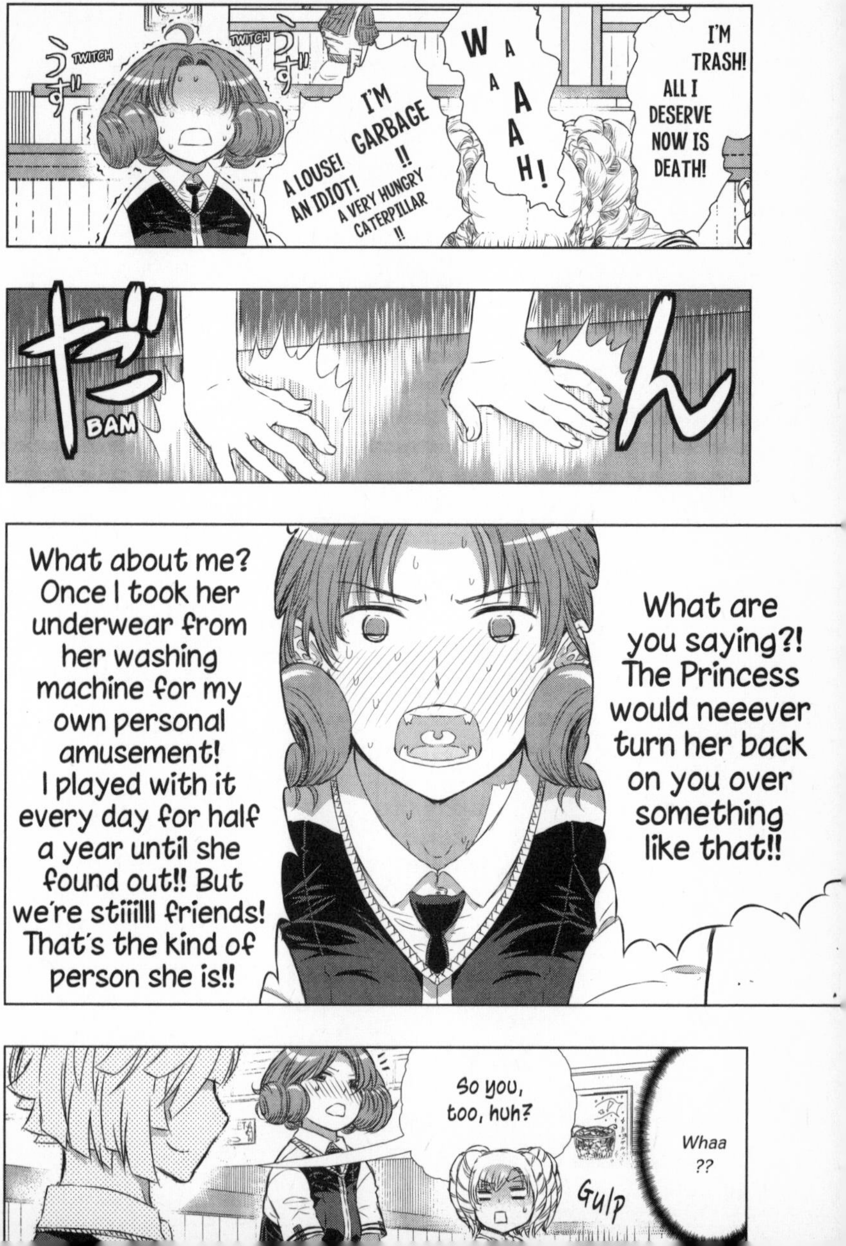
I'M TRASH! ALL I DESERVE NOW IS DEATH!
WAAAH!
I'M GARBAGE!!
A LOUSE! AN IDIOT!
A VERY HUNGRY CATERPILLAR!!
うずうず
TWITCH
TWITCH
だーん
BAM
What are you saying?! The Princess would neeever turn her back on you over something like that!!
What about me? Once I took her underwear from her washing machine for my own personal amusement! I played with it every day for half a year until she found out!! But we're stiiilll friends! That's the kind of person she is!!
Whaa ??
So you, too, huh?
Gulp

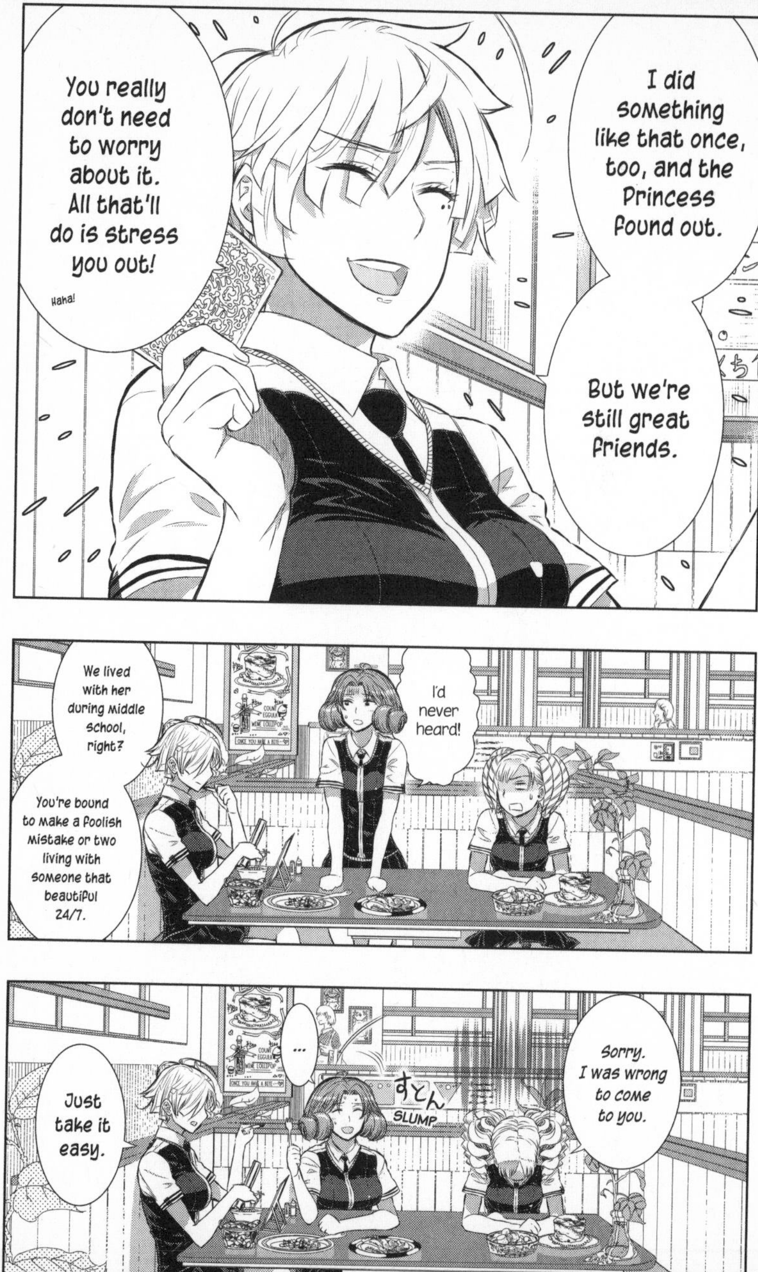
I did something like that once, too, and the Princess found out.
But we're still great friends.
You really don't need to worry about it. All that'll do is stress you out!
Haha!
I'd never heard!
We lived with her during middle school, right?
You're bound to make a foolish mistake or two living with someone that beautiful 24/7.
Sorry. I was wrong to come to you.
すとん
SLUMP
...
Just take it easy.

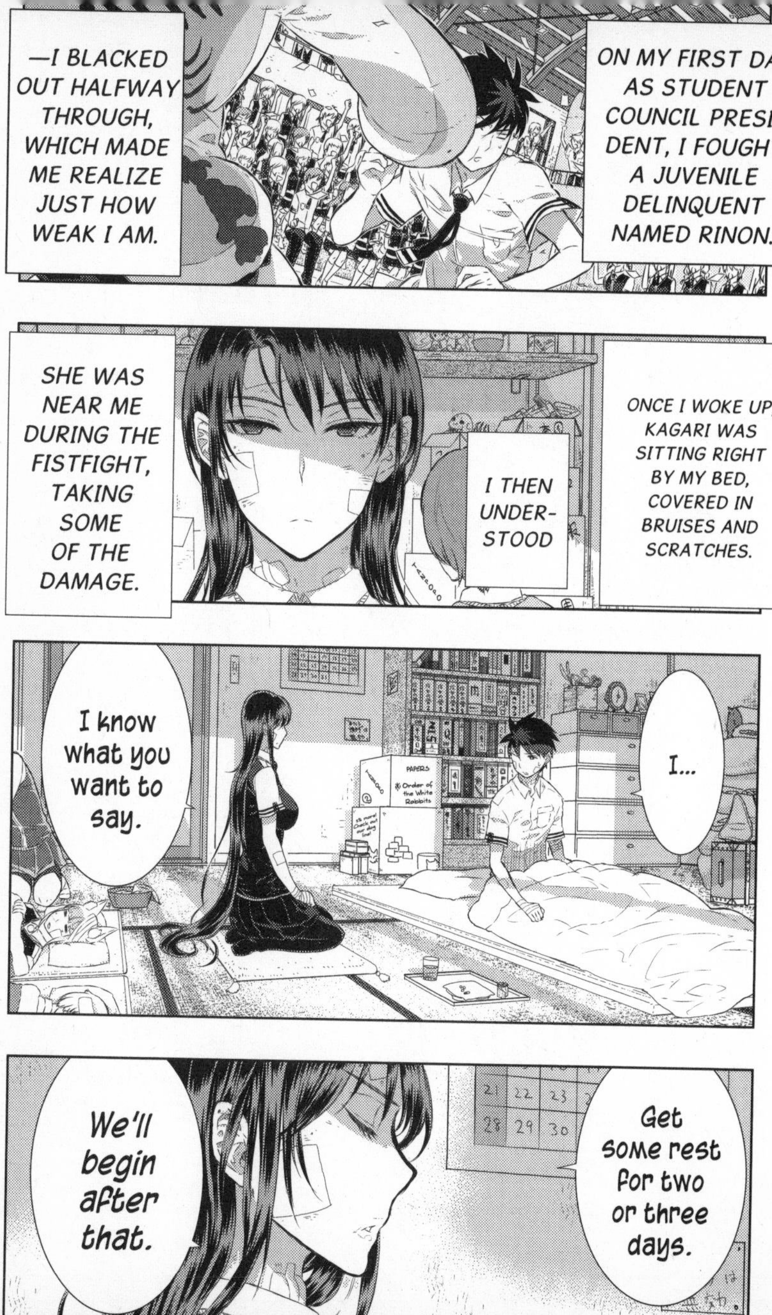
ON MY FIRST DAY AS STUDENT COUNCIL PRESIDENT, I FOUGHT A JUVENILE DELINQUENT NAMED RINON.
—I BLACKED OUT HALFWAY THROUGH, WHICH MADE ME REALIZE JUST HOW WEAK I AM.
ONCE I WOKE UP, KAGARI WAS SITTING RIGHT BY MY BED, COVERED IN BRUISES AND SCRATCHES.
I THEN UNDERSTOOD
SHE WAS NEAR ME DURING THE FISTFIGHT, TAKING SOME OF THE DAMAGE.
I...
PAPERS
Order of the White Rabbits
I know what you want to say.
Get some rest for two or three days.
We'll begin after that.

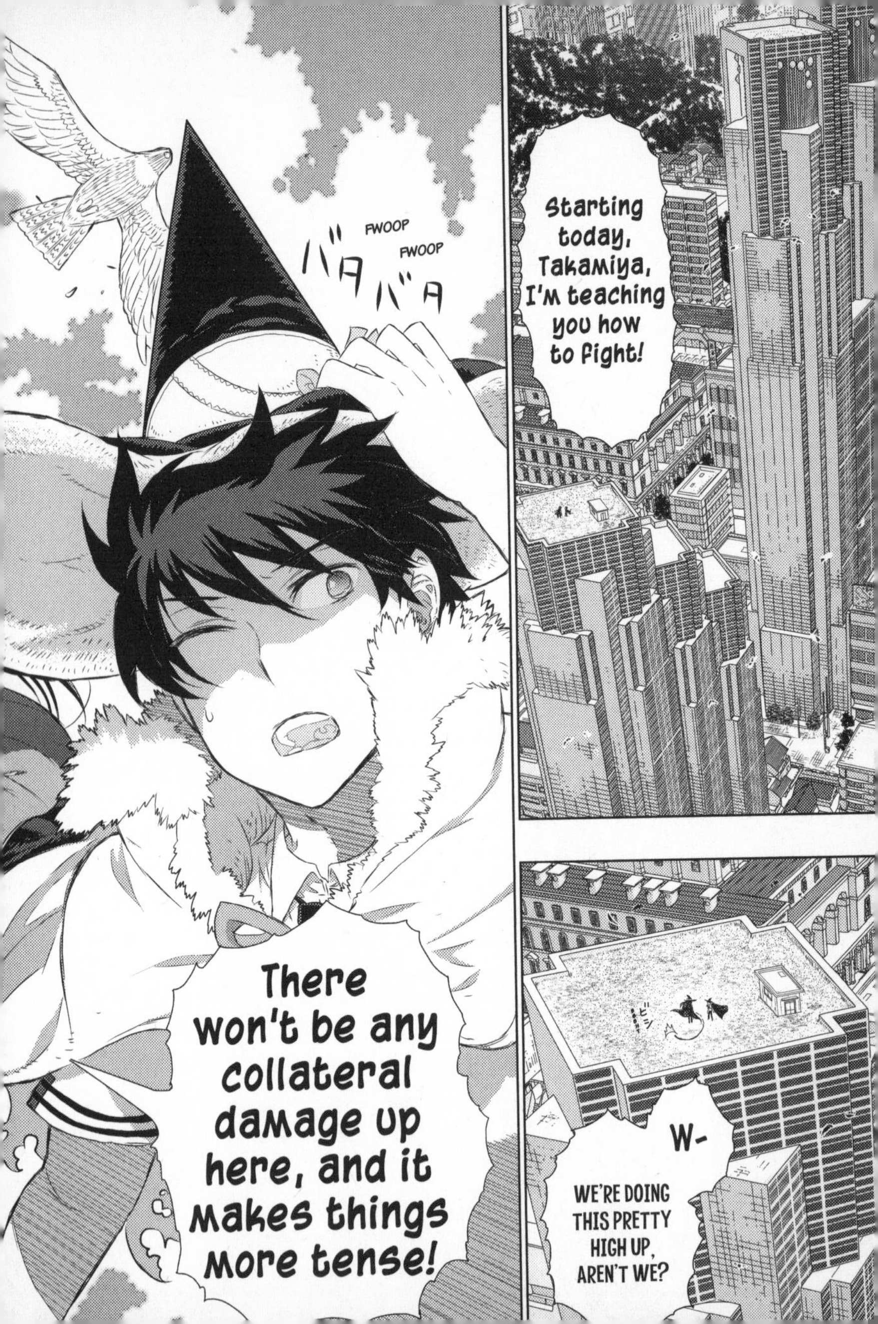
Starting today, Takamiya, I'm teaching you how to fight!
W-
WE'RE DOING THIS PRETTY HIGH UP, AREN'T WE?
バタバタ
FWOOP FWOOP
There won't be any collateral damage up here, and it makes things more tense!

CHAPTER 16 Takamiya and Kagari's After-School Lessons Part 2

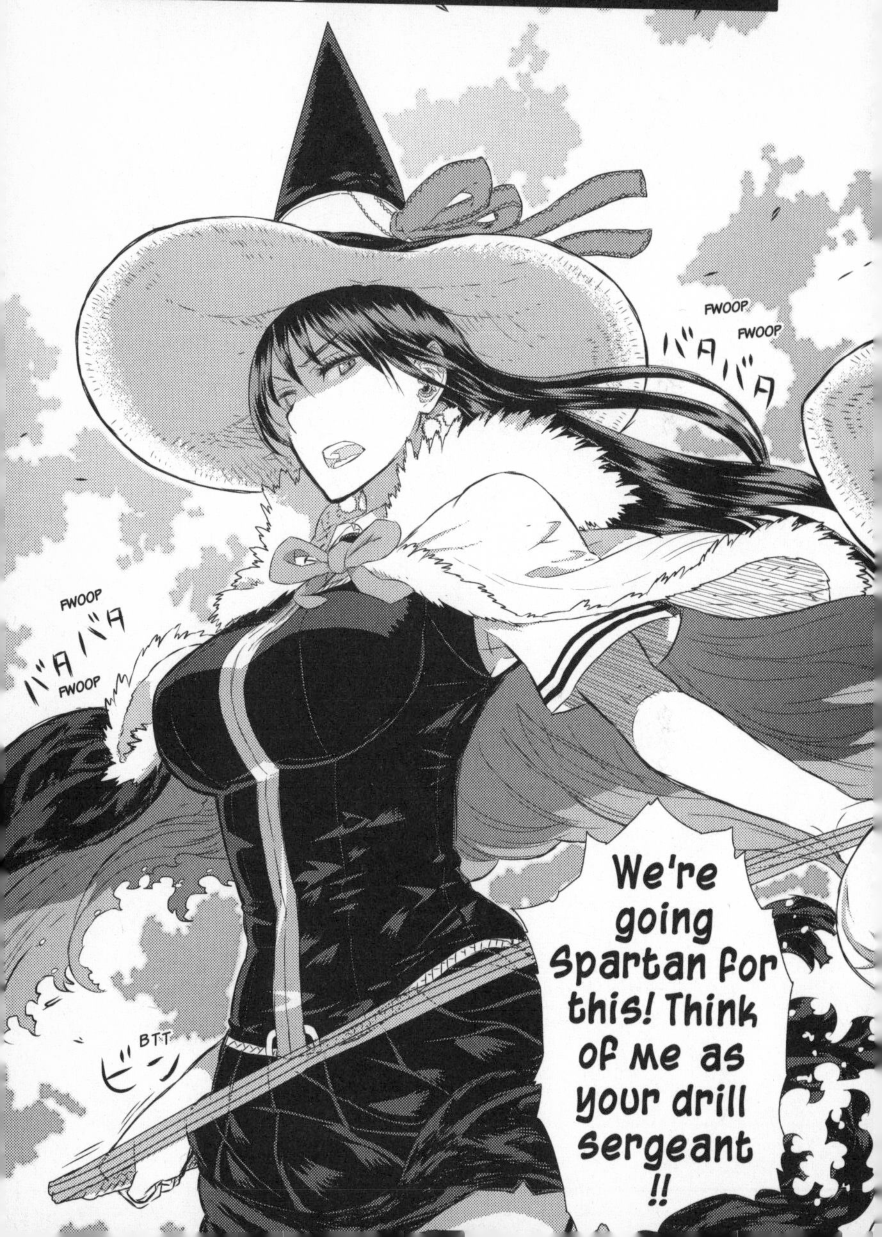
FWOOP FWOOP
バタバタ
FWOOP
バタバタ
FWOOP
We're going Spartan for this! Think of me as your drill sergeant!!
BTT
ビーン

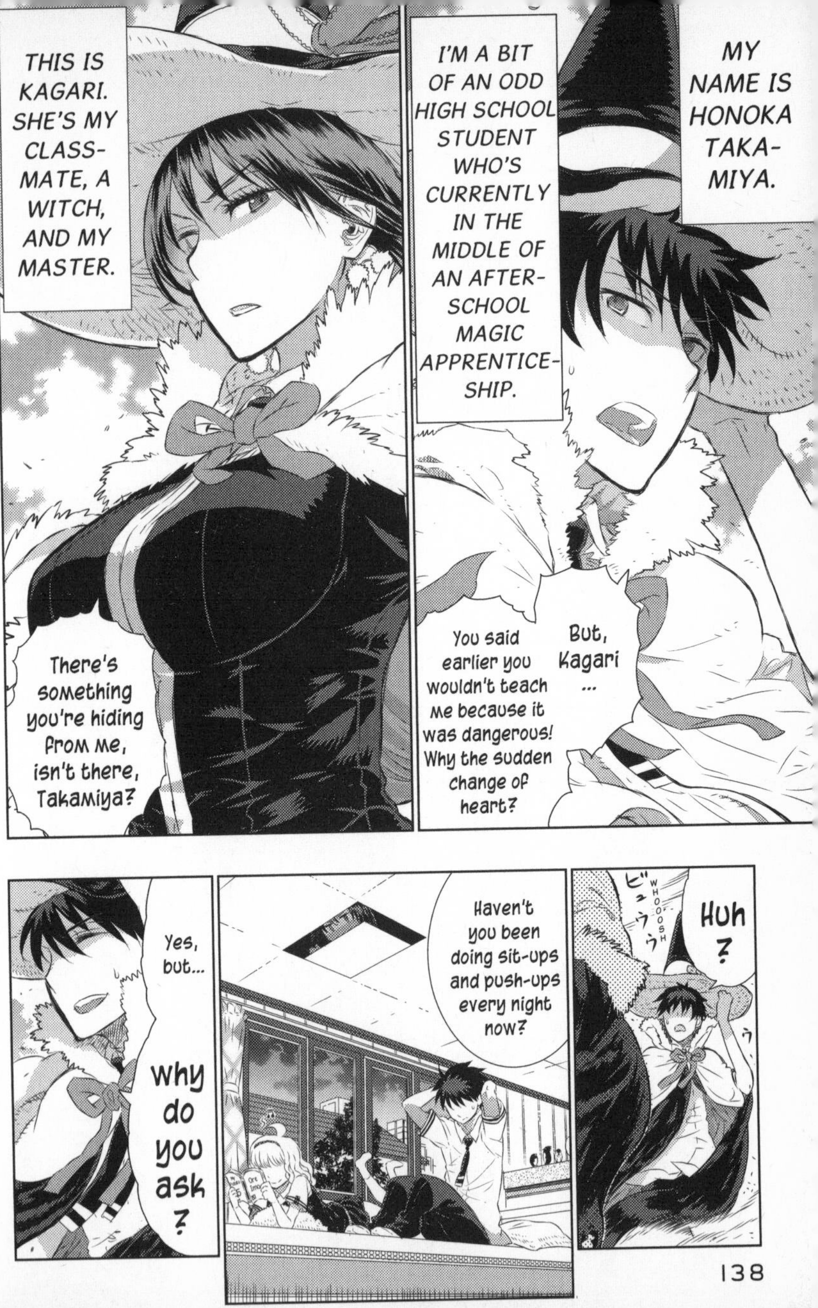
MY NAME IS HONOKA TAKAMIYA.
I'M A BIT OF AN ODD HIGH SCHOOL STUDENT WHO'S CURRENTLY IN THE MIDDLE OF AN AFTER-SCHOOL MAGIC APPRENTICESHIP.
But, Kagari...
You said earlier you wouldn't teach me because it was dangerous! Why the sudden change of heart?
THIS IS KAGARI. SHE'S MY CLASSMATE, A WITCH, AND MY MASTER.
There's something you're hiding from me, isn't there, Takamiya?
ビュウウ
WHOOOSH
Huh?
Haven't you been doing sit-ups and push-ups every night now?
Yes, but...
Why do you ask?

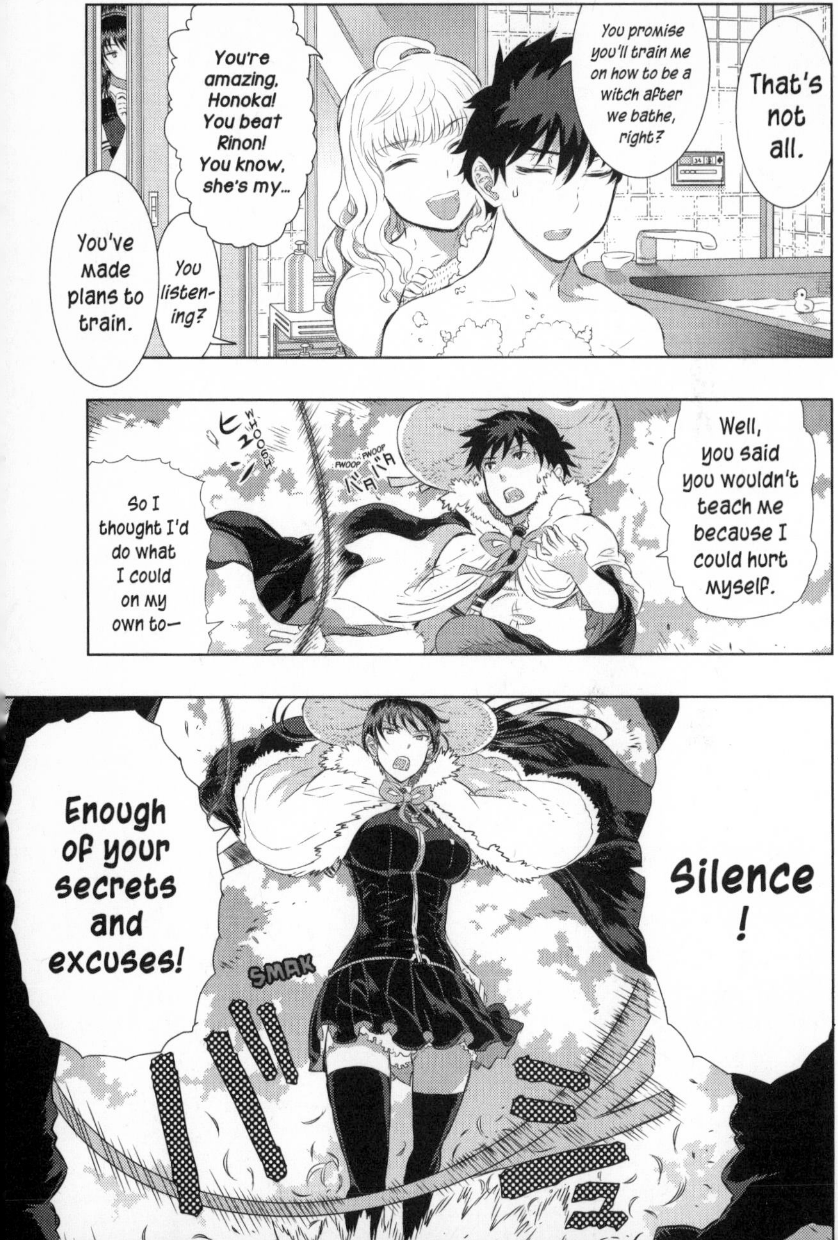
That's not all.
You promise you'll train me on how to be a witch after we bathe, right?
You're amazing, Honoka! You beat Rinon! You know, she's my...
You listen-ing?
You've made plans to train.
Well, you said you wouldn't teach me because I could hurt myself.
FWOOP FWOOP
WHOOSH
So I thought I'd do what I could on my own to—
Silence!
Enough of your secrets and excuses!
SMAK

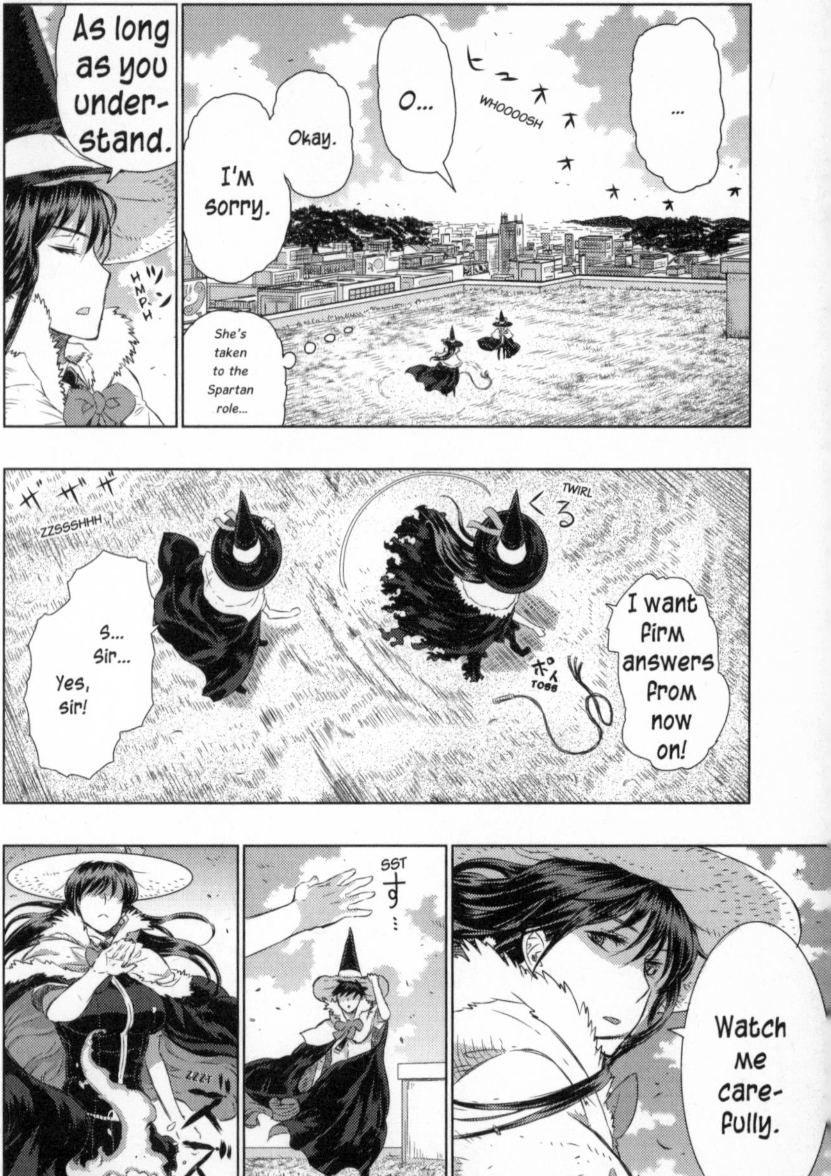
...
WHOOOOSH
O...
Okay.
I'm sorry.
She's taken to the Spartan role...
As long as you under-stand.
HMPH
I want firm answers from now on!
TWIRL
TOSS
S... Sir... Yes, sir!
ZZSSSHHH
Watch me care-fully.
SST

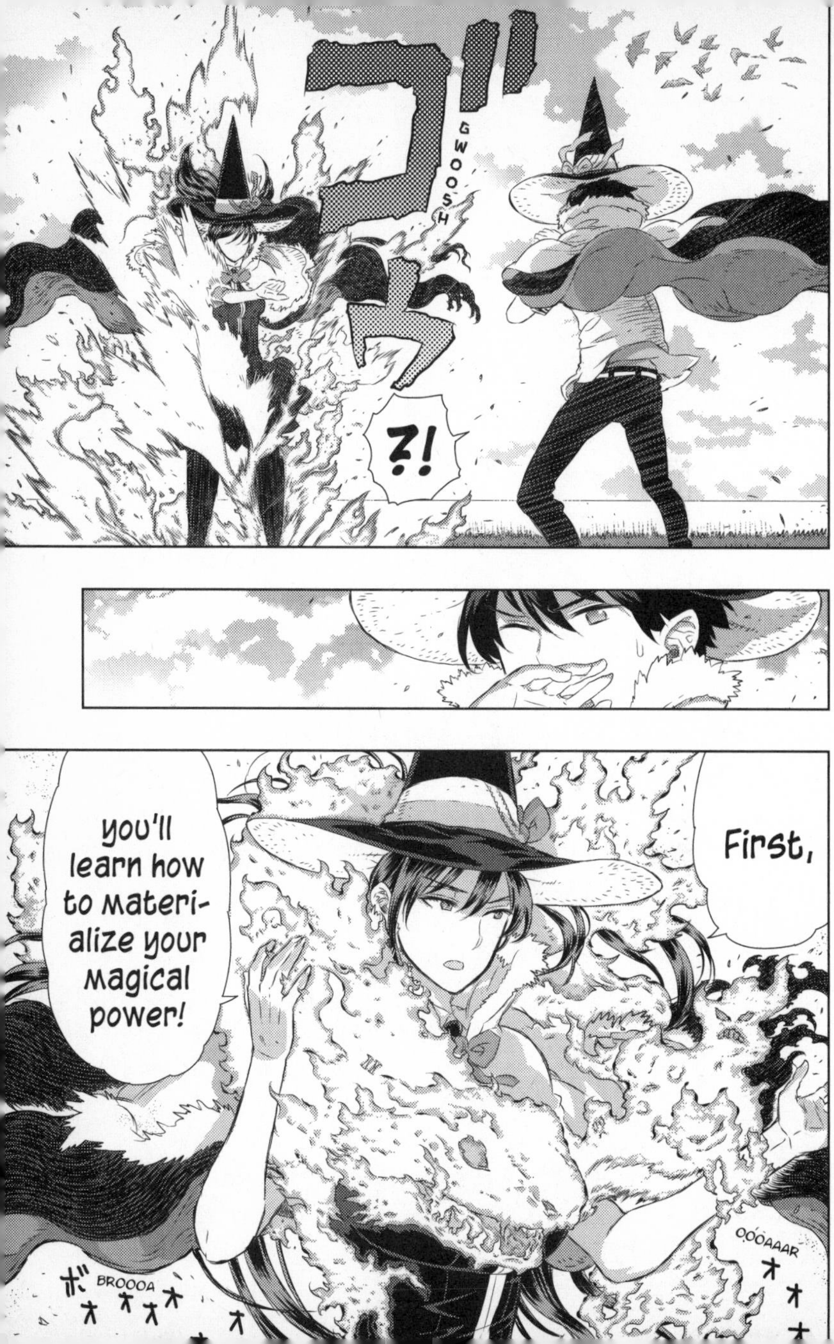
ゴッ
GWOOSH
?!
First,
you'll learn how to materi-alize your magical power!
OOOAAAR
オオオ
ボオオオオ
BROOOA

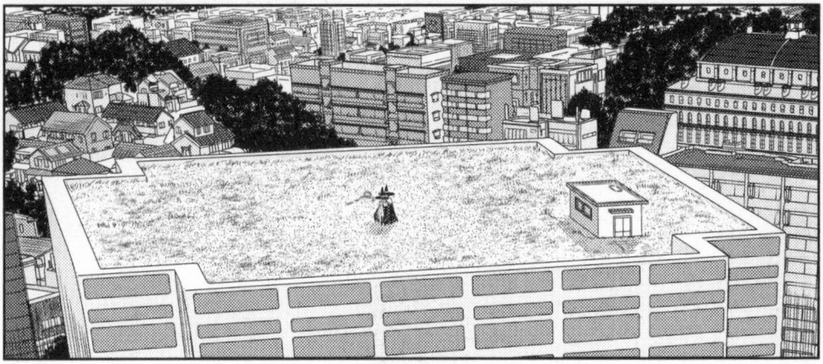

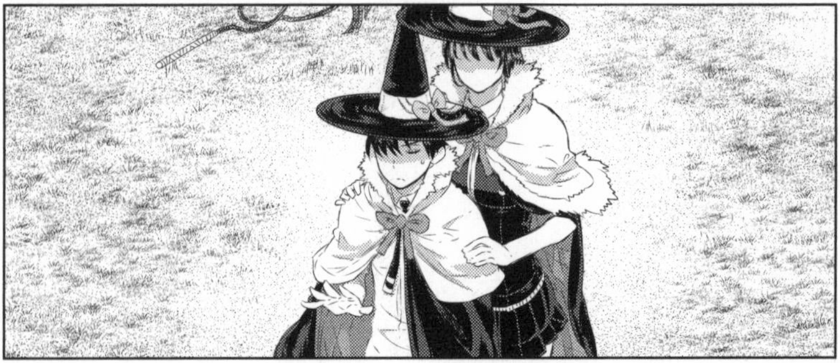

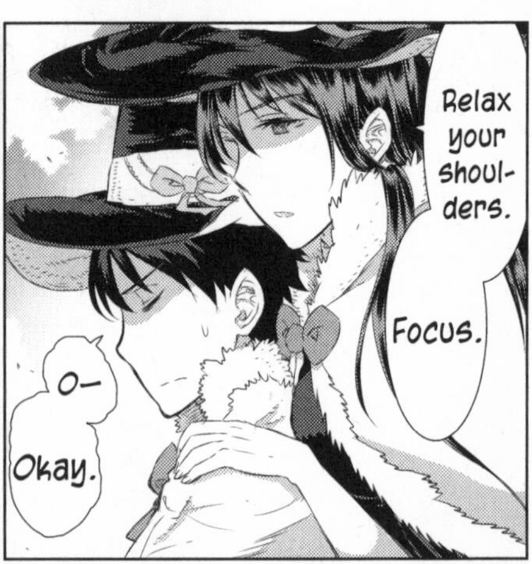
Relax your shoul-ders.
Focus.
O—
Okay.

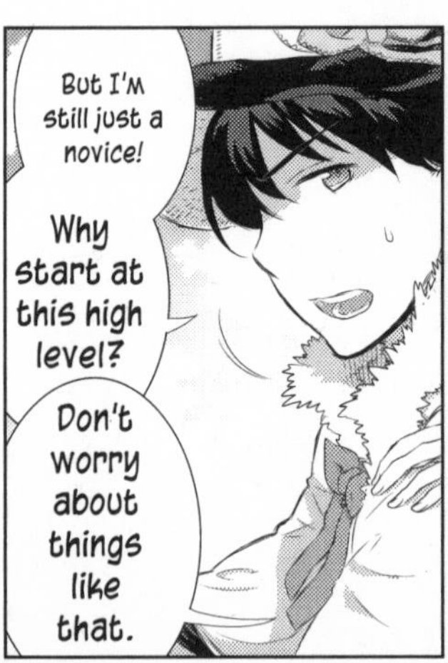
But I'm still just a novice!
Why start at this high level?
Don't worry about things like that.

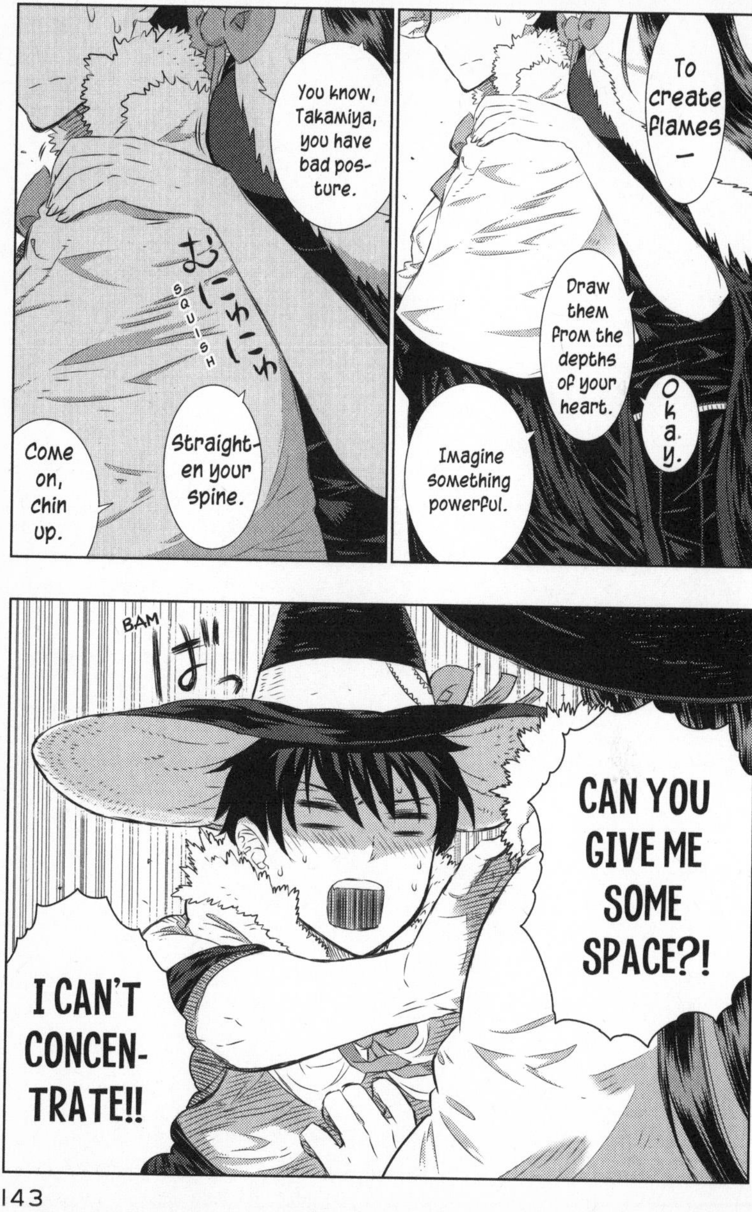
To create flames —
Draw them from the depths of your heart.
Okay.
Imagine something powerful.
You know, Takamiya, you have bad posture.
おにゅにゅ
SQUISH
Straighten your spine.
Come on, chin up.
ばっ
BAM
CAN YOU GIVE ME SOME SPACE?!
I CAN'T CONCENTRATE!!

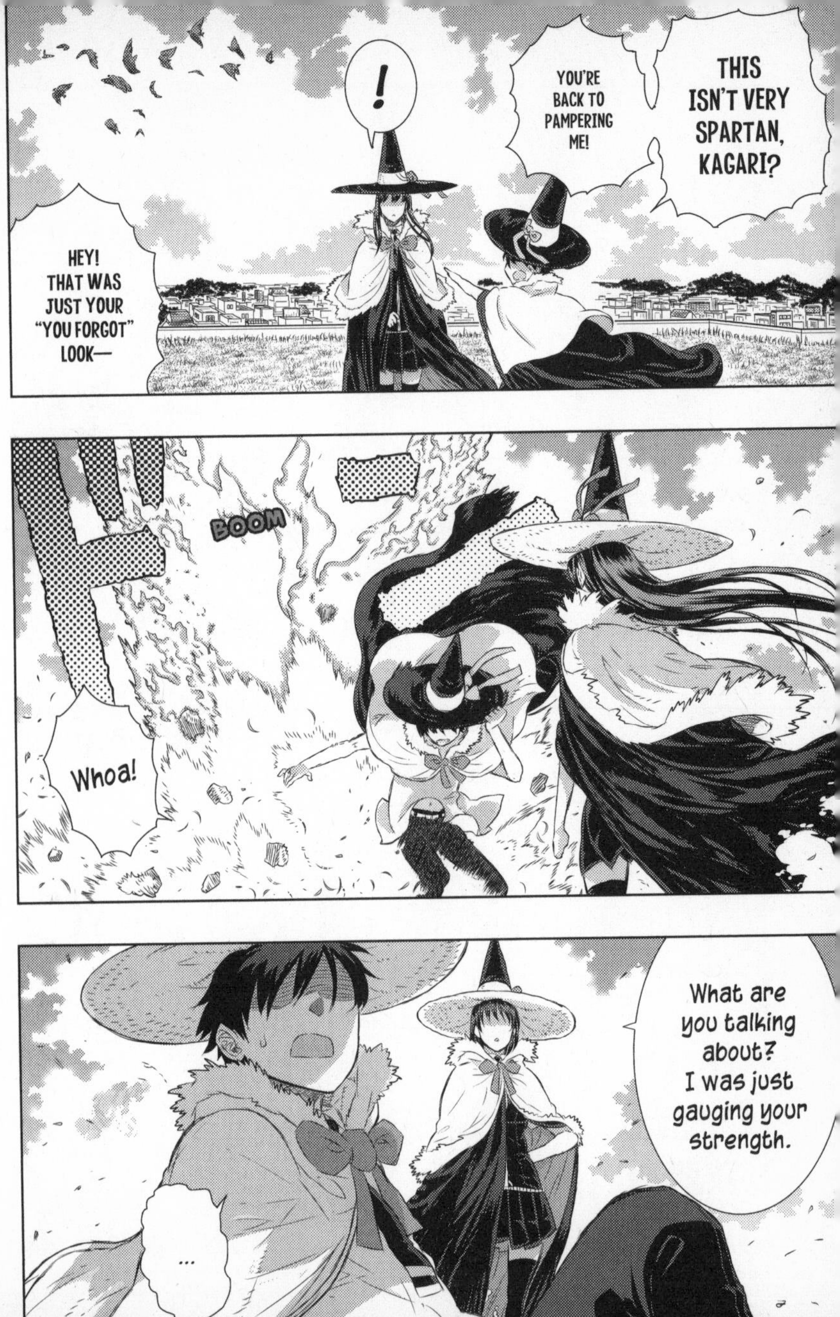
THIS ISN'T VERY SPARTAN, KAGARI?
YOU'RE BACK TO PAMPERING ME!
!
HEY! THAT WAS JUST YOUR "YOU FORGOT" LOOK—
BOOM
Whoa!
What are you talking about? I was just gauging your strength.
...

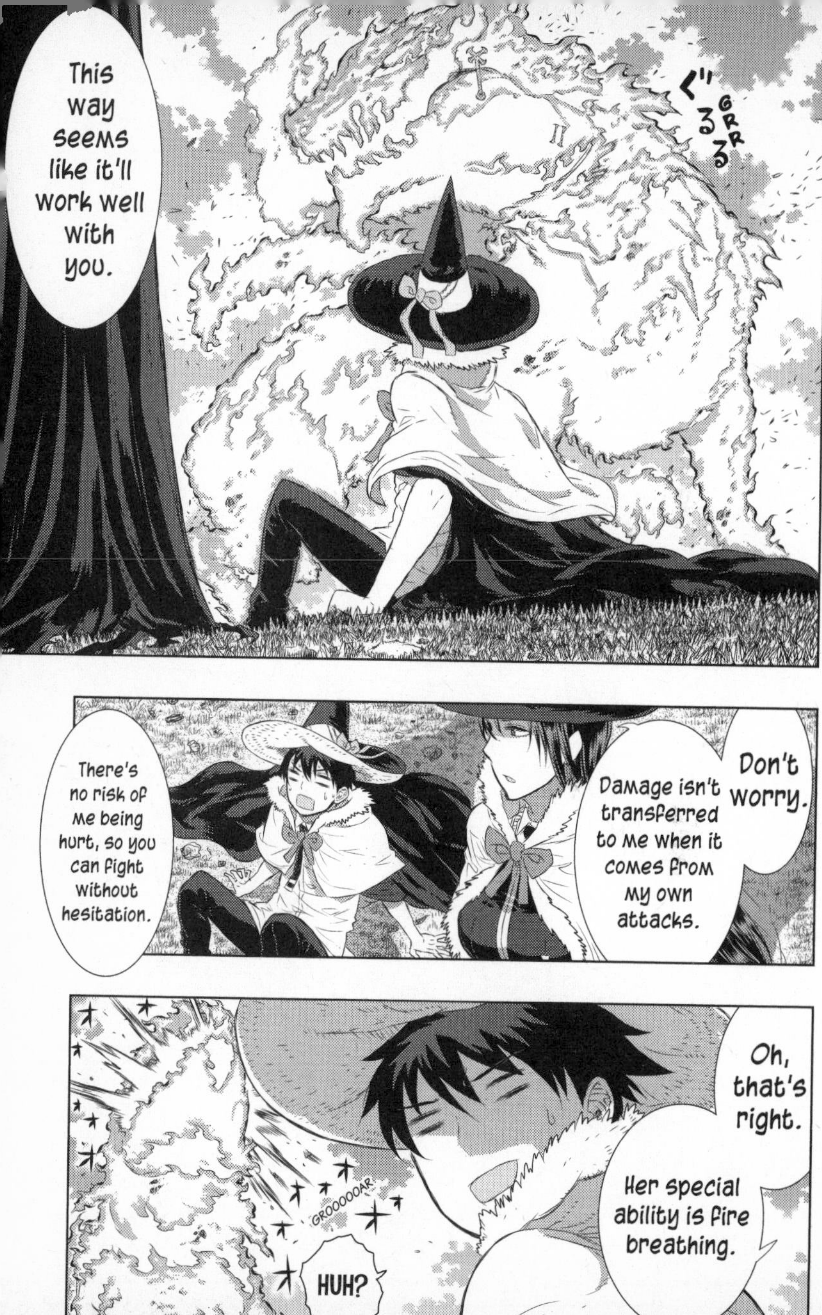
ぐるる
GRR
This way seems like it'll work well with you.
Don't worry.
Damage isn't transferred to me when it comes from my own attacks.
There's no risk of me being hurt, so you can fight without hesitation.
Oh, that's right.
Her special ability is fire breathing.
GROOOOOAR
HUH?

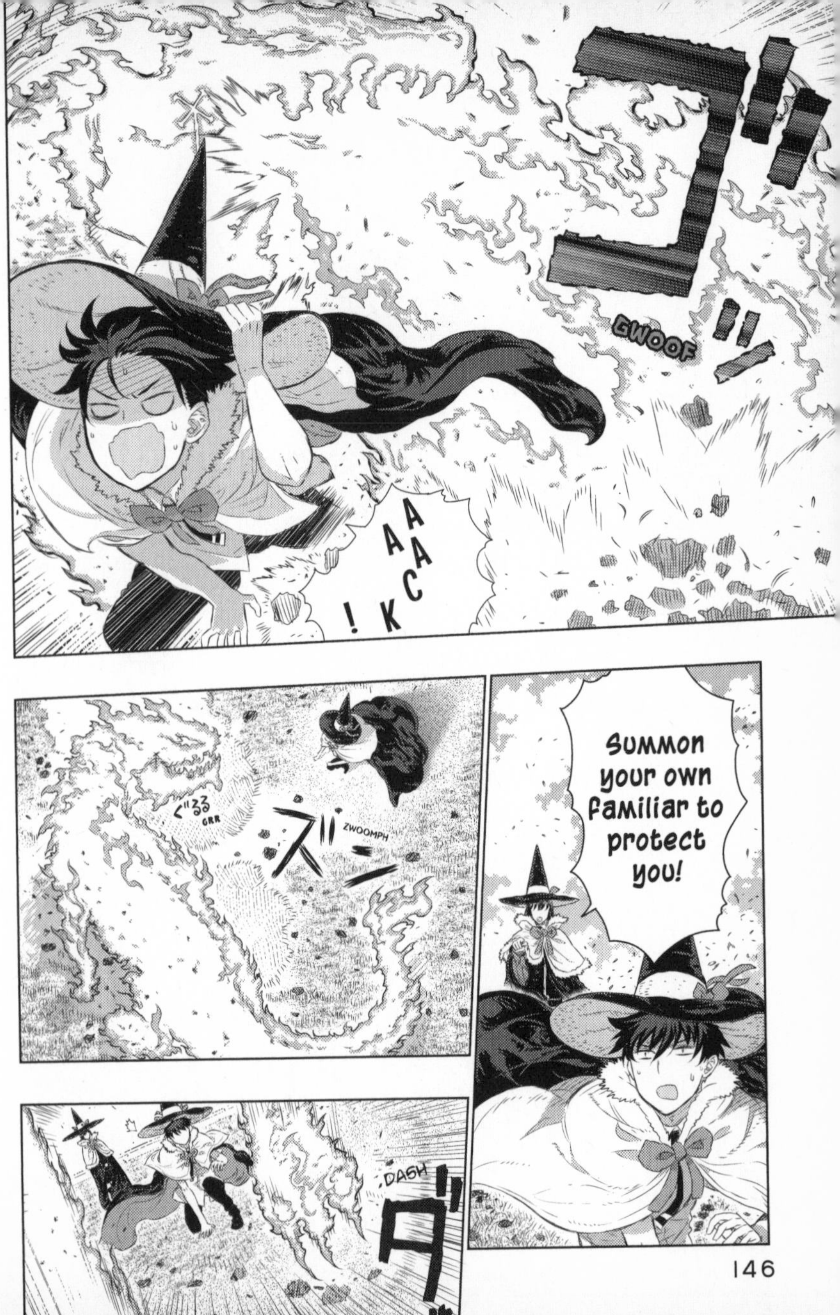
GWOOF
AAACK!
Summon your own familiar to protect you!
GRR
ZWOOMPH
DASH

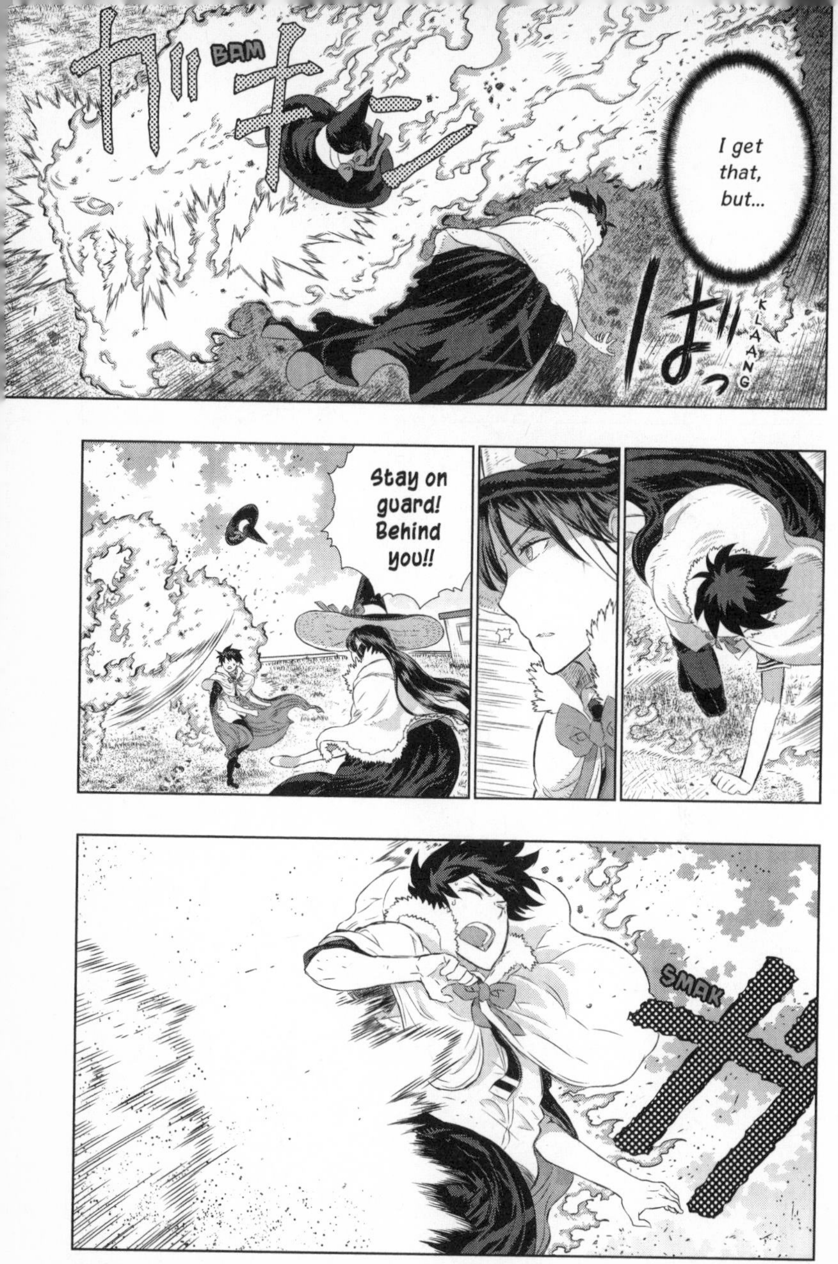
I get that, but...
BAM
KLAANG
Stay on guard! Behind you!!
SMAK

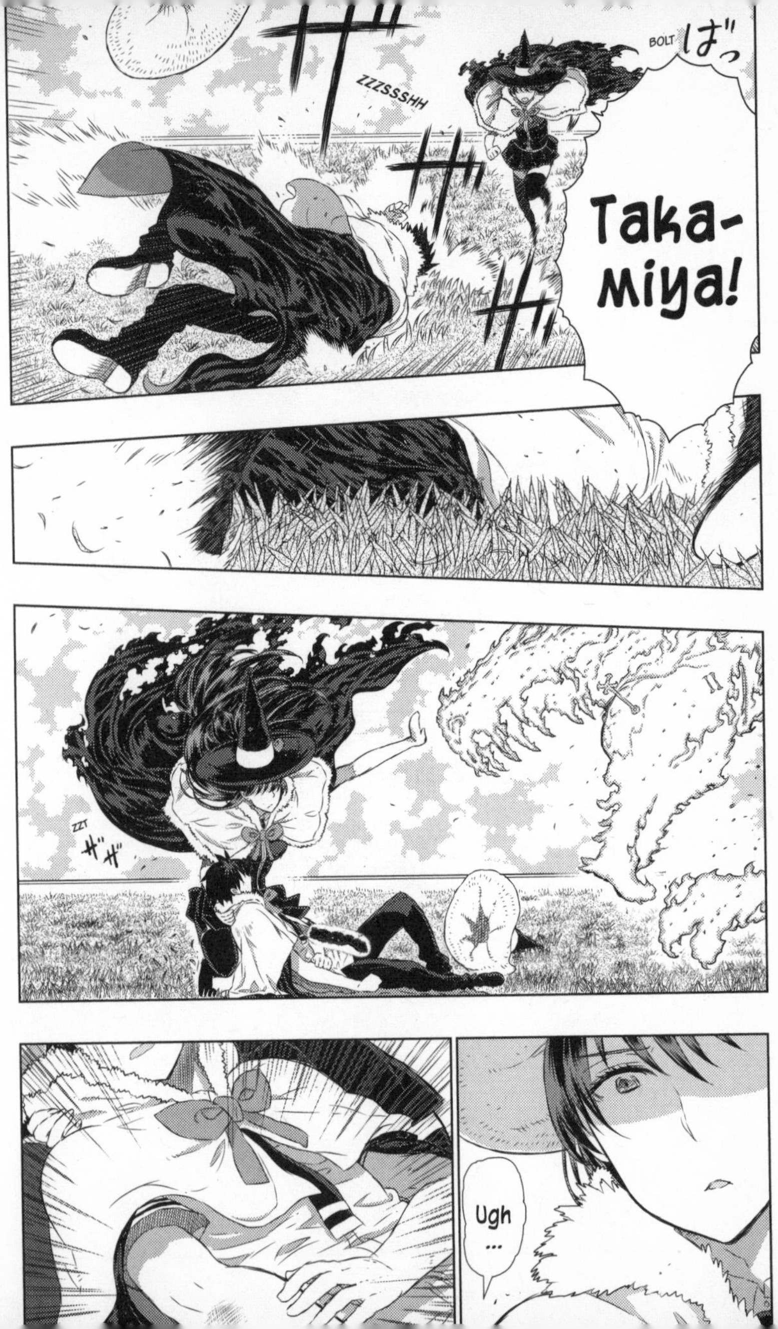
BOLT ばっ
ZZZSSSHH
Taka-miya!
ZZT ザザ
Ugh ...

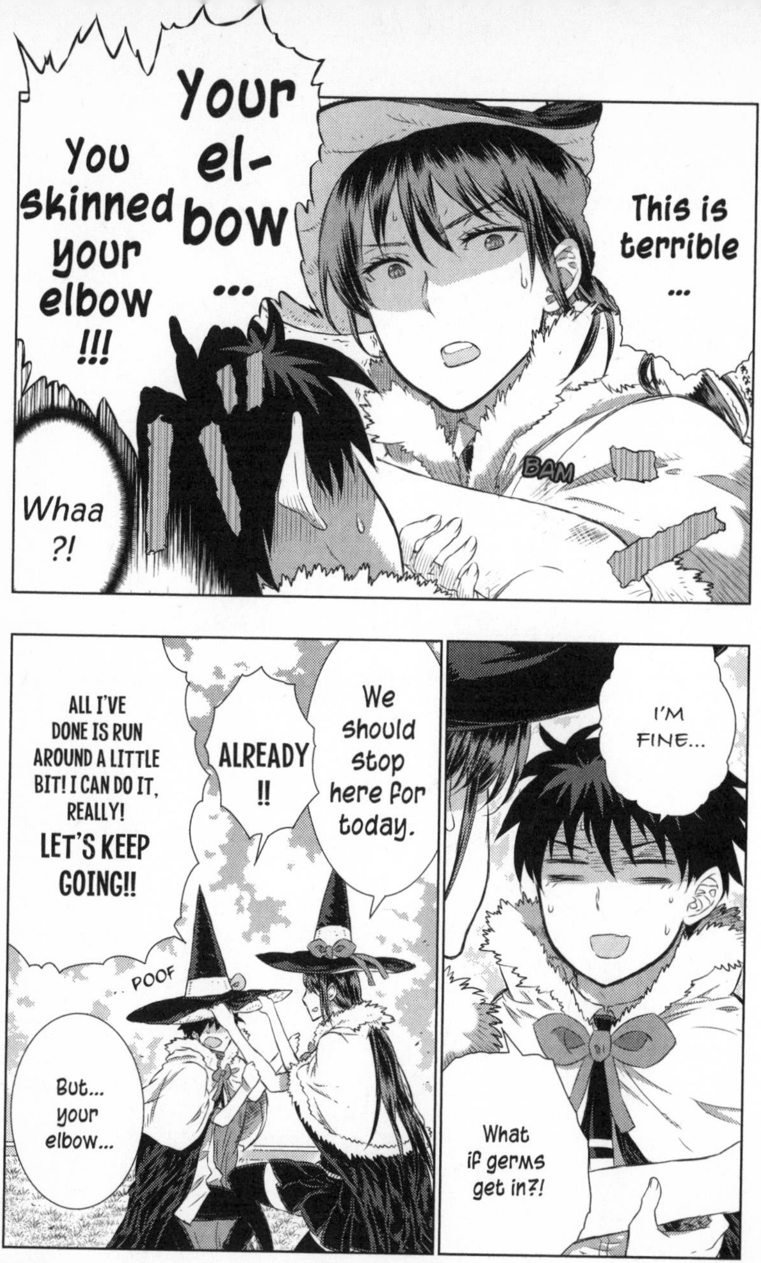
This is terrible ...
Your el-bow ...
You skinned your elbow !!!
BAM
Whaa ?!
I'M FINE...
What if germs get in?!
We should stop here for today.
ALREADY !!
ALL I'VE DONE IS RUN AROUND A LITTLE BIT! I CAN DO IT, REALLY!
LET'S KEEP GOING!!
POOF
But... your elbow...

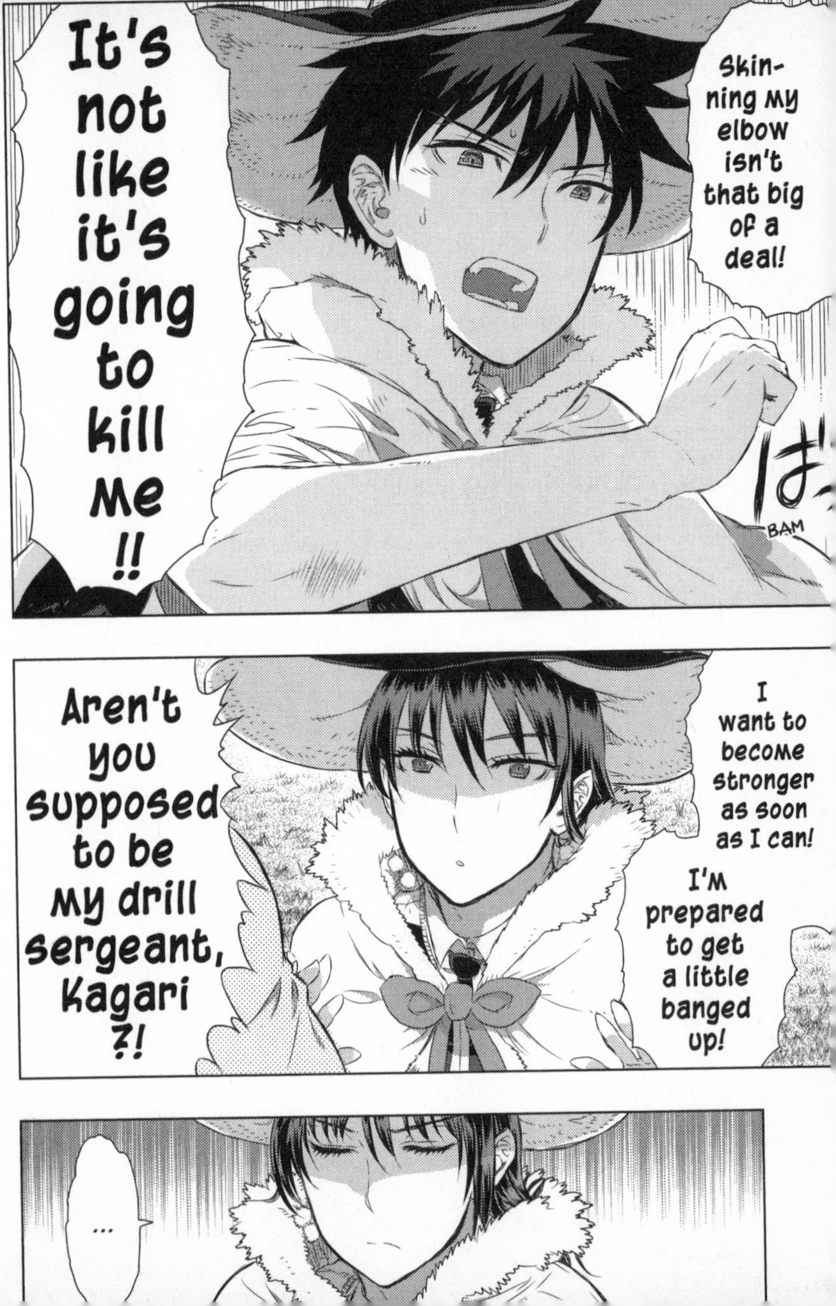
Skinning my elbow isn't that big of a deal!
It's not like it's going to kill me!!
ぱっ
BAM
I want to become stronger as soon as I can!
I'm prepared to get a little banged up!
Aren't you supposed to be my drill sergeant, Kagari?!
...

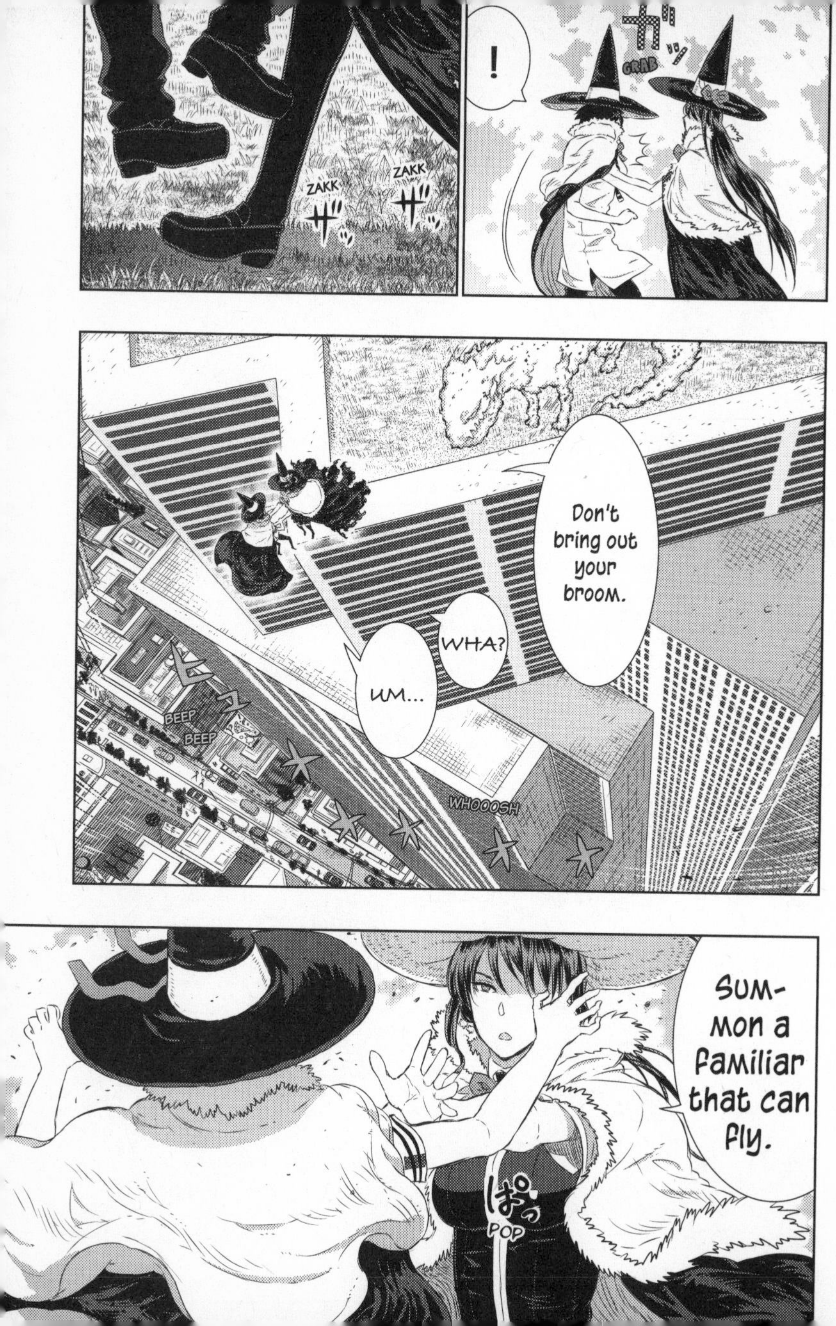
!
GRAB
ZAKK
ZAKK
Don't bring out your broom.
WHA?
UM...
BEEP
BEEP
WHOOOSH
Sum-mon a familiar that can fly.
POP

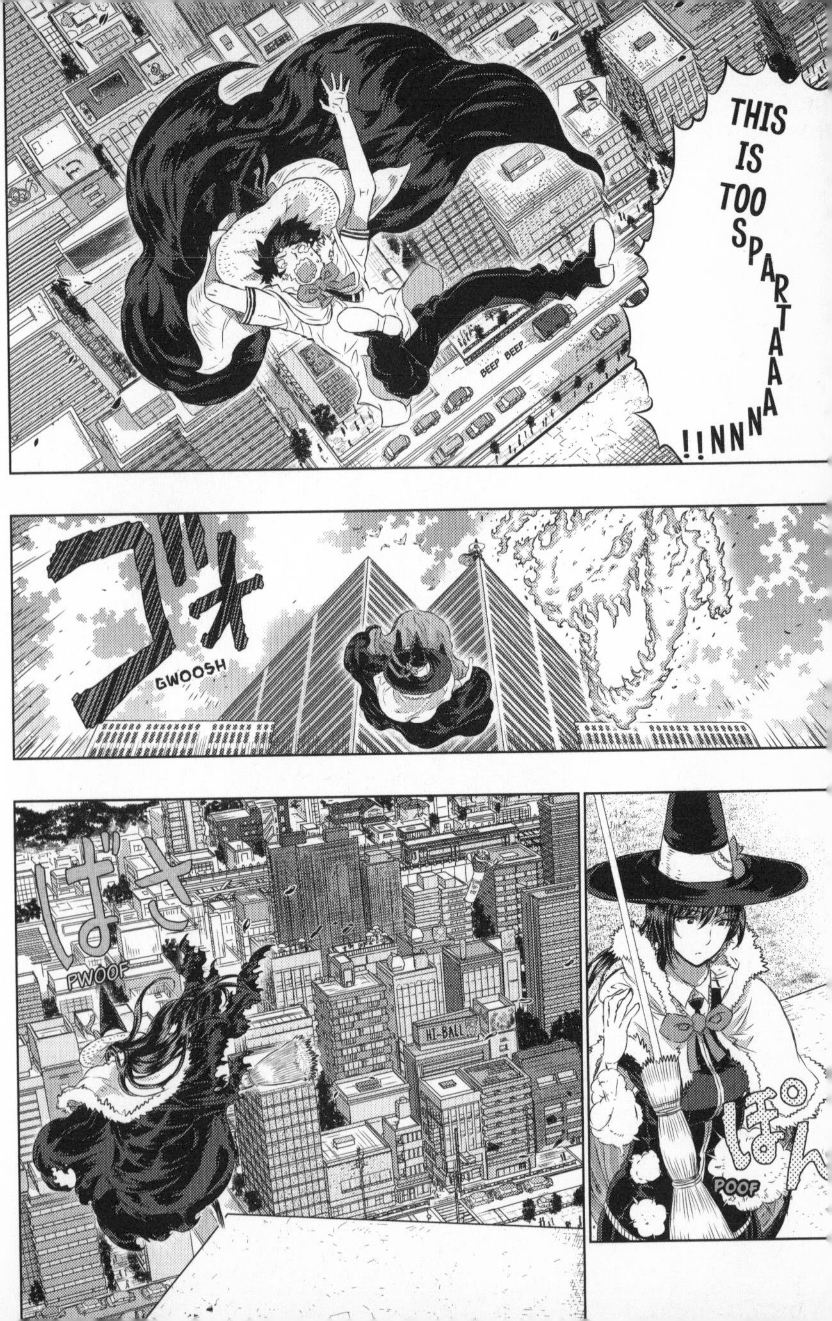
THIS IS TOO SPARTAAANNN!!
BEEP BEEP
ゴォ
GWOOSH
ぽん
POOF
ばさ
PWOOF
HI-BALL

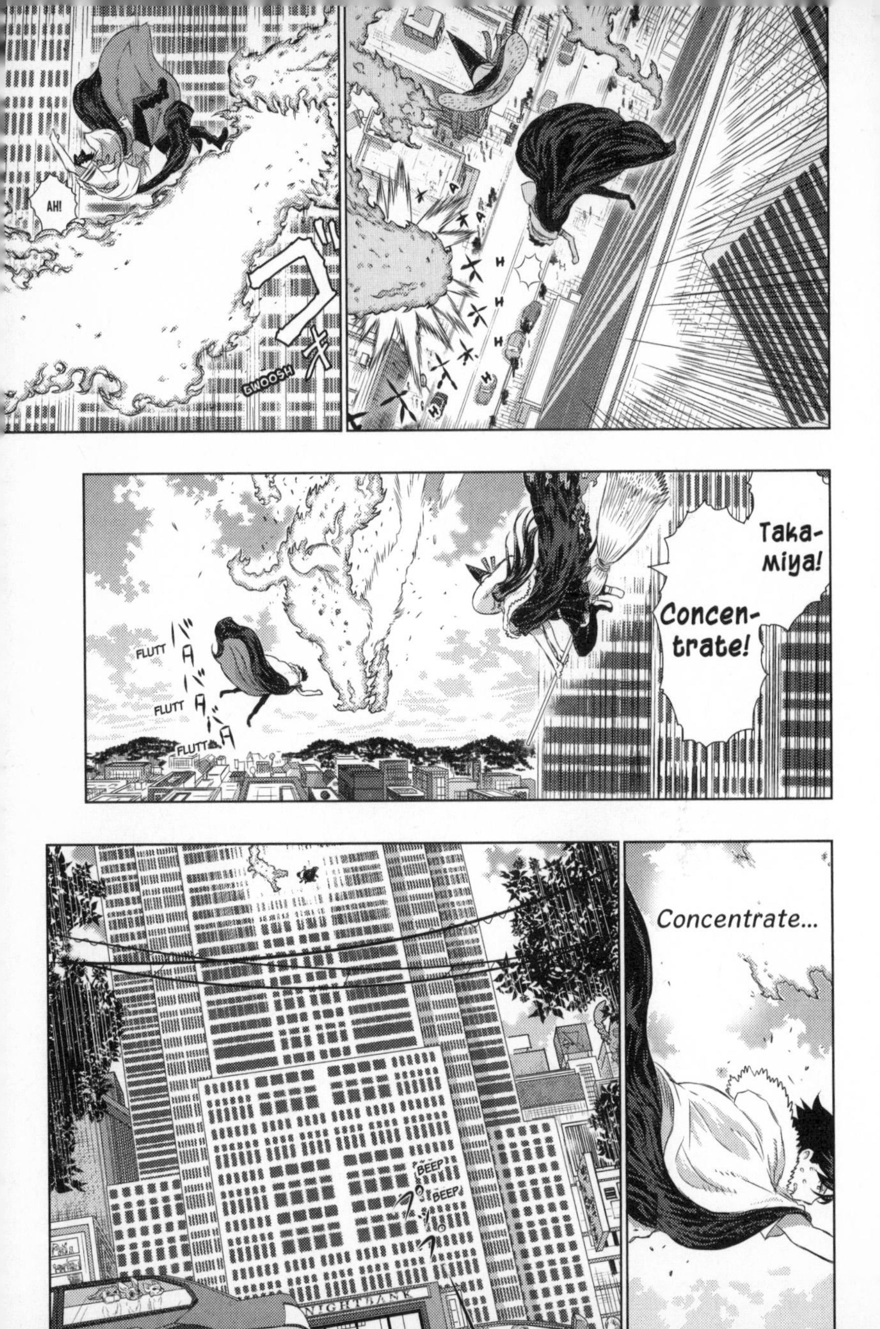
AH!
GWOOSH
Taka-miya!
Concen-trate!
FLUTT
FLUTT
FLUTT
Concentrate...
BEEP
BEEP

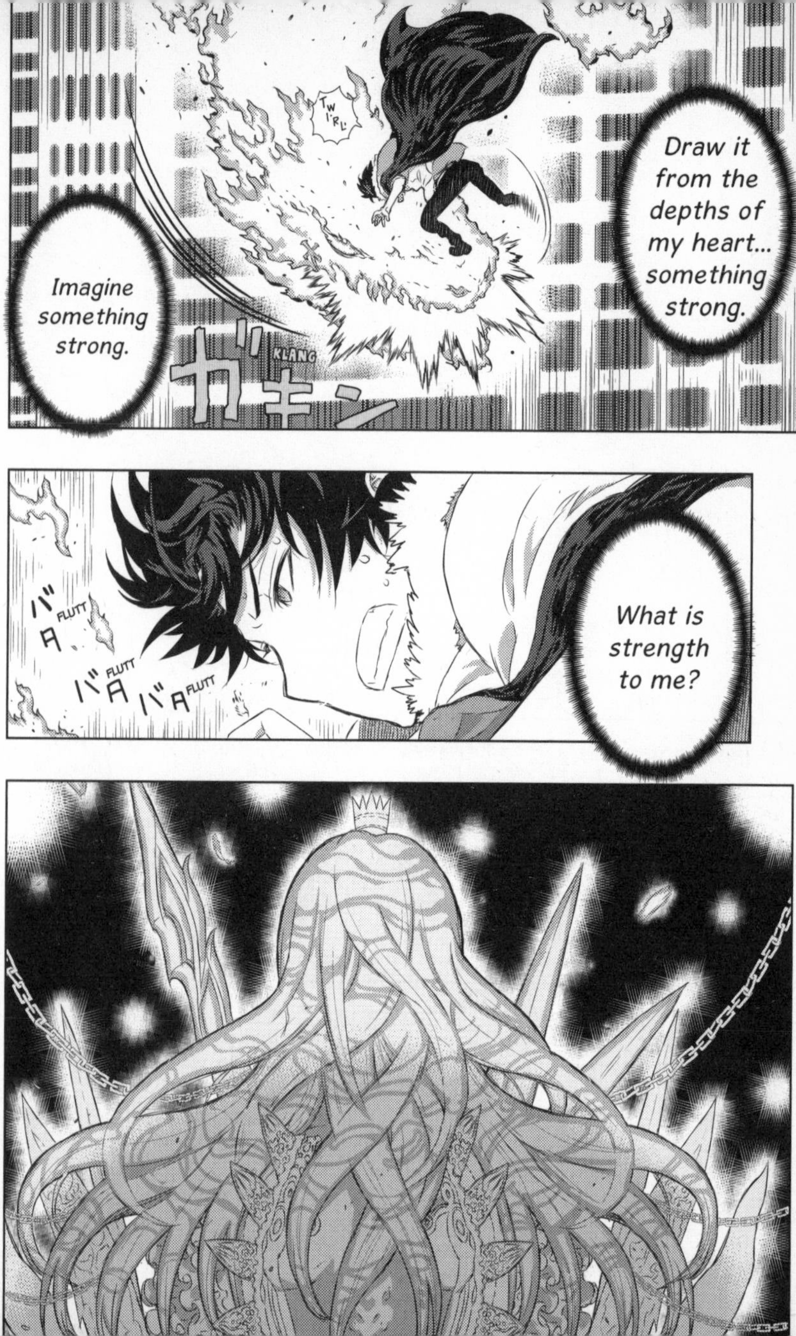
Draw it from the depths of my heart... something strong.
TW I'RL'
Imagine something strong.
ガキン KLANG
What is strength to me?
バ FLUTT
バ FLUTT
バ FLUTT

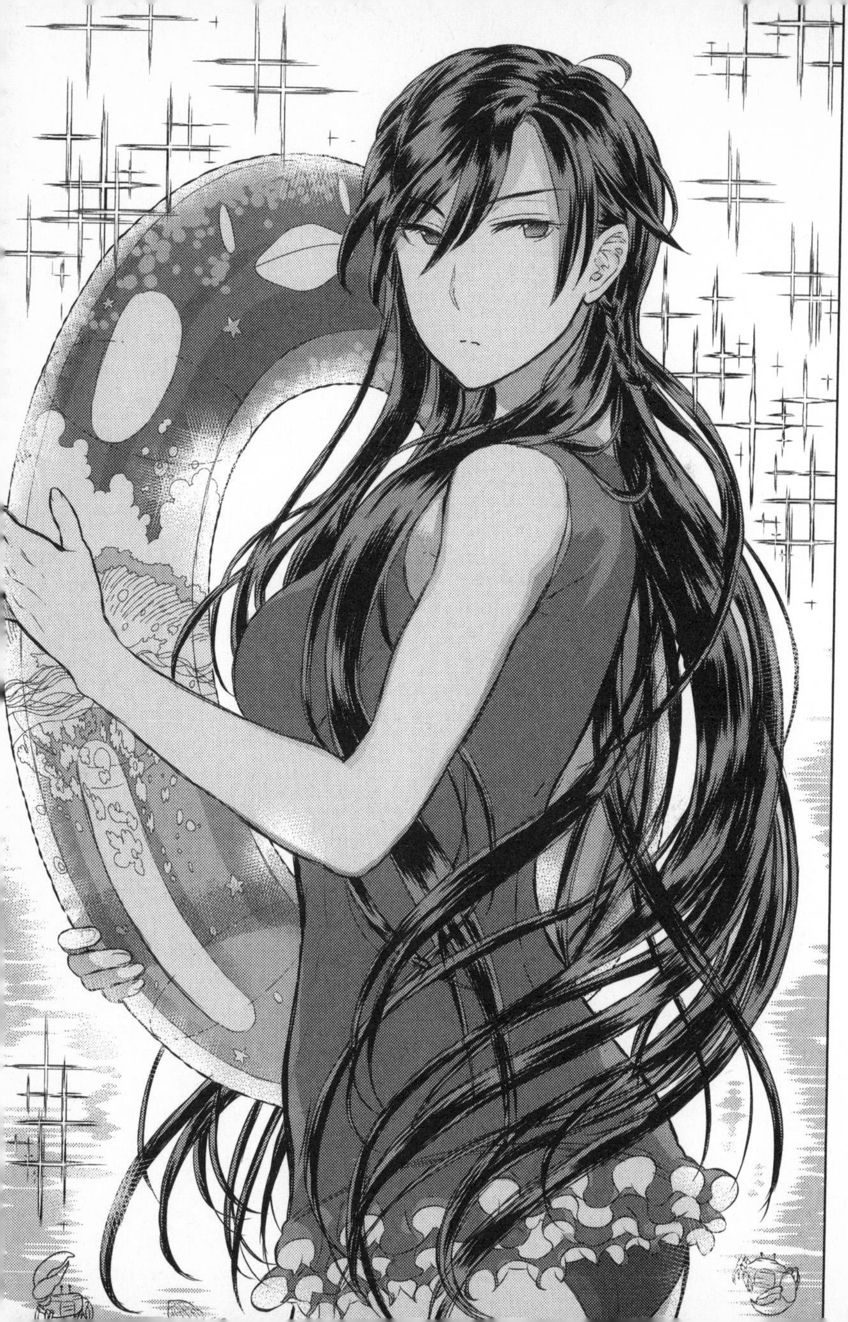

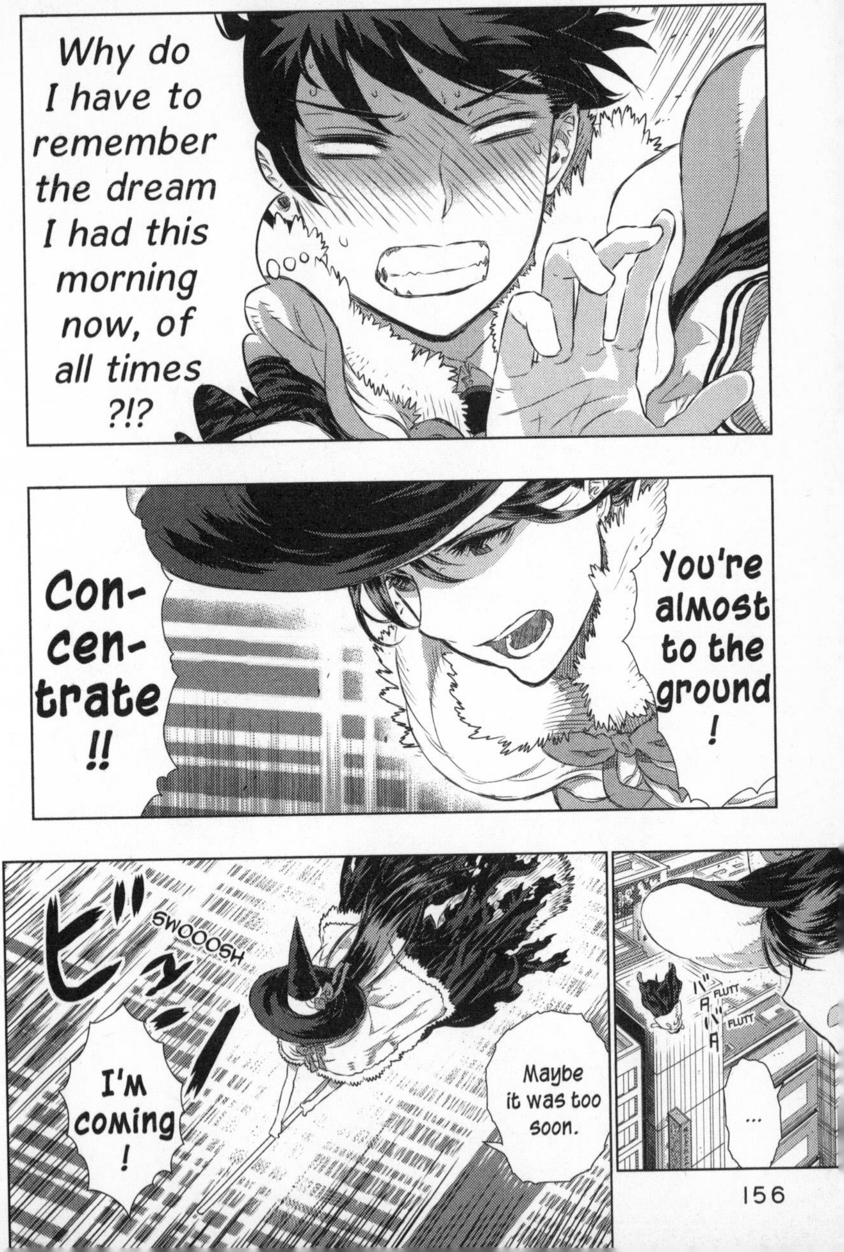
Why do I have to remember the dream I had this morning now, of all times ?!?
You're almost to the ground !
Con-cen-trate !!
FLUTT
FLUTT
...
Maybe it was too soon.
ビュッ
SWOOOSH
I'M coming !

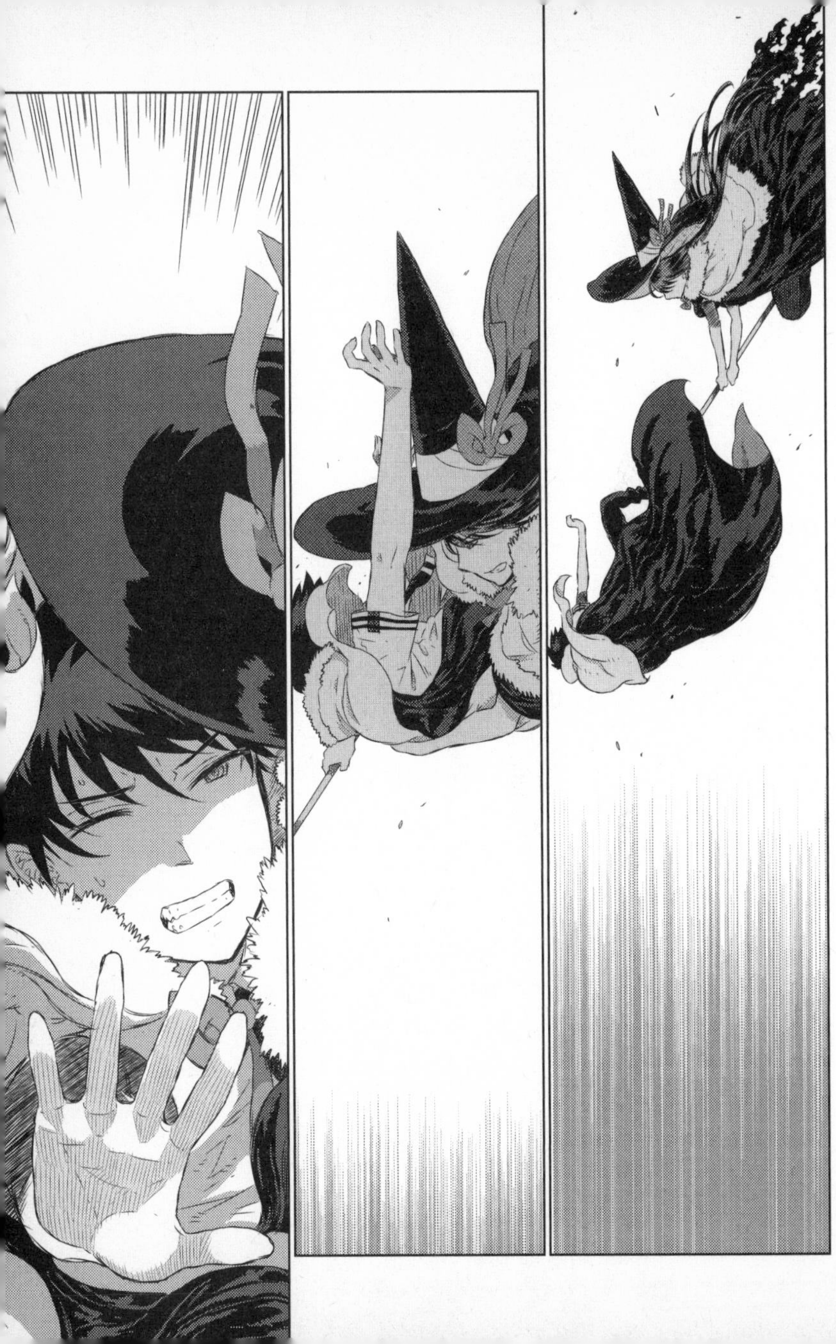

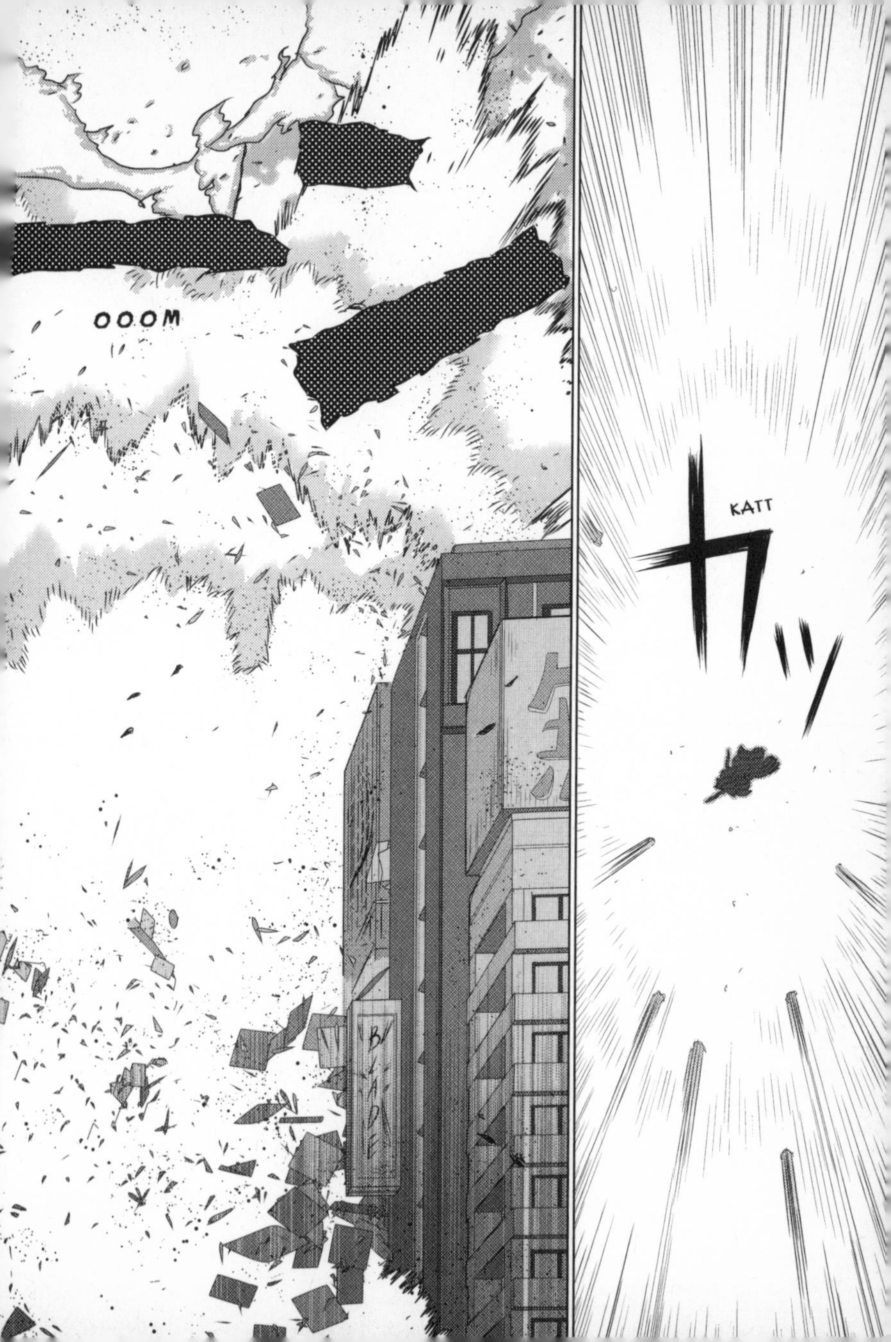
KATT
カッ
OOOM

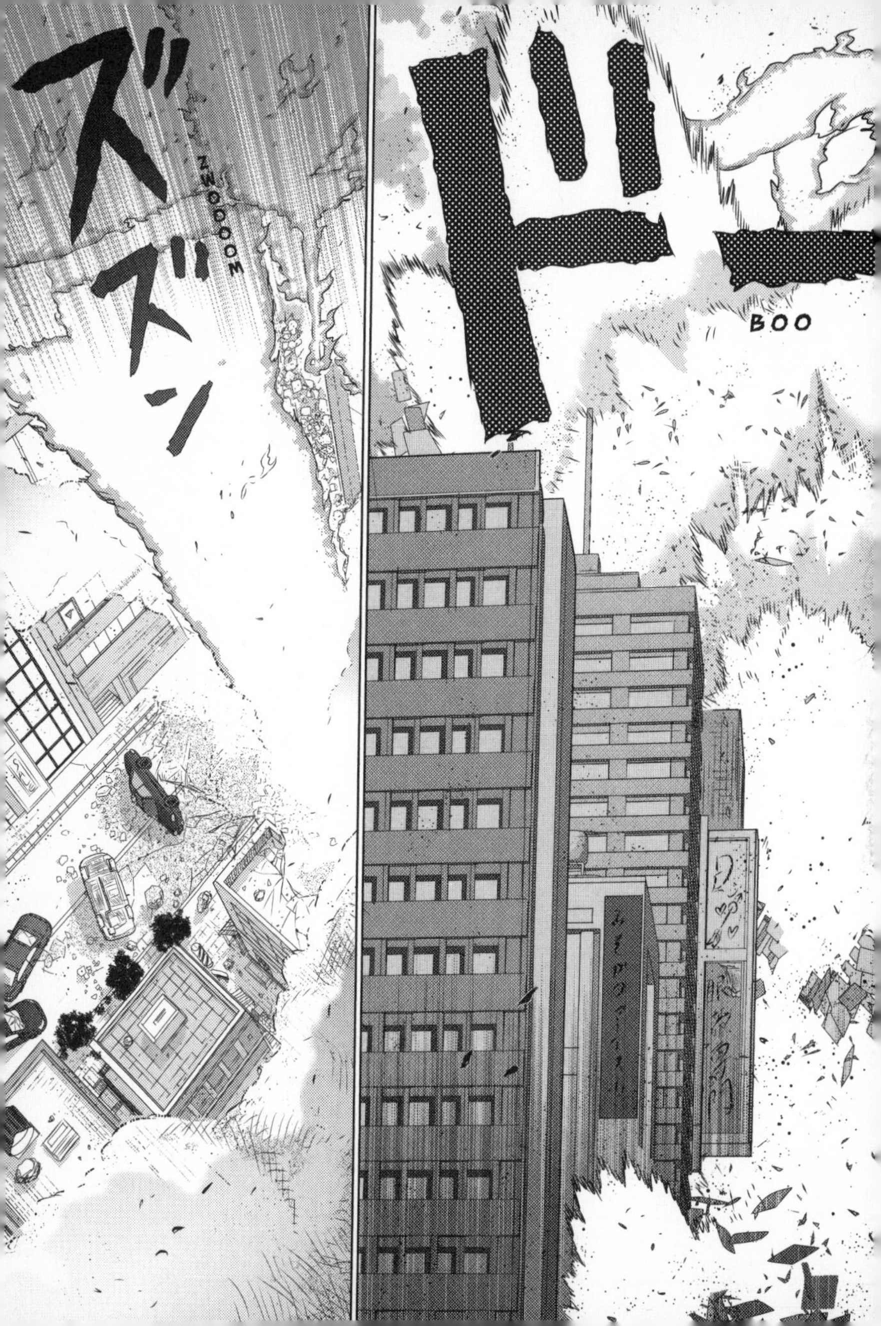
ドー
BOO
ズズン
ZWOOOOOM

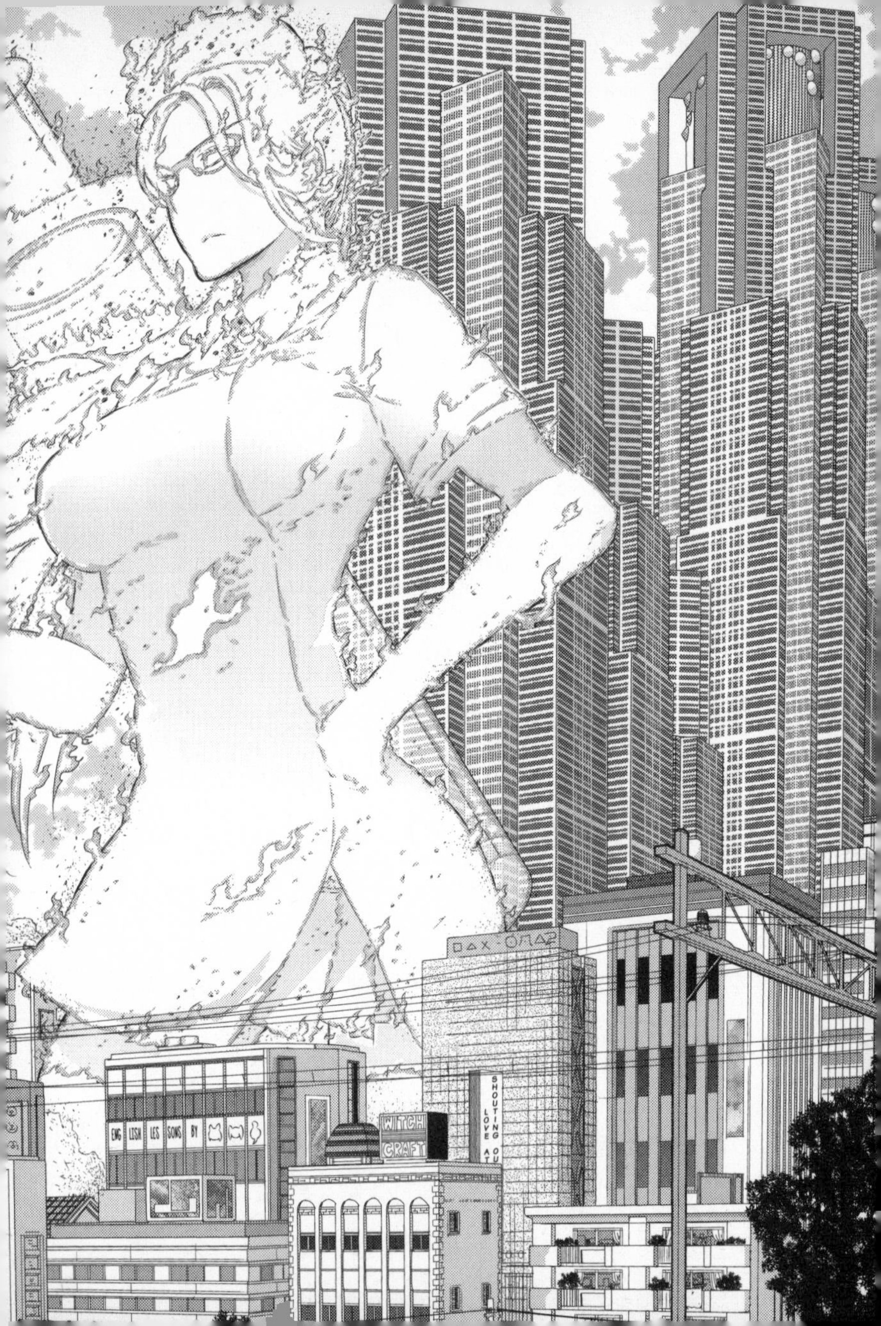
ENG LISH LES SONS BY
WITCH CRAFT
SHOUTING OU
LOVE AT

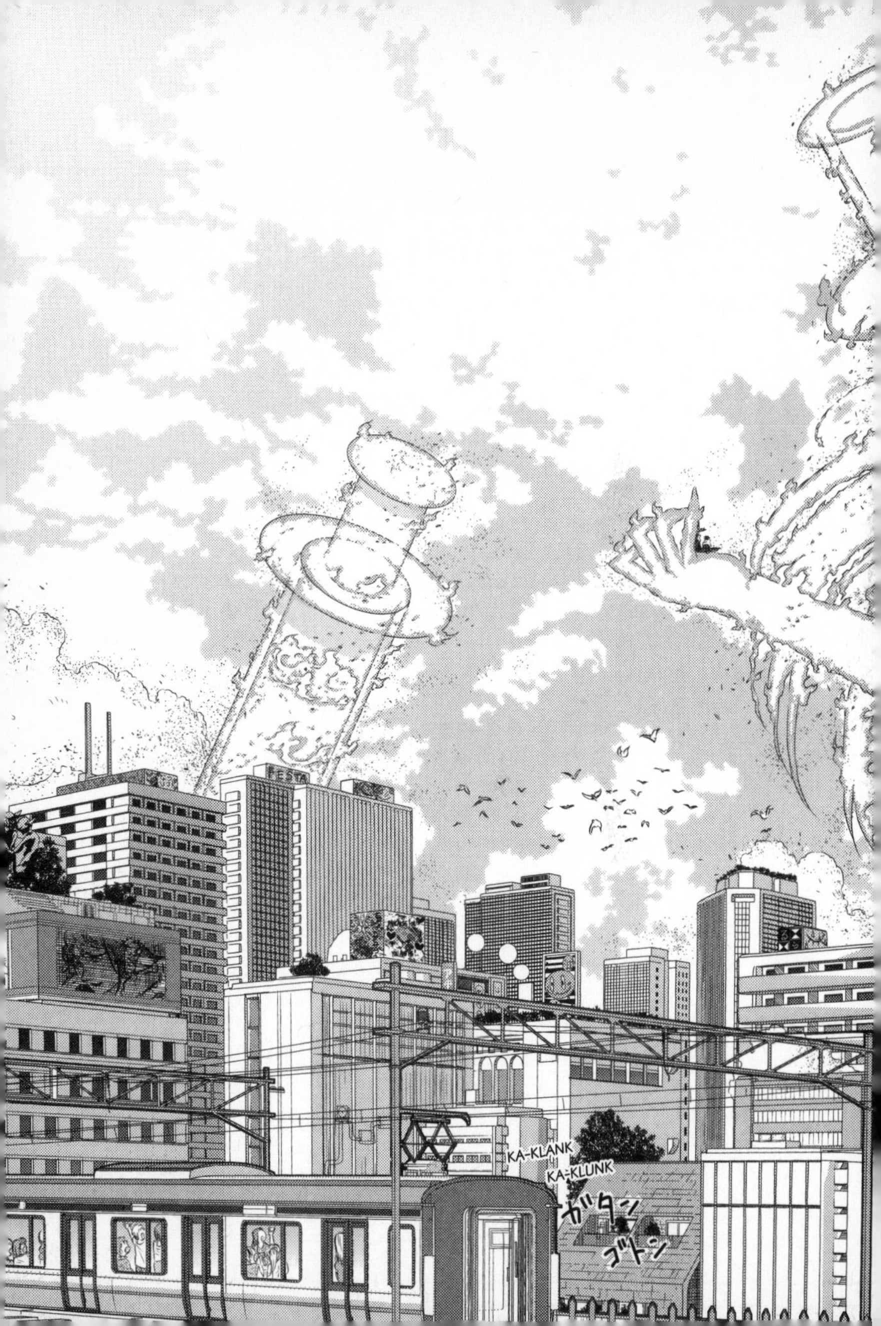
FESTA
KA-KLANK
KA-KLUNK
ガタン
ゴトン

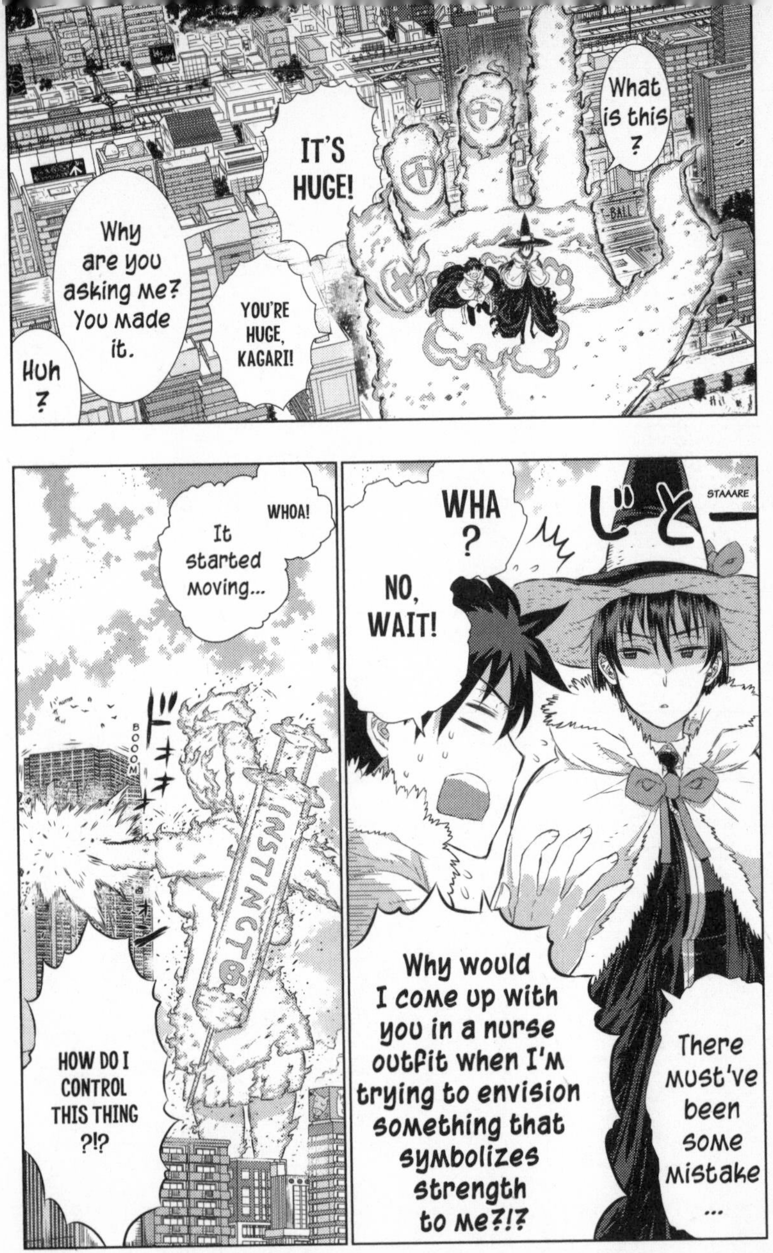
What is this?
IT'S HUGE!
YOU'RE HUGE, KAGARI!
Why are you asking me? You made it.
Huh?
じとー
STAAARE
WHA?
NO, WAIT!
There must've been some mistake...
Why would I come up with you in a nurse outfit when I'm trying to envision something that symbolizes strength to me?!?
WHOA!
It started moving...
ドォォ
BOOOOM
HOW DO I CONTROL THIS THING?!?

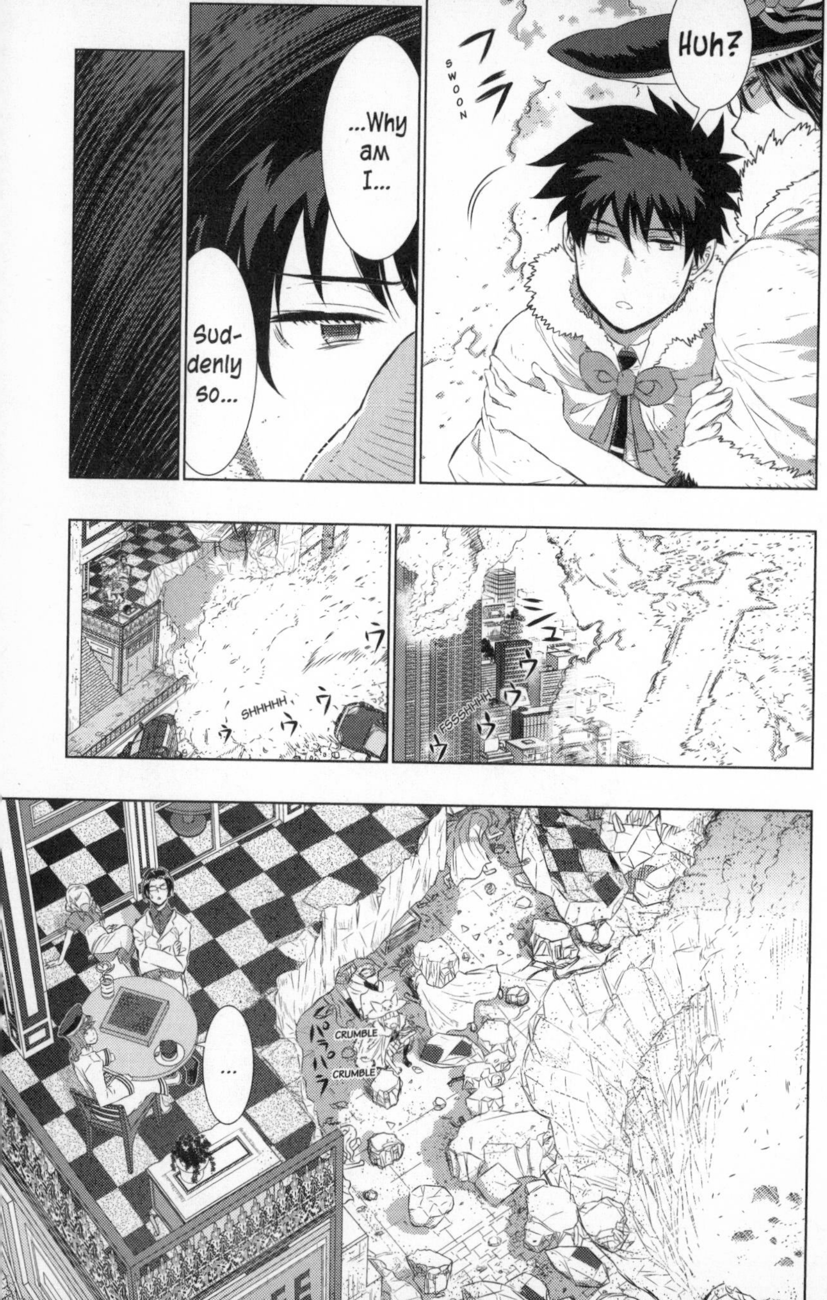
Huh?
SWOON
...Why am I...
Sud-denly so...
FSSSHHHH
SHHHHH
CRUMBLE
CRUMBLE
...

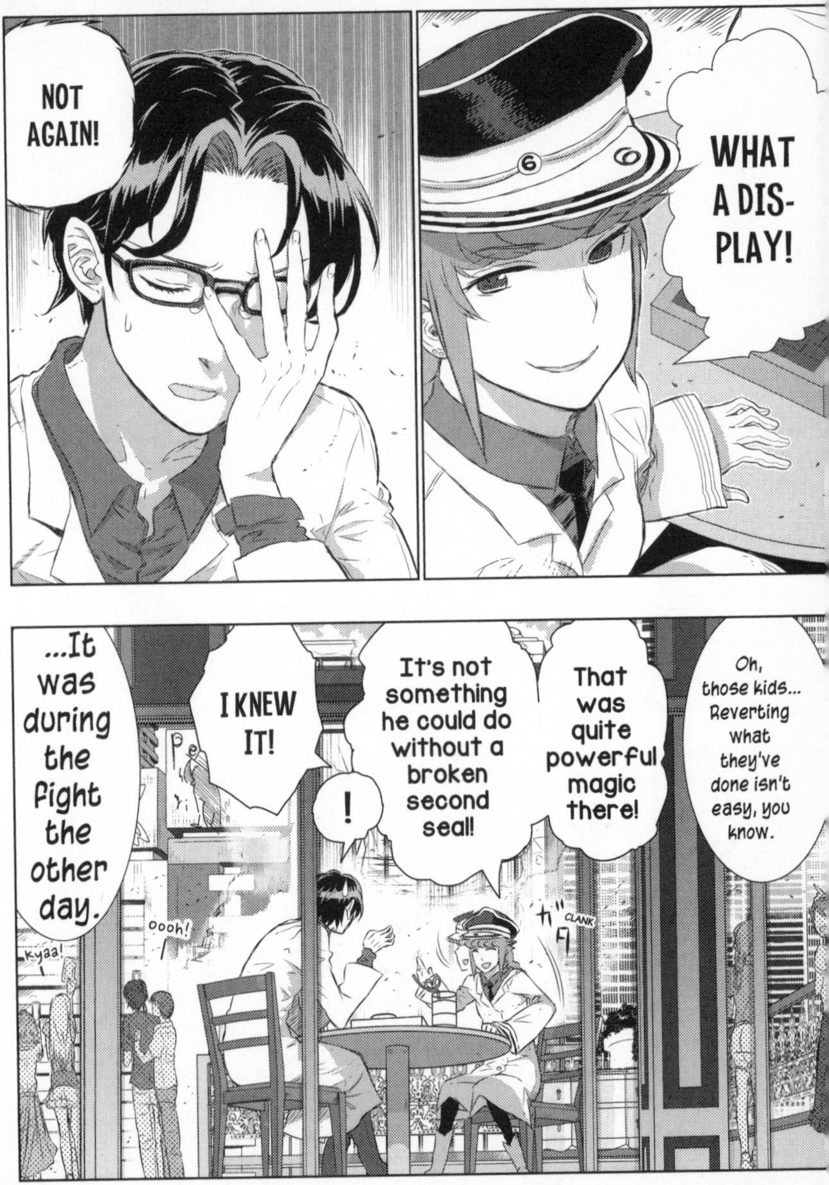
WHAT A DIS-PLAY!
NOT AGAIN!
Oh, those kids... Reverting what they've done isn't easy, you know.
That was quite powerful magic there!
It's not something he could do without a broken second seal!
!
I KNEW IT!
...It was during the fight the other day.
CLANK
oooh!
kyaa!

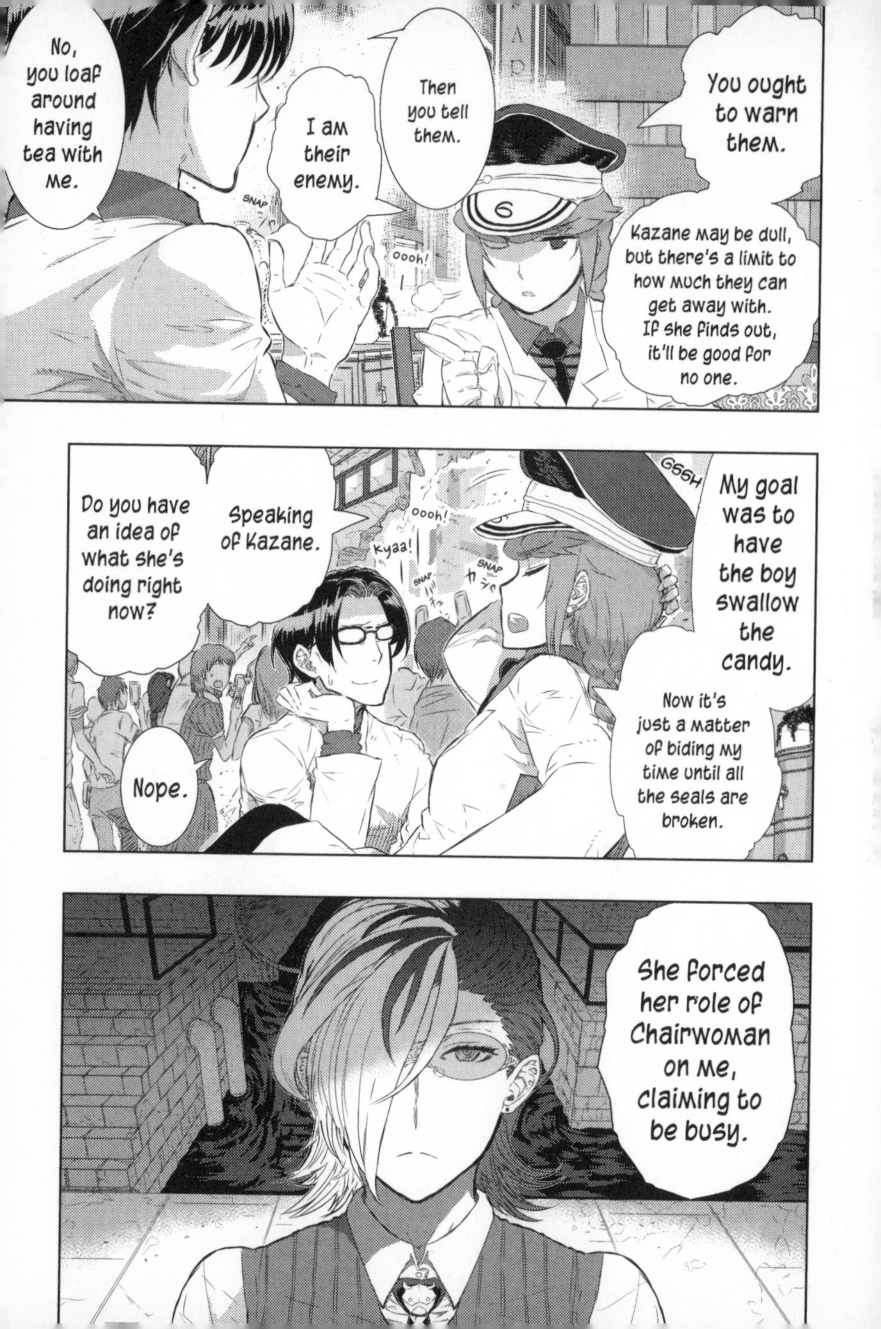
You ought to warn them.
Kazane may be dull, but there's a limit to how much they can get away with. If she finds out, it'll be good for no one.
Oooh!
Then you tell them.
I am their enemy.
SNAP
No, you loaf around having tea with me.
GSSH
My goal was to have the boy swallow the candy.
Now it's just a matter of biding my time until all the seals are broken.
SNAP
Oooh!
Kyaa!
SNAP
Speaking of Kazane.
Do you have an idea of what she's doing right now?
Nope.
She forced her role of Chairwoman on me, claiming to be busy.

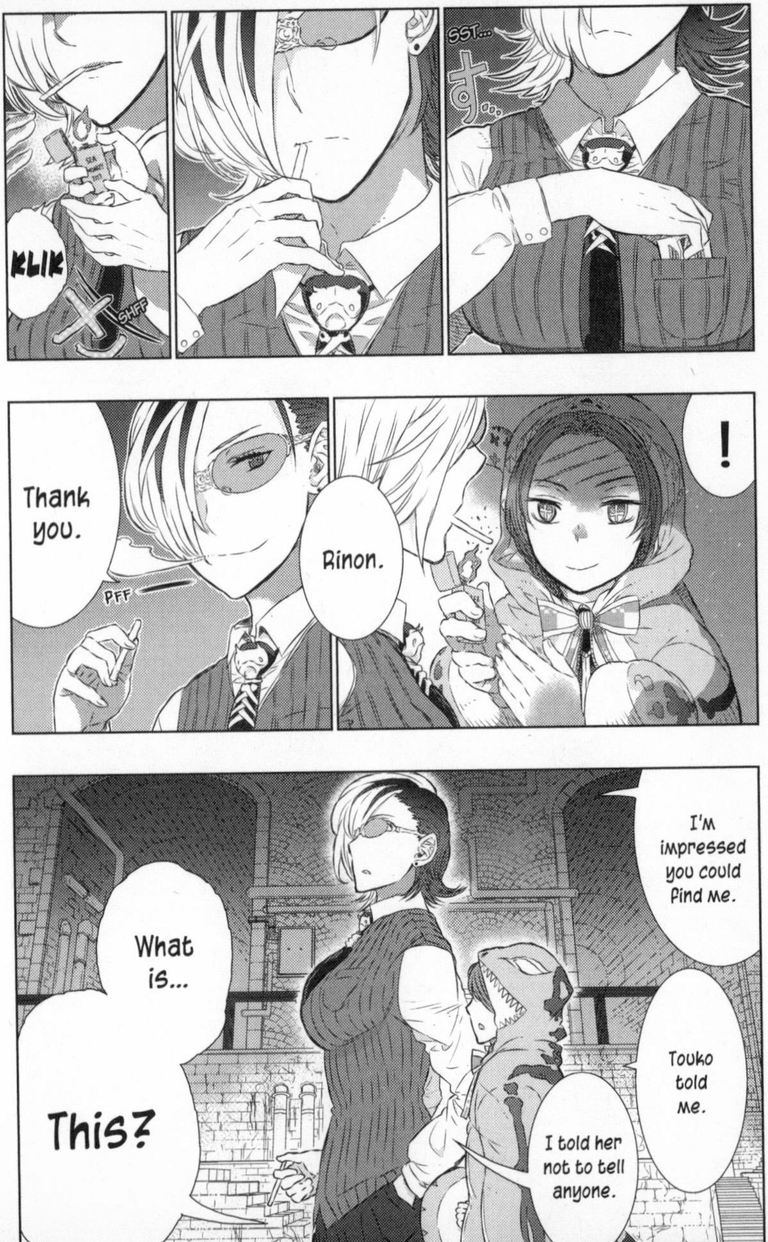
SST...
す...
KLIK
SHFF
!
Rinon.
Thank you.
PFF
I'm impressed you could find me.
Touko told me.
I told her not to tell anyone.
What is...
This?

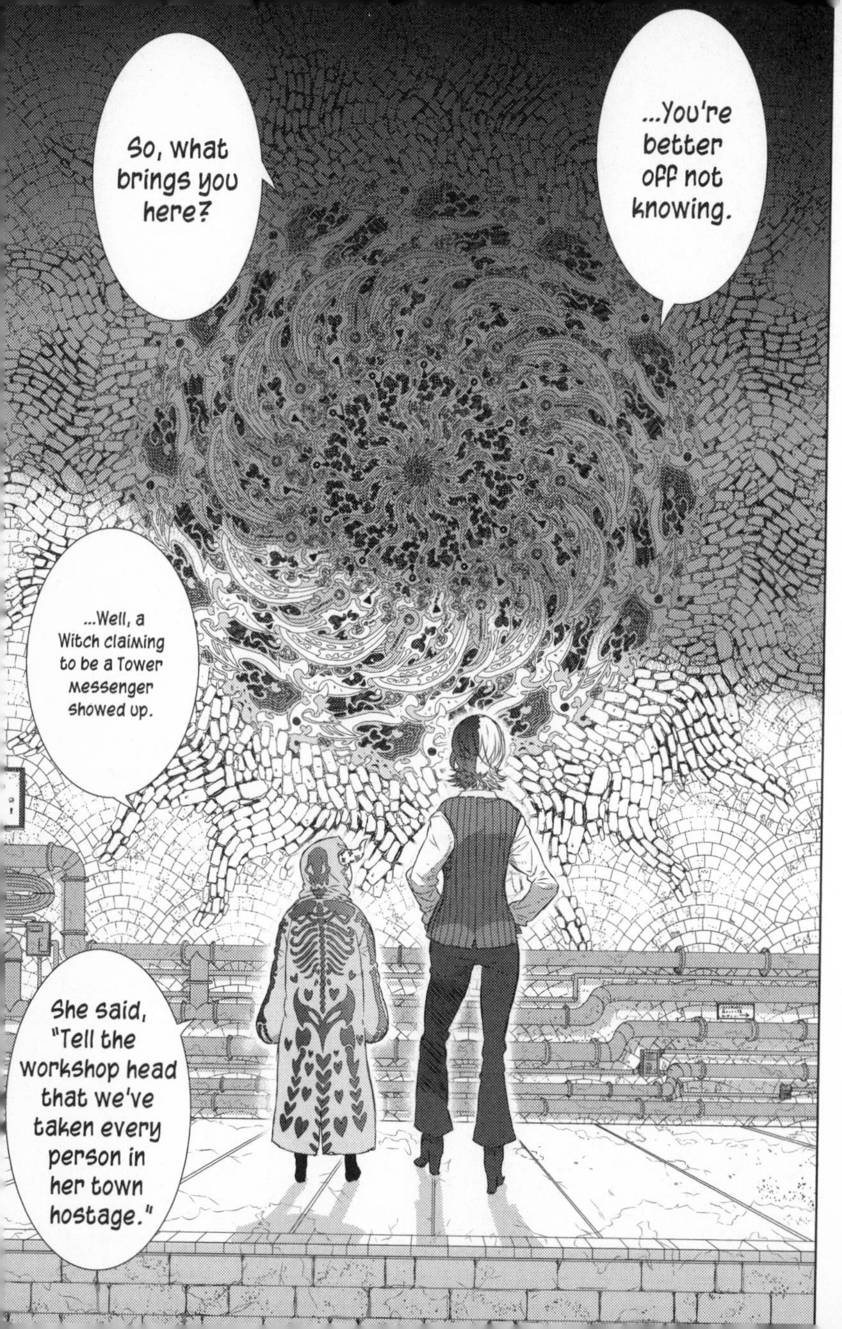
...You're better off not knowing.
So, what brings you here?
...Well, a Witch claiming to be a Tower messenger showed up.
She said, "Tell the workshop head that we've taken every person in her town hostage."

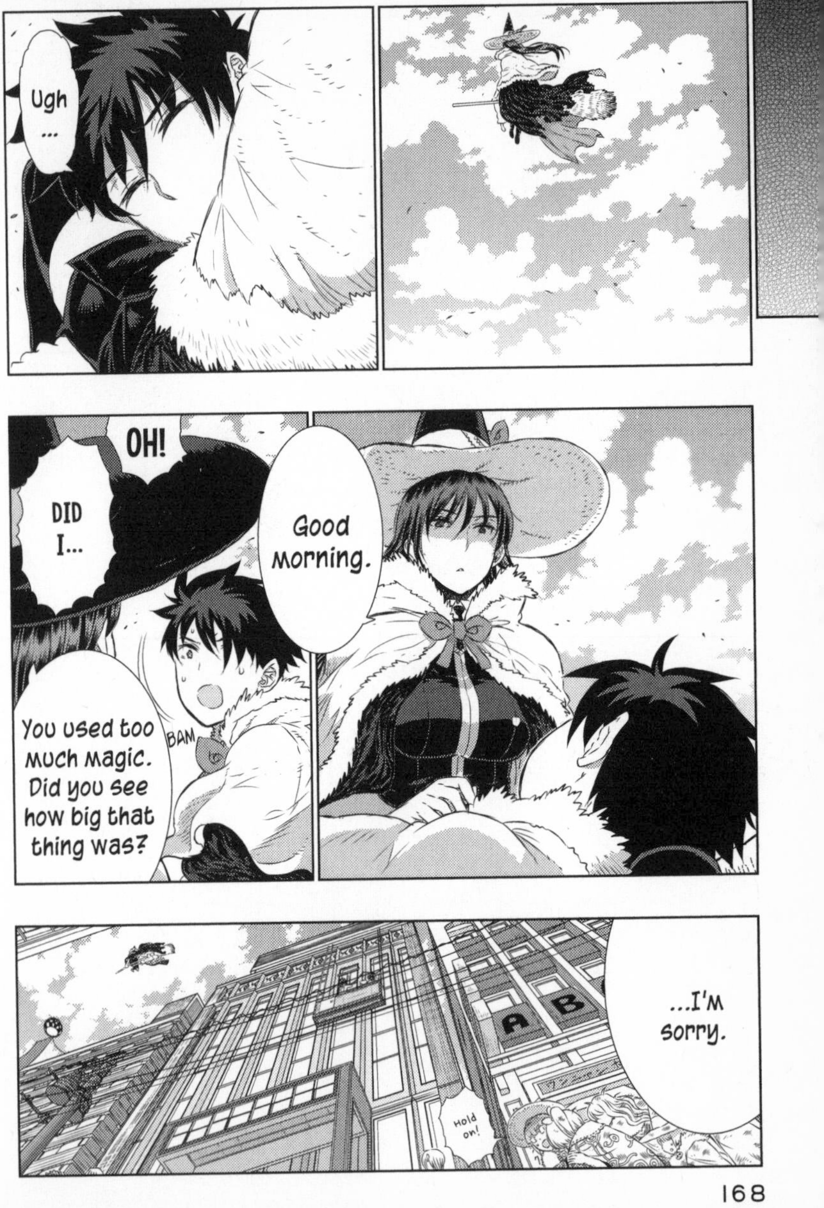
Ugh ...
Good morning.
OH!
DID I...
BAM
You used too much magic. Did you see how big that thing was?
...I'M sorry.
Hold on!

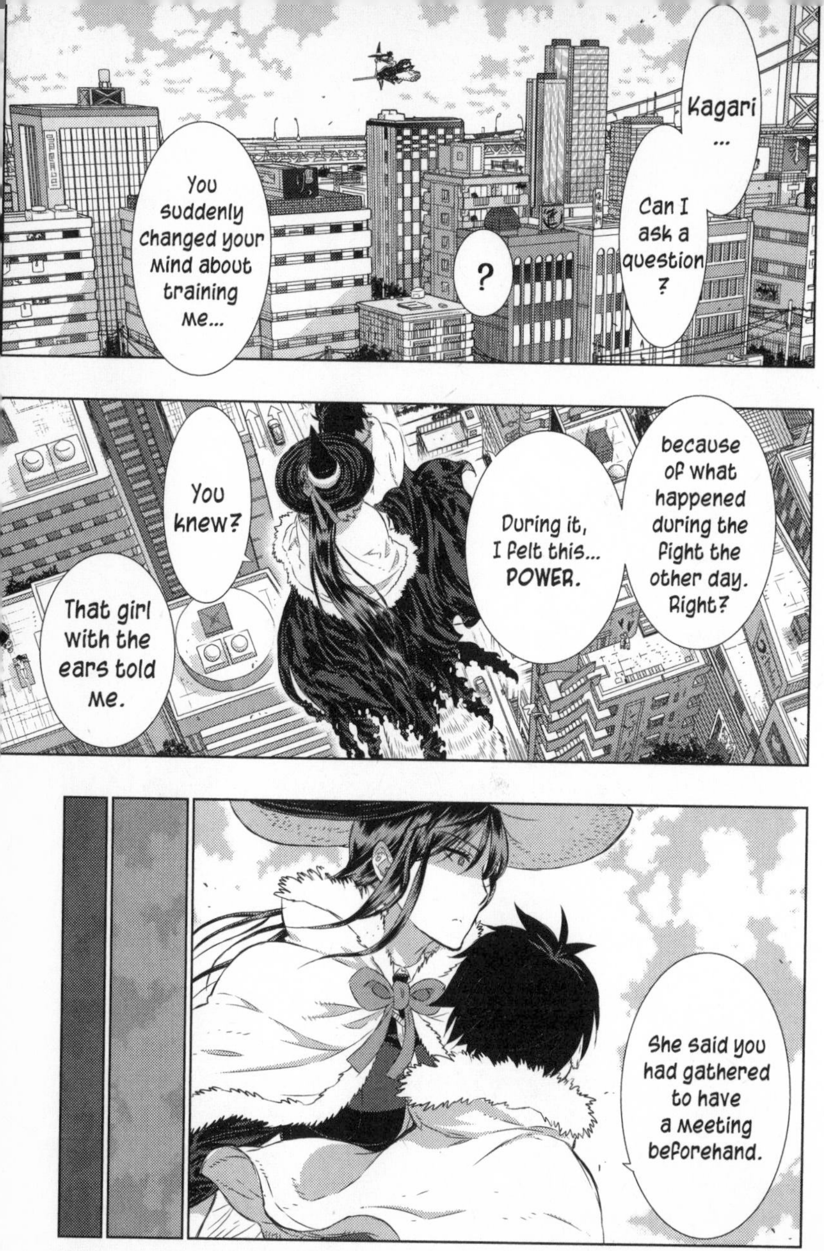
Kagari...
Can I ask a question?
?
You suddenly changed your mind about training me...
because of what happened during the fight the other day. Right?
During it, I felt this... POWER.
You knew?
That girl with the ears told me.
She said you had gathered to have a meeting beforehand.

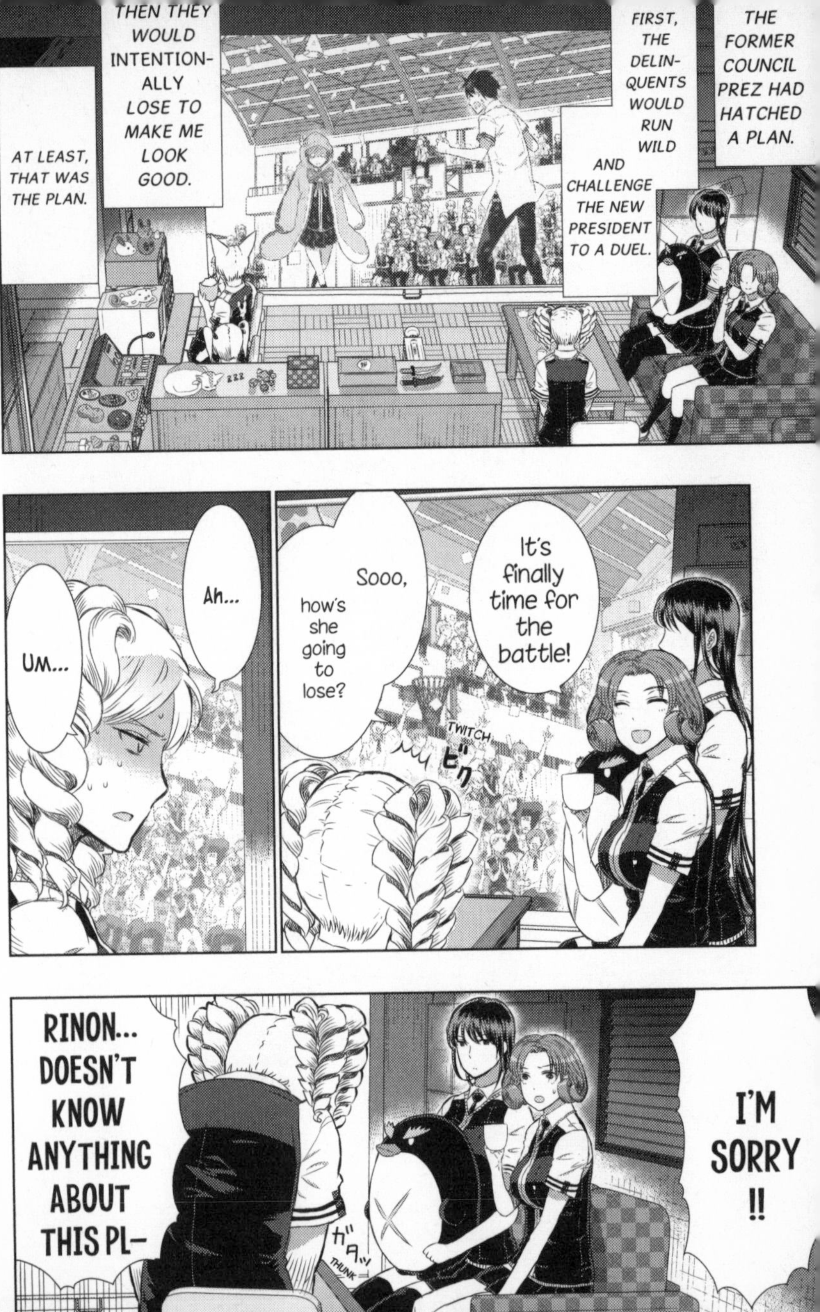
THE FORMER COUNCIL PREZ HAD HATCHED A PLAN.
FIRST, THE DELIN-QUENTS WOULD RUN WILD
AND CHALLENGE THE NEW PRESIDENT TO A DUEL.
THEN THEY WOULD INTENTION-ALLY LOSE TO MAKE ME LOOK GOOD.
AT LEAST, THAT WAS THE PLAN.
It's finally time for the battle!
Sooo,
how's she going to lose?
TWITCH
Ah...
Um...
I'M SORRY!!
RINON... DOESN'T KNOW ANYTHING ABOUT THIS PL-
THUNK

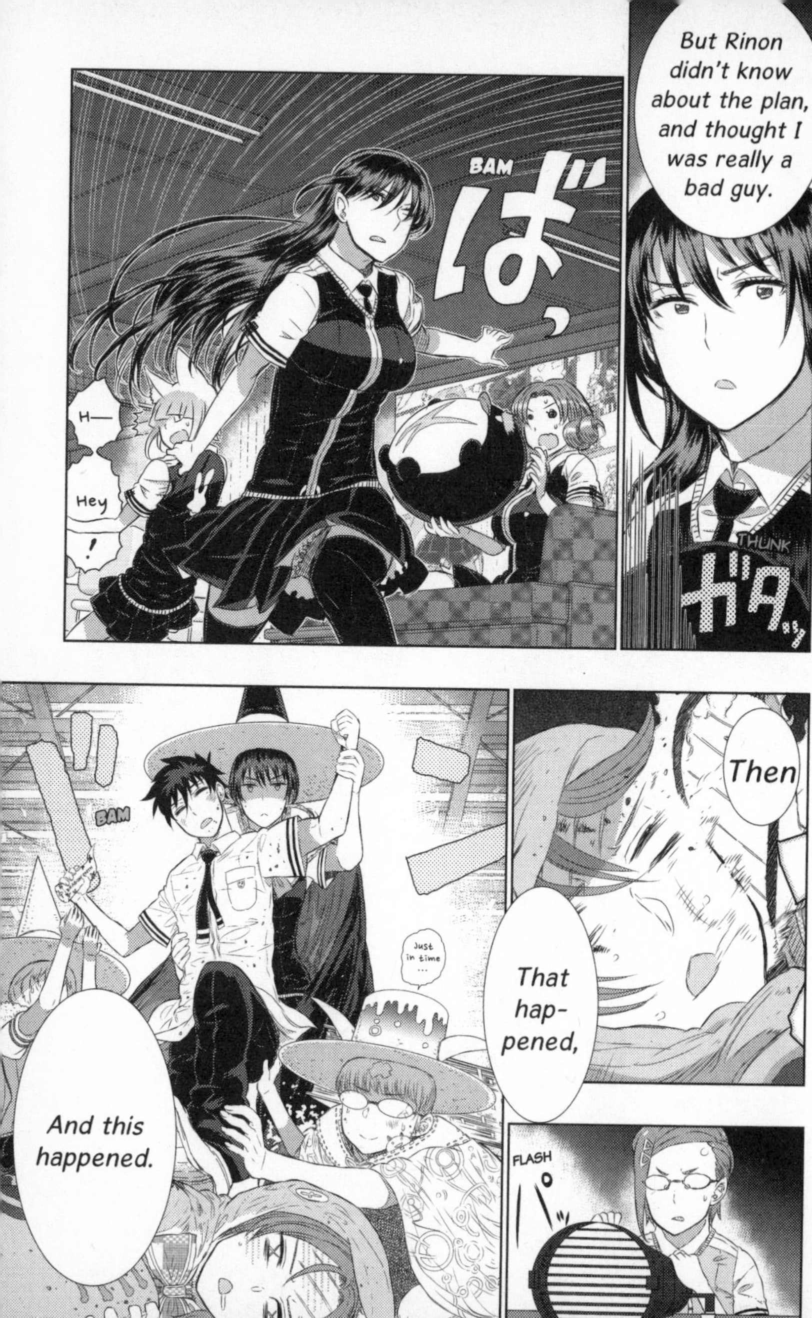
But Rinon didn't know about the plan, and thought I was really a bad guy.
THUNK
ガタッ
BAM
ばっ
H—
Hey
!
Then
That hap-pened,
FLASH
バッ
BAM
Just in time...
And this happened.

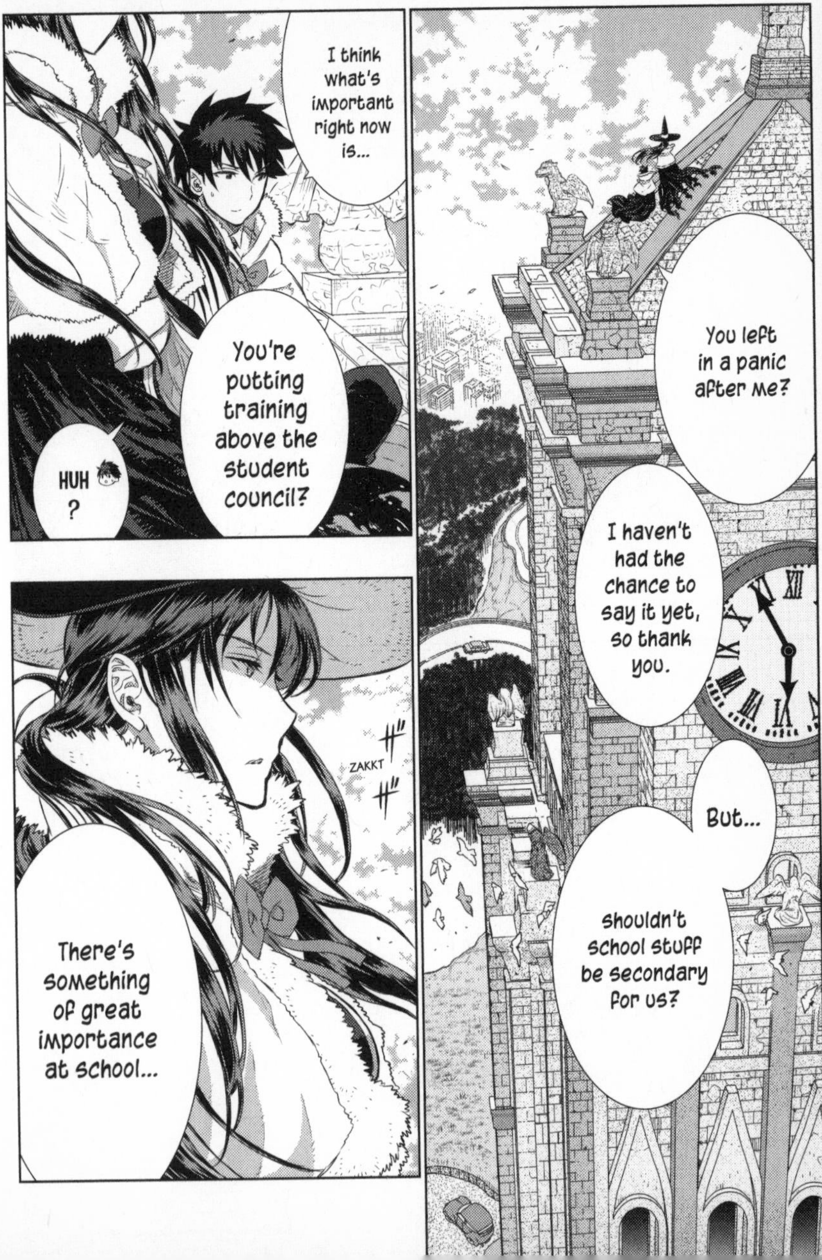
You left in a panic after me?
I haven't had the chance to say it yet, so thank you.
But...
Shouldn't school stuff be secondary for us?
I think what's important right now is...
You're putting training above the student council?
HUH ?
ZAKKT
There's something of great importance at school...

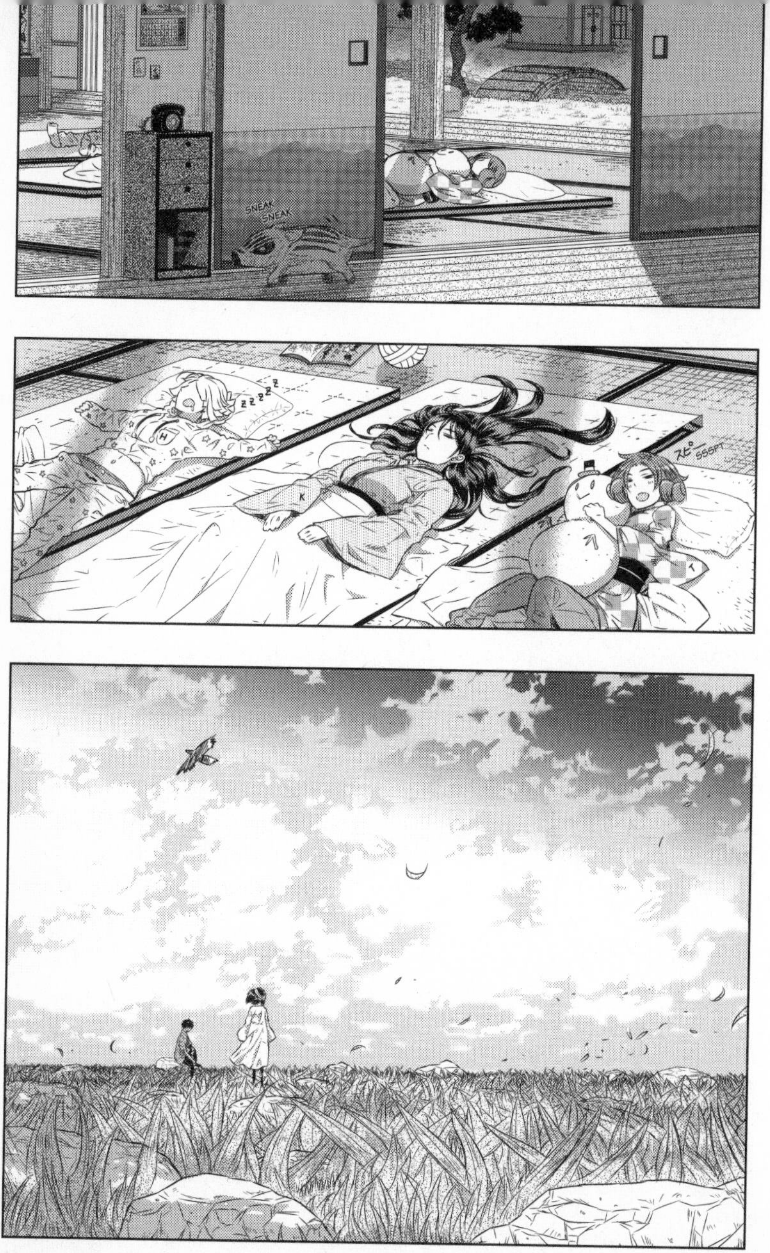
SNEAK
SNEAK
スピー
SSSPT

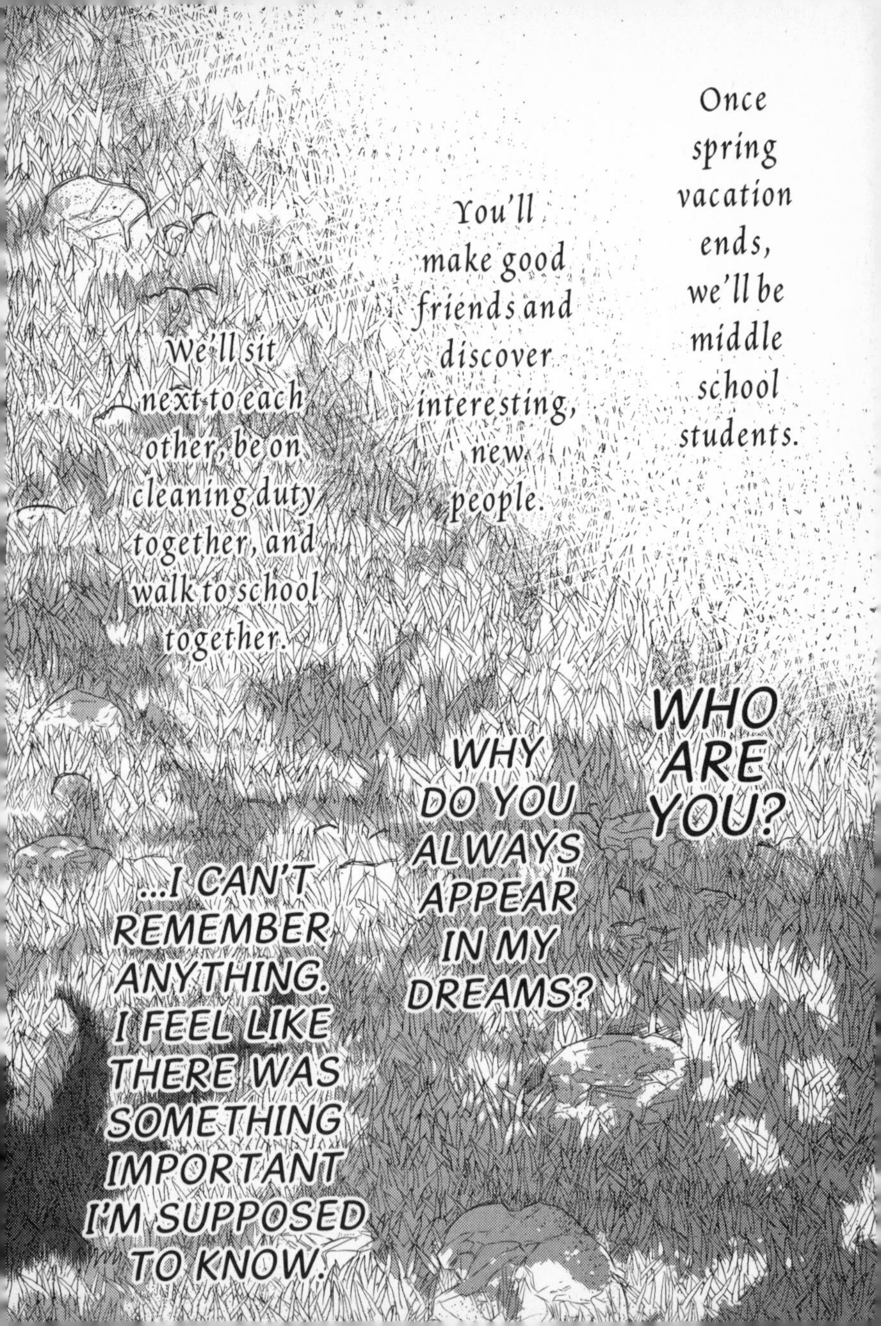
Once spring vacation ends, we'll be middle school students.
You'll make good friends and discover interesting, new people.
We'll sit next to each other, be on cleaning duty together, and walk to school together.
WHO ARE YOU?
WHY DO YOU ALWAYS APPEAR IN MY DREAMS?
...I CAN'T REMEMBER ANYTHING. I FEEL LIKE THERE WAS SOMETHING IMPORTANT I'M SUPPOSED TO KNOW.

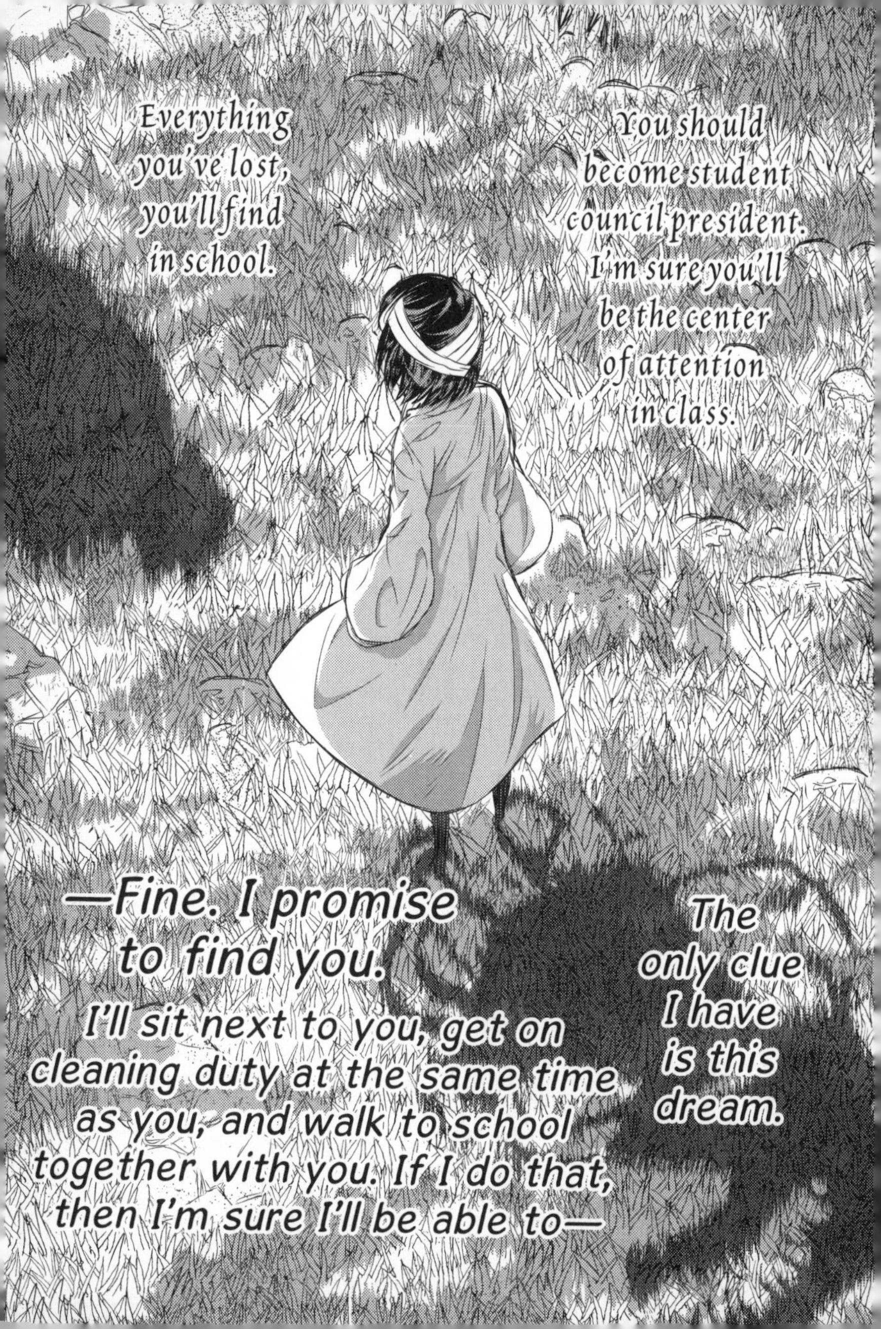
You should become student council president. I'm sure you'll be the center of attention in class.
Everything you've lost, you'll find in school.
The only clue I have is this dream.
—Fine. I promise to find you.
I'll sit next to you, get on cleaning duty at the same time as you, and walk to school together with you. If I do that, then I'm sure I'll be able to—

It's nothing...

I was just remembering a dream I had some time ago.

Ka-gari?

Anyway, Takamiya... Finals are next week.

And those are far more important than witches!

POOF
ぽん

CHAPTER 16 END

THE PASSION OF THE FURRY-EARS

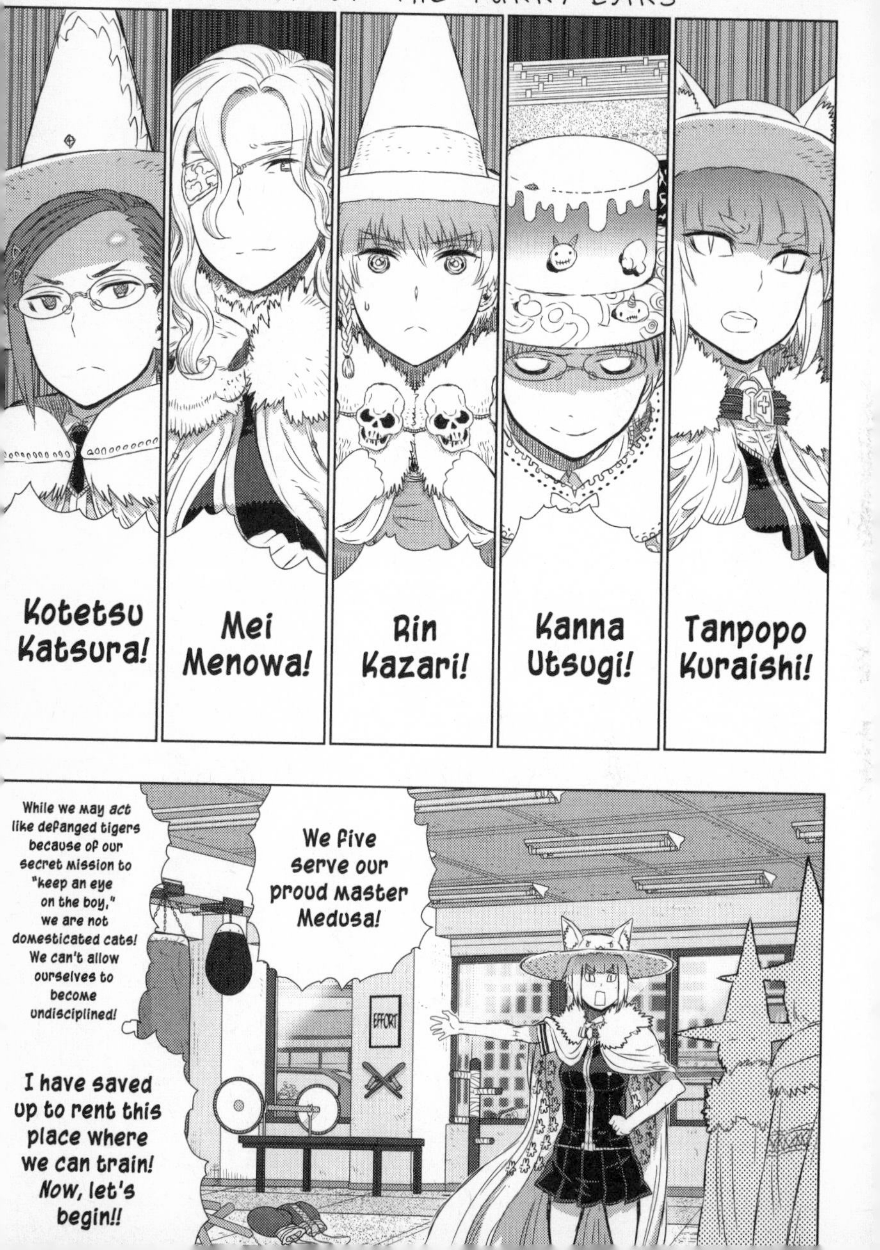
Tanpopo Kuraishi!
Kanna Utsugi!
Rin Kazari!
Mei Menowa!
Kotetsu Katsura!
We five serve our proud master Medusa!
While we may act like defanged tigers because of our secret mission to "keep an eye on the boy," we are not domesticated cats! We can't allow ourselves to become undisciplined!
I have saved up to rent this place where we can train! Now, let's begin!!
EFFORT

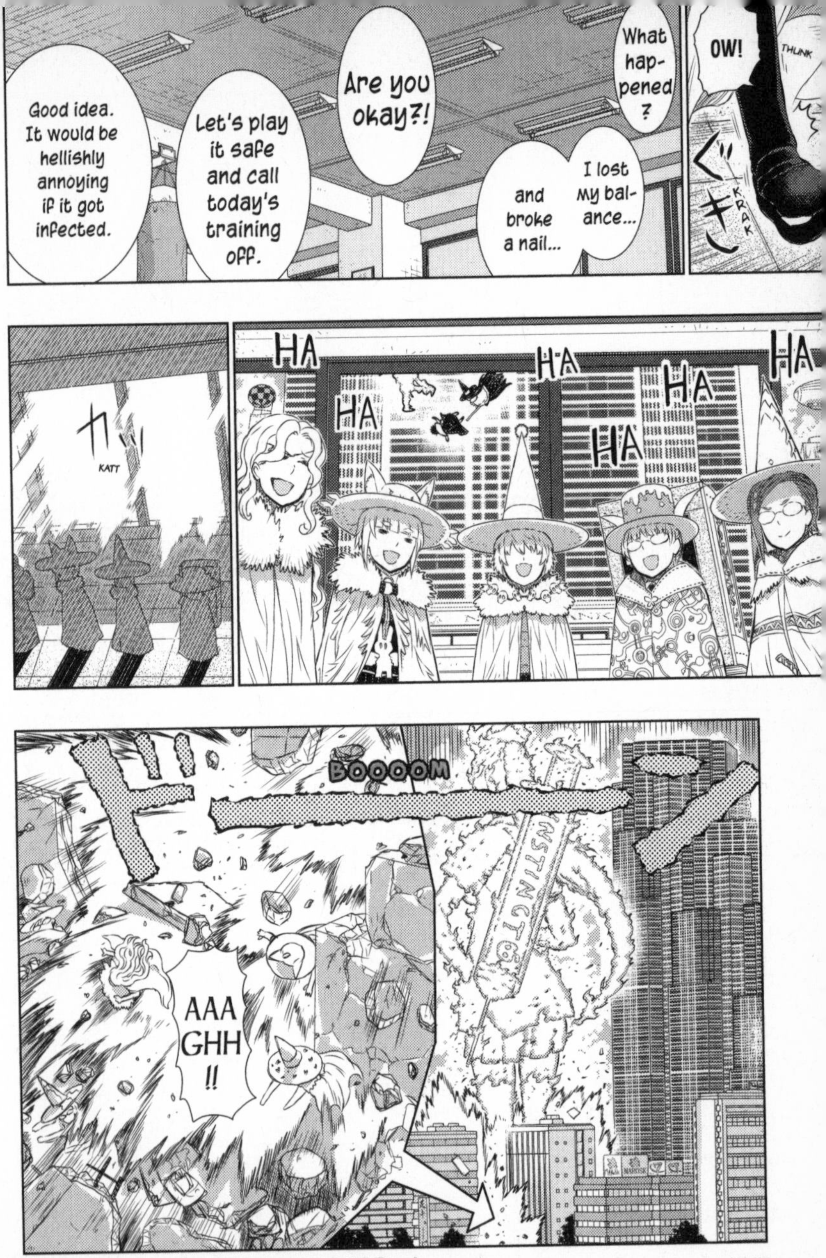
OW!
THUNK
KRAK
What hap-pened?
I lost my bal-ance...
and broke a nail...
Are you okay?!
Let's play it safe and call today's training off.
Good idea. It would be hellishly annoying if it got infected.
HA
HA
HA
HA
HA
HA
KATT
BOOOOM
AAAGHH!!

WITCHCRAFT WORKS 4: END

Assistants:
Shinobu
Takumi
Ricchan
Tamocchan

Afterword

Hello, Mizunagi here. Four volumes of Witchcraft Works already. Yaaay.

My editor told me that plans for an anime adaptation were moving forward. It's hard to explain how amazing it feels as a creator to know that a huge group of people are going to work to make characters you created "move" and "speak."

In this volume, we saw a giant Kagari, in a swimsuit, and the development of a new enemy. Please look forward to the next volume!

Ryu Mizunagi

LITTLE SISTER THEATER

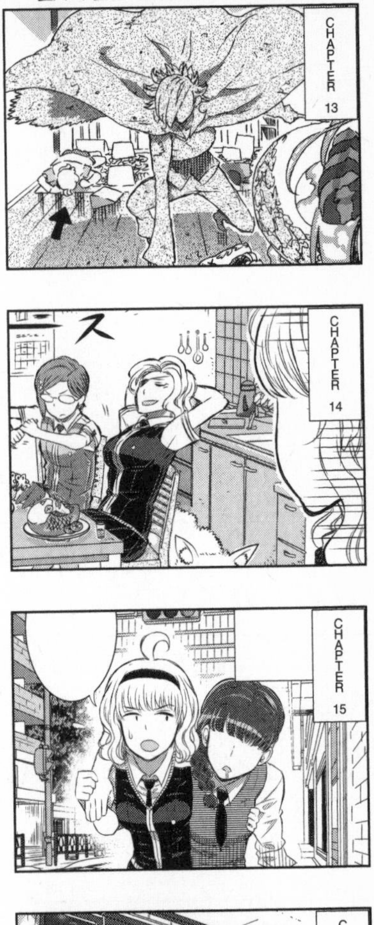

CHAPTER 13
CHAPTER 14
ス
CHAPTER 15
CHAPTER 16

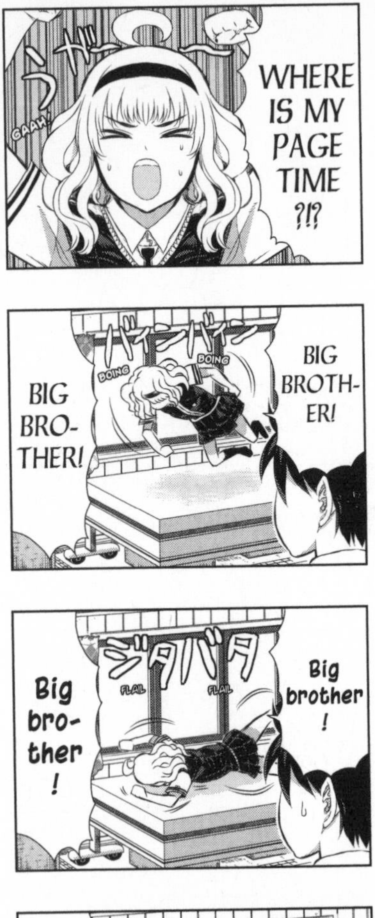

WHERE IS MY PAGE TIME ?!?
GAAH!
BIG BROTHER!
BIG BROTHER!
バインバイン
BOING BOING
Big brother!
Big brother!
ジタバタ
FLAIL FLAIL
...Big brother!
すやすや
ZZZ...

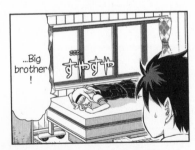

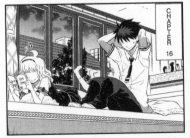

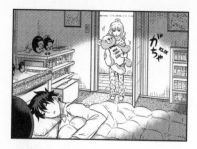

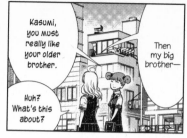

Then my big brother—
Kasumi, you must really like your older brother.
Huh? What's this about?
That lame, boring, useless brother of mine?
Everyone else in the world hates him, so I'm just paying attention to him out of pity.
Hehe. Well...
I like him.
Okay, you're excom-muni-cated.
Bye Forever.
AAHHH!! NOOO!
IT TOOK TWO WEEKS FOR THEM TO MAKE UP.
ぴゅー
PYOOO

がちゃ
KLIK
もぞもぞ
SNUGGLE
SNUGGLE
GOOD NIGHT, BIG BROTHER.

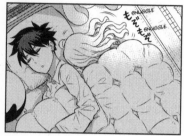

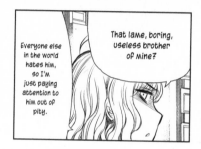

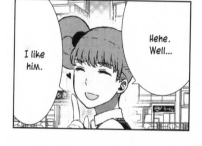

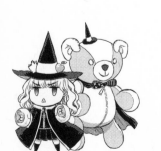

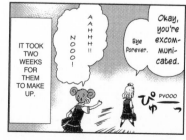

Witchcraft Works

WITCHCRAFT WORKS

CHAPTER 16 BONUS: THE TRUTH BEHIND THE DREAM

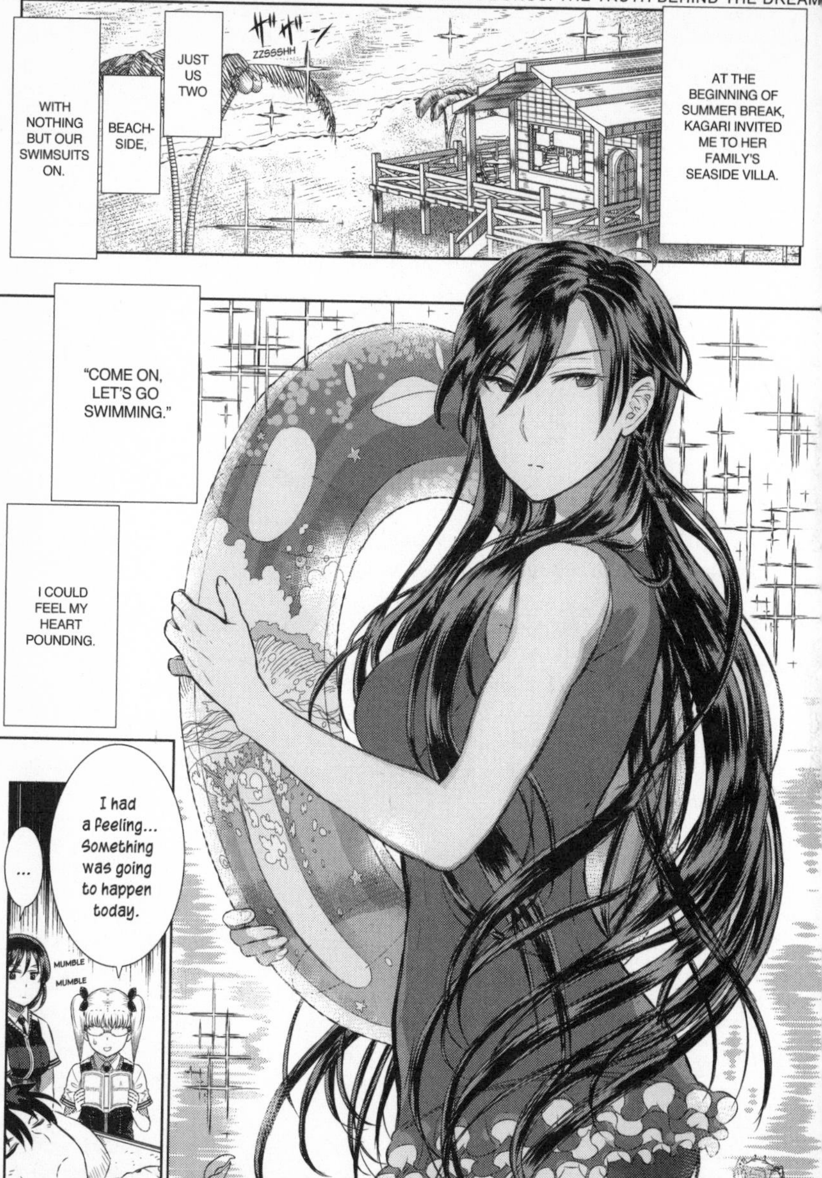
AT THE BEGINNING OF SUMMER BREAK, KAGARI INVITED ME TO HER FAMILY'S SEASIDE VILLA.
ZZSSSHH
JUST US TWO
BEACH-SIDE,
WITH NOTHING BUT OUR SWIMSUITS ON.
"COME ON, LET'S GO SWIMMING."
I COULD FEEL MY HEART POUNDING.
I had a feeling... Something was going to happen today.
...
MUMBLE
MUMBLE

IT WAS KANNA'S LATEST STORY.

Witchcraft Works | SETTING + SECRETS

These pages are a collection of behind-the-scenes character and story elements that probably won't affect or appear in the main story, as well as comments by the author. If you finish reading the story and think, "I want to know more!" then we hope you enjoy the information here.

Chapter 13: Takamiya and Noblesse Oblige

★ Noblesse Oblige
A pact (custom) among witches that states, "Strength comes from dignity and beauty."
An old pact that was formerly important when masters made agreements with familiars, knights, and so on. The effects are as follows.

A witch gains the protection of Noblesse Oblige when she acts with dignity and beauty.
When a witch has the protection of Noblesse Oblige, her magical power is increased tenfold.
When a witch loses the protection of Noblesse Oblige, her magical power is reduced by nine tenths, and any special abilities are limited (※) Invincibility, damage transfer.

In short, it is a pact that allows a witch to wield powerful magic so long as she acts with grace.

More details about the pact will eventually be revealed in the series.
Kagari violated the pact this time around by forming two simultaneous contracts, considered an act of infidelity.

The only way to regain its lost effects is to once again act properly in a disciplined way over a long period of time. However, we see Kagari immediately regaining her power in this chapter.
This is because before getting thrown into jail, the Chairwoman used her ridiculous powers to return Kagari's contract to normal. She then scolded her daughter

saying, "This is the only time I'm doing this."

★ Location Exchange
Magic that allows a retainer to exchange places with their master when their master is put in danger. A high-level form of damage transfer, it can only be used by Takamiya, the master in the contract.

★ The Apple of Discord
A fruit from the Garden of the Hesperides, found at the end of the world. It allows two witches to temporarily fuse their power. While Kagari says that Medusa "left her body," in reality, time simply ran out. The Apple works for about an hour.

★ The Punishment Room
You can tell by the graffiti on the wall that Kagari has been here a number of times in the past.

• Kazane Kagari
Grows horns when angered. She has an extremely haphazard personality, sometimes ignoring the custom of leaving the protection of the town to five high school students, and also allowing Tower Witches to do as they please until they cause trouble. Some Workshop heads will not even tolerate the presence of a Tower Witch in their domain.

• Ayaka Kagari
Holds ear picks strangely; in her left hand, at that.

• Laurent and Vine of Rothenberg
"Tattooed Witches" sent from the German Workshop responsible for managing Medusa. They ride a large bird known as a rukh.
Currently searching for Medusa.

• Medusa
In seclusion for the time being, as she'd be found if she returned to Tougetsu.

Chapter 14: Takamiya and Kagari's Wound

A story about Kagari's middle school days.

This story begins during the spring vacation immediately before Ayaka enters middle school. Kanae Hoozuki and Touko Hio, Ayaka's relatives, are ordered by the feared head of the Kagari household, Kazane Kagari, to look after her daughter. The story itself takes place in Tougetsu Girls Middle School.

• Ayaka Kagari
Starts off confused by school, then one day begins to seclude herself in the library. She then finally starts to go around visiting different schools, all while also working to improve herself.
These actions are driven by a dream Ayaka has every night, some of which we learn about in chapter 16.
When she finds Takamiya, Ayaka holds her hand to an old scar on her stomach and grimaces.

★ Old scar
There is a large scar on Kagari's stomach.

★ Waking from a dream
In one scene, Kagari gets out of bed, leaves the room once, then re-enters. Something is slightly different about her when she comes back in.

• Kanae Hoozuki
Dislikes Kagari at first, but gradually comes to accept her. After entering high school, she takes on the role of her manager, as the head of her elite guard. Is not happy about Takamiya, who appeared from nowhere and stole away the school's princess.

• Touko Hio
Eats ice cream as a staple food. Loves winter. Creates aggressive snowmen when she's scared, and snowmen for hugging when she's sleepy. Loves Kagari a little too much.

• Mr. Mikage
Teacher for class 1-B. He infiltrates the middle school in order to scout future witches.
Natsume Mikage, one of his relatives, is also enrolled at the school.

• Furry-ears
These girls can be seen here and there during their middle school years, as well.

- Sasukee

A Naruto meme based on a line Itachi says, kind of like the Japanese version of the "Good Naruto, you look kind of cool" meme.

- Wanigawa

A prodigy whose grades are third in her class. She can be found all throughout the chapter. Looks like a regular crocodile, but becomes more humanoid as she matures. She shows up during high school in the volume 3 bonus as one of the three seniors that Kasumi beats up. May or may not have fallen in love at first sight with the gentleman crocodile who works for Chronoire.

- Gang of delinquents

A group of delinquents who look somewhat familiar. As they're poor students, many of them went on to enroll at St. Jural Girls Academy, not Tougetsu Academy.

Chapter 15: Takamiya and the Strong-Armed Witch

- Takamiya

While Takamiya normally acts the part of the loser, in this chapter, he works hard to live up to his role as student council president. Of course, he does end up breaking his second seal during the battle with Rinon without even noticing it... Kagari probably decided to teach him how to fight in chapter 16 after seeing this and deciding that if he was going to let his power run wild, he might as well know how to use it.

- Kagari

Nurse Kagari makes an appearance this chapter. It's important to note that she's wearing her school uniform under the nurse outfit. Kagari is the type that favors form over function.

- The former student council president, now the vice-vice-vice student council president

She proposed the plan to set up a duel. Plans to ask for her good friend Rinon's help, but strays from the path of good and causes her friend to go insane instead. A former *yankii*, she seems to be embarrassed about her past.

- Chronoire Schwarz VI

Becomes the substitute chairwoman when Kazane Kagari is out. She wholeheartedly believes that "Youth is violence" and "Justice is power."

• Rinon Otometachibana

A bearslayer with strong arms and iron fists, she is the leader of the pajama
wearing, problem-causing, costumed killers known as Tenjiku. The current
bancho-style boss of Tougetsu city. She wears the Dragon's Tooth, given to
bancho as proof of their battles, on her head like a horn.

She's a Workshop witch with a focus on power, and has three honorary scars
on her forehead from her battle against a tiger. When blood rushes to her head,
these scars open and ooze blood. A gang boss by day and witch by night, she is
one of the five witches who protect the town.

• Kasumi

Leaves school early in the morning and doesn't know about Rinon's girls running wild as a result. She's shocked when she sees her bruised and battered
brother that night and asks him what happened, but he doesn't tell her anything,
leaving her annoyed.

Heard a rumor, the next day at school, that her brother won a duel against Rinon.

★ Normal students can't see witches when they wear robes, so the few student
witches who were in attendance know the truth behind the fight.

Chapter 16: Takamiya and Kagari's After-School Lessons Part 2

Our second training chapter.

• Takamiya

As part of learning how to fight, Takamiya is trained in how to summon a familiar.

This ends up with him fighting a familiar summoned by Kagari, but (as Kagari
also says), damage transfer does not work here as it normally would.

Self-inflicted injuries and damage from a retainer are not transferred, so when he
fights his retainer Kagari's familiar, no damage will be transferred to her. This
allows Takamiya to fight without having to worry about Kagari.

• Kagari

A pampering drill sergeant. We see different Kagari variations in this chapter,
such as giant Kagari and swimsuit Kagari.

While she also says something similar at the end of volume 1, we learn what she
sees as important here.

• Kasumi

Tends to spend a lot of time in her older brother's room. Tricks him into bathing with her, too.

Begins to tell her brother something about her and Rinon, so we can conclude that the two have some sort of relationship.

• Mr. Mikage + Chronoire Schwarz VI

Tea for two. Mr. Mikage is responsible for various tasks given to him directly by the chairwoman, and he befriends Chronoire while helping her during her time as substitute chairwoman.

• Kazane Kagari & Rinon Otometachibana

The magic square placed in the sewers, and the message Rinon was given that "Every person in town is a hostage."

At last, a wicked Tower assassin makes her appearance next volume...! I hope you're looking forward to it.

• Furry-ears

We finally learn all of their full names here in volume 4.

Under orders by Medusa to keep an eye on Takamiya (so that other Tower witches don't steal him away), they have no choice but to work with him.

As always, they're leading easygoing lives, getting beaten up by Rinon and watching their training room be destroyed.

Witchcraft Works, volume 4

A Vertical Comics Edition

Translation: Ko Ransom
Production: Risa Cho
          Melissa DeJesus

Copyright © 2015 Ryu Mizunagi. All rights reserved.
First published in Japan in 2012 by Kodansha, Ltd., Tokyo
Publication rights for this English edition arranged through Kodansha, Ltd., Tokyo
English language version produced by Vertical, Inc., New York

Translation provided by Vertical Comics, 2015
Published by Vertical, Inc., New York

Originally published in Japanese as *Uicchi Kurafuto Waakusu 4* by Kodansha, Ltd., 2012
Uicchi Kurafuto Waakusu first serialized in *good! Afternoon*, Kodansha, Ltd., 2010-

This is a work of fiction.

ISBN: 978-1-941220-18-4

Manufactured in Canada

First Edition

Vertical, Inc.
451 Park Avenue South
7th Floor
New York, NY 10016
www.vertical-inc.com

Vertical books are distributed through Penguin-Random House Publisher Services.